THE
FUTURE
OF
MAKING

Making things is what makes us human.

The tools we first used were a natural fit.

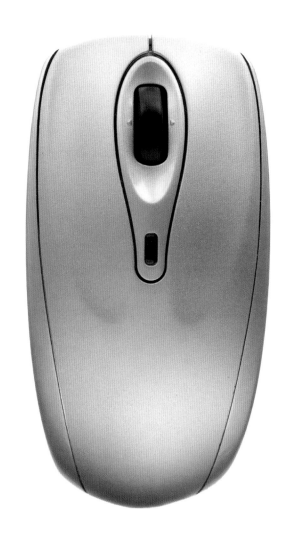

They still are.

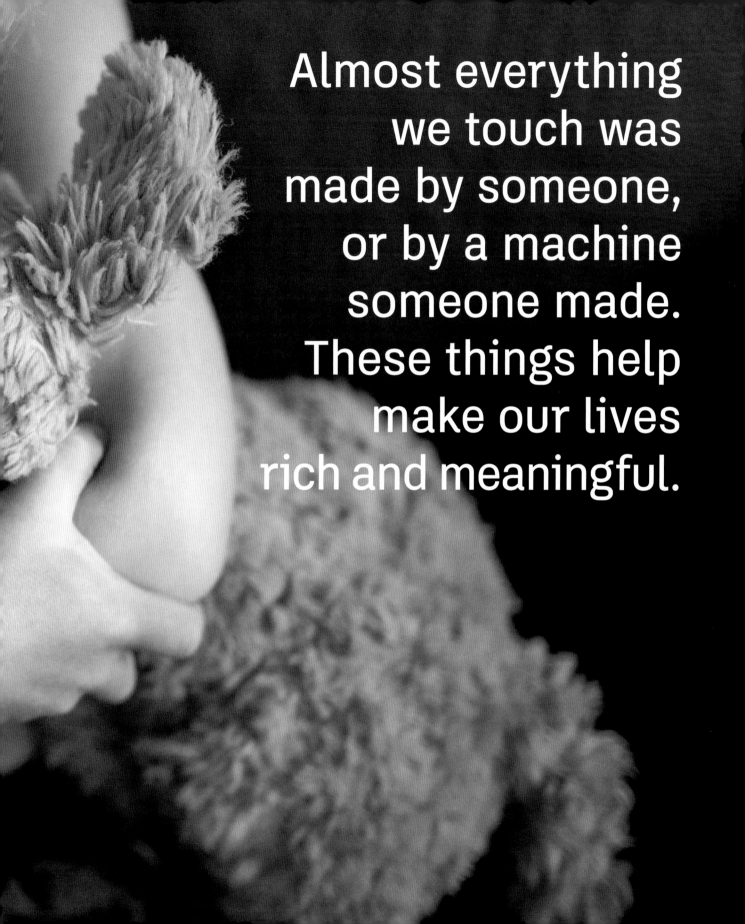

Almost everything
we touch was
made by someone,
or by a machine
someone made.
These things help
make our lives
rich and meaningful.

But the ways
we make things
can be toxic,
ugly, or lifeless.
They threaten
our planet and
our happiness.

Now, as our digital
and physical worlds
grow more linked...

...new technologies
are transforming
how we make
things—and what
we make.

This is the future
of making things.
This is the
future of us.

Contents

Foreword
by Carl Bass, CEO Emeritus

Making is the bedrock of our modern world. It gives us things like buildings, automobiles, infrastructure, and phones. Making gives us our privileged lives. Without it, there would be no housing, fast transportation, clothing, nor modern machines. And although it drives business at Autodesk, it's also a personal undertaking.

I started out as a mathematician. I was intrigued by problem-solving. It was only a matter of time before I started applying a systematic approach to making things like boats, bowls, tables, lamps, chairs, and electric go-karts. When I joined Autodesk, computers were still in their infancy. They were primarily a documentation tool. Now with approaches like generative design, the computer is becoming my partner as we make things together.

When I began computer programming, it was all about the algorithms. How can the code be the most efficient? How can it use the least amount of memory? Today, it's all about big data and near-infinite computing power. With the advances in cloud computing and machine learning, success depends on how much data is available and how many banks of servers are at one's disposal. And that will remain with us into the future.

At Autodesk, we are focused squarely on improving the future of making: creating tools to help millions of people design, make, and use places, things, and media to imagine, design, and create a better world. From what I can see, odds are that the future not only looks better, but brighter. Well, maybe that's just the mathematician in me.

We hope this book will inspire you to rethink the ways you make. If you are a professional designer, learn about the amazing technologies that are changing how and what we make. If you are starting out, get inspired to design something, join a club, and apply your energy to creating something. It's really rewarding.

Go ahead. Make something.

Preface:
The Forces of Change

Tom Wujec, Autodesk Fellow

In a world of exponential growth, technology seems to advance slowly, then lurch forward suddenly. Six years ago, when Autodesk launched its first book, *Imagine, Design, Create*, 3D printing was a quick and dirty prototyping tool; the cloud was a term used for weather; and Uber was just a weird German word.

Today, these and many other technologies are rocketing forward at an ever-more-blistering pace. Autodesk makes software for people who make things. The industries we serve—architecture, engineering, construction, and manufacturing, as well as media and entertainment—are being transformed by many new tools. We felt it was time to describe what they are, how they are playing out, and what they mean for makers.

In these pages, you will read stories of remarkable people and firms that are taking advantage of these new technologies to make better things. Some come from within Autodesk; most come from the global community of designers, architects, engineers, and other makers. You will meet a man who lost his legs in a teenage climbing accident but restored his ability to walk, run, dance, and climb. You will meet a "technology whisperer" who digitally captures spacecraft and prints turtle shells to protect threatened species. You will meet architects who produce fantastical buildings by computationally exploring the boring alternatives, scientists who can now design viruses, designers who invent shoes for top Olympic athletes, programmers who teach algorithms to create beauty, roboticists who are taking on multinational corporations, and amateur makers who are building things we couldn't have imagined just a few years ago. It all seems to be the stuff of science fiction. But it is real.

Creating *The Future of Making* was a deeply collaborative undertaking. The ideas presented here were gathered, shaped, and developed through hundreds of conversations with people working at the sharp edges of technology and innovation inside and outside of Autodesk. The conversations became storyboards, themes became chapters, and stories brought life to the technologies by featuring real people tackling real problems.

During the process, we felt the pace of change accelerate. As we settled on one story of innovation, three more appeared. Since predicting the future is always a precarious undertaking, we focused on exploring how fundamental classes of technology that support making are evolving and connecting together. Though specific examples will come and go, the sets of tools to design, make, and operate things will persist.

To keep current on the future of making and to download free tools, workshop planners, presentations, videos, and examples of evolving technologies, visit *autodesk.com/future-of-making-book*.

We hope *The Future of Making* inspires you to participate fully in the fourth industrial revolution, rethink how and what you design, and make something that's just amazing.

MAK

KING

The
Big Picture

Making is as old as humanity. Millennia before the dawn of writing, early makers took advantage of the properties of locally available materials to make things that improved their lives.

The earliest known arrowhead, more than 60,000 years old and found in modern-day Armenia, was chiseled from flint and attached to a wood shaft with bone marrow glue. To make this object, our ancestor took several steps: envisioning an object to serve a purpose; planning a sequence of actions to make it; gathering and working the raw materials; assembling, testing, and reworking it until it did its job; and, finally, putting it to good use. These fundamental acts that convert an intangible idea into a tangible thing are the essence of making.

The art and science of making evolved slowly. The first musical instrument was made about 42,000 years ago; ceremonial masks, 9,000 years; leather shoes, 5,500 years. As makers grew more capable, invented and used more sophisticated tools and materials, and coordinated with others, they created things that met the kaleidoscope of human needs, including warmth, protection, shelter, convenience, luxury, and joy.

Today, making has evolved into an impossibly inter-connected network of material extractors, designers, architects, engineers, manufacturers, builders, assemblers, distributors, and retailers. Collectively, global manufacturing and construction employs one quarter of the world's population and generates more than $30 trillion of value each year.

EVERYTHING COMES FROM SOMEWHERE

Look around. Every manufactured object you see—desk, chair, floor, window, light fixtures, the physical book or electronic device you are holding—was envisioned, designed, fabricated, assembled, and transported to where it is now.

Some objects take relatively short journeys: They are simple, made from one or two materials. The hand-carved hardwood bowl or the glass vase followed a narrow route along its supply chain and passed through only a few people's hands. These objects, considered simple and authentic, are cherished for their craftsmanship.

Other objects emerge from supply chains that look more like tangled spiderwebs. A refrigerator needs several hundred parts from dozens of manufacturers. Modern cars can have more than 30,000 individual components, each produced hundreds or thousands of miles from the factory floor. Mobile phones contain elements from over half the periodic table, including unpronounceable ones such as yttrium, lanthanum, praseodymium, and neodymium, all mined from remote locations.

THE PRESSING NEED TO MAKE BETTER THINGS IN BETTER WAYS

It's a complex and sometimes fragile system that depends on traditional methods of extraction and labor. And it cannot last.

In 30 years, the earth's population is set to grow by 2 billion, while the global middle class is predicted to increase by a factor of five, mostly in developing countries. Each freshly affluent family will want a car, a bigger home, computers, and televisions. The amount of energy we produce will need to double to support the needs of this emerging middle class. Meanwhile, in China and India, 400 million people will move from rural villages to cities in the next two decades, creating the need to build more infrastructure than has been constructed in the past century.

And as more people enjoy affluence and education, they will exercise their tastes, individuality, and power of choice, demanding things that are personally suited, but made at scale, at lightning speeds, and for an affordable price. These forces are creating vast new opportunities for makers. But they also highlight the many hidden costs of making—and how those add up.

The way we make things needs a major upgrade. The stakes are high: Continue to make things as we have, and we will stall economies and irrevocably damage our planet. Reinvent them, and we will have the potential to meet the needs of our advancing civilization while working within the limits of our environment.

MAKING REVOLUTIONS

Although the abstract process of making has been constant, the actual practice has seen massive changes. In early historical times, making stepped forward with the periodic discovery of new tools and materials—giving names to the Stone, Bronze, and Iron ages. In each of those eras, making was a local, personal, and skilled craft; it produced one object at a time, usually made uniquely for one person.

That ended when the first industrial revolution arrived in the 18th century. Steam and water power let textile mills, steel foundries, and industrial machines work at unprecedented scales. The second industrial revolution emerged in the late 19th century, when interchangeable parts, new steelmaking processes, and the moving assembly line launched the age of mass production. Electrically powered factories turned immense supply chains into endless, identical products. A third industrial revolution took hold by the 1970s, propelled by digital tools that helped plan, manage, and execute manufacturing as well as all other aspects of business.

Each revolution improved efficiency. And each produced better products: safer, more stylish cars, cheaper clothing, more secure and longer lasting homes. As factories churned out vast amounts of finished goods, they greatly improved our material standard of living.

NOW, REVOLUTION NO. 4

We are entering a fourth industrial revolution. It is not driven by a single force, but by a combination of technologies, including sensors, algorithms, and robotics. Though in use for decades, their combined low cost, broad access, high speed, fine precision, and interconnectivity have opened the door to a new reality. Their synthesis is connecting all parts of making—people, processes, materials—in surprising ways, creating far more than the sum of their constituent parts.

The transformation is sweeping. Technology is changing how we make things, who makes things, and the very nature of what we make.

This new industrial revolution is unfolding much faster than any of the previous, and it brings more profound implications. It will affect every industry that makes things and eventually touch every person involved in making. It will change our personal lives as well as our vocations. And it is happening because of the proliferation of one thing: the transistor.

This year, more transistors will be produced than grains of rice harvested—and at a lower cost. Let that fact sink in for a moment.

We produce 13 trillion transistors per second. That adds up to 400 billion billion in a year. Transistors are now so small that millions could fit into the period at the end of this sentence. A typical smartphone contains about 1.5 billion.

Because of the unique properties of the semiconducting material silicon dioxide, transistors can store and route minuscule amounts of electrical charge in predictable patterns. This gives transistors, when artfully arranged into microprocessors, RAM, and the

other chips that go into our digital devices, the capacity to capture, manipulate, and share information. They create a computable world of bits.

We are all familiar with the result: global telecommunications networks; the Internet available on our smartphones; the ability to call a taxi or reserve a hotel room from virtually anywhere in the world.

MAKING BECOMES DIGITIZED

The rise of digital tools and products is proving to be more disruptive than the previous industrial shifts—which were truly revolutionary in their own right. At the core of this disruption is computability—our ability to work on a problem within a computer, rather than in the physical world.

When an industry becomes computable, it is forever changed. For example, when music became computable—as songs became digitized, shareable, and searchable—the entire recording industry was disrupted. Value shifted from the physical production

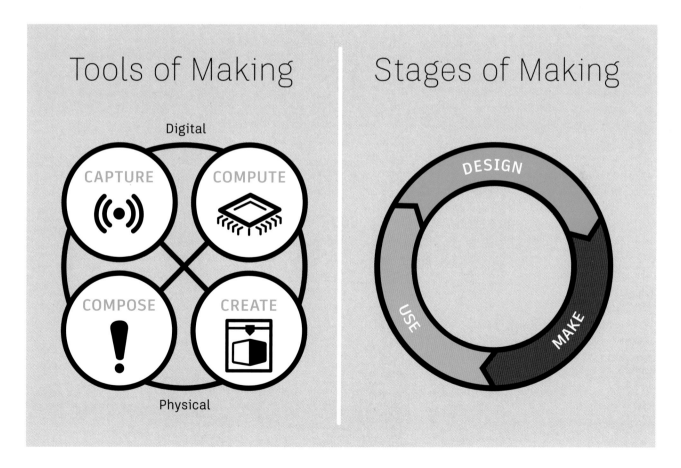

of records and CDs to online music platforms. Sales of physical products plummeted—but the shift also allowed almost any musician to participate in new online markets. This pattern of digitization, disruption, and democratization has been repeated in the realms of photography, books, classified ads, financial markets, and many others.

The world of making has now become computable.

When an industry becomes computable, it is forever changed.

Computation introduces new methods of production, changes distribution channels, and creates novel business models that generate new kinds of value. This disruption follows an exponential growth curve. It happens slowly at first, and then suddenly. As computation accrues, as networks branch out, as fast computers build even faster computers, as more people get access to these powerful and inexpensive tools, change catapults forward.

Four broad classes of technology are driving this fourth revolution: sensors, computers, robotics, and materials science. These technologies augment the four basic actions performed when making anything: capture, compute, create, and compose.

Capture: sensors record properties of things and convert them into digital data.
Compute: algorithms process this data and help us figure out exactly what to make and how to make it.
Create: machines follow digital instructions to shape things into precise forms.
Compose: better materials are brought together to make up better things.

CAPTURE

Sensors capture the physical properties and behaviors of objects and convert them into a torrent of useful data. Cameras, microphones, heat sensors, laser scanners, and many other sensing technologies see, hear, and locate things in the real world, often better than we can, and place them into the parallel digital world. Sensors can pinpoint the dimensions and movements of an athlete's foot, for example, or the soil conditions and microclimate of a building site. Once in digital format, this captured information establishes a detailed and accurate framework to make a running shoe that fits and performs better, or a building that is more resilient and efficient. Increasingly, sensors provide data from a wider range of relevant sources, including the flow of materials through a supply chain or the buying patterns of consumers. Unlike physical objects, data becomes permanent and computable.

Imagine when sensors are so cheap that they are embedded into everything we make—clothing, furniture, appliances, perhaps even our bodies. The emerging data will give manufacturers (and us) insight into how their products actually perform and help anticipate what we need next.

Sensors will provide unprecedented information. But they will also raise new questions concerning privacy and security. What will it mean when the things we own can sense how they are used? Will the data grow more valuable than the objects? Who owns this data? Who will buy it, sell it, and use it?

COMPUTE

Computation is problem-solving. Start with inputs and use algorithms to calculate intelligent outputs. What shape should a piece take? How much should it weigh? How much torque should it be able to withstand? How should it be assembled and shipped?

These questions have long been answered by building a parade of prototypes. Today, those are increasingly digital: Dozens, hundreds, and now even millions of digital prototypes are visualized, explored, tested, and finalized for a product.

Virtually infinite computing power is allowing designers to digitize the entire manufacturing process, with staggering results and implications. Each new generation of digital prototypes reveals more detail and realism and embodies more intelligence, making manufactured objects and buildings more computable and therefore more testable.

The most important news, though, is that new classes of algorithms are doing more creative work. Able to process data vastly beyond the capacity of the human brain, new software will learn from the real world, optimize trade-offs, and generate new solutions.

These new algorithms will be welcomed as they reduce the drudgery of mundane work. But as machine learning encroaches on our most cherished creative skills, it will shake our assumptions about what it means to design. If a computer designs a beautiful bridge, who owns that design? Who is responsible if something goes wrong? If an algorithm produces a solution more elegant and sublime than humans can, what does that mean for our creativity?

CREATE

We create with our bare hands, simple tools, machines, and, increasingly, robots. Robots are digitally controlled devices that faithfully follow detailed instructions to move, bend, and shape materials; cut, sculpt, or drill them away; or add to them via 3D printing.

Robots are becoming safer, faster, more reliable, and, most important, intelligent, as increased computation power enables them to sense their environments and respond quickly and accurately. They have already superseded human dexterity and are established as fixtures in automobile, aerospace, and countless manufacturing facilities. But as they evolve, and especially as they become cheaper and more adaptable, they will move from secured enclosures to a bigger world.

What will it mean for people, businesses, and countries when robots do most of the making? What does automation mean for craftsmanship? As some jobs inevitably disappear, new ones will appear—just as they did in the previous industrial revolutions. But once the new ways are in place, we never go back.

COMPOSE

As emerging technologies are digitizing materials, the very matter we make things with has become computable. And as with any industry that becomes computable, disruption follows. It is now routine to discern the detailed properties of familiar substances—wood, stone, glass, cement, plastics—and use them in more precise and thoughtful ways. But it is also possible to design new materials from scratch, identifying desired properties and engineering substances to embody these characteristics.

This emerging capacity to manipulate matter is allowing designers to rethink what they want their materials to do. It affects everyday objects—such as sports helmets and cars—as well as exotic things like advanced electronics and spacecraft. What seemed impossible will become ordinary as new materials are invented that can clean themselves, heal themselves, even assemble themselves into more complicated shapes. It is now even possible to program living materials: reading, understanding, and writing DNA to create things that have even more remarkable properties.

Materials advancements are central to the well-being of our world. What materials will we invent to make things that last longer, require less maintenance, and use less energy to create and operate? What will it mean when we create a better design not by changing a form, but by changing the stuff the form is made from? What might this mean for clothing and infrastructure? The choices we make will affect how we address many of the grand challenges humanity faces.

WHAT LIES AHEAD

The synthesis of these four technologies is creating new, integrated systems of making. These extend far beyond manufacturing lines. As digital information is intelligently ferried among people, processes, and products, once disparate domains become connected. Sensors will inform designers how well products work and who is using them. Artificial intelligence will help designers manufacture parts in optimal ways. This will connect the design with actual operation, and manufacturing with distribution, integrating the entire value-creation process.

A running shoe that once took a year and a half to design and make can now be produced in days, soon hours. Jet engine parts that needed to be grinded, milled, and polished are now made by growing metal. Work done by more than a hundred carpenters can be done by ten—faster and more accurately. Start-ups of four people can challenge entrenched industries.

The future of making is already here. With today's technologies, and powered by the creativity of manufacturers, builders, and makers, we are now able to design and fabricate just about anything.

The question becomes, if we can make anything, what should we make?

CHAPTER 1

We are just at the start of the sensor revolution. By 2022, a *trillion* connected sensors will populate our world. Most will be embedded into the things we make.

Some will inform our designs. Others will make machines better fabricators. These sensors will capture much of what we can see, hear, touch, smell, and taste—and increasingly what we can't. All together, they will help bridge the gap between the physical world and the digital one—ushering in new ways of designing for both realms.

MAKING SENSE OF THE WORLD

Makers know what to pay attention to. Architects visit sites, survey environments, and observe people to understand the physical, social, and economic environments of the buildings they will create. Product designers do the same: They learn as much as possible by measuring, touching, and recording the world as it is, then wonder what it could be.

Taking stock of the world and the objects in it has always been a manual undertaking. Recording sizes, distances, weights, and stresses is a time-consuming and error-prone process. That is, until computers gained senses via components that could measure all of that and more. Digital sensors are enhancing and expanding human perception, broadening our ability to make sense of things.

Think of sensors as the eyes, ears, and fingertips of computers. By continually capturing accurate information about the physical world, sensors provide on-ramps into the digital world. What once needed to be entered manually now gushes freely, providing vast reservoirs of data. Images, temperature, physical stresses, motion, atmospheric pressure, infrared radiation—all of the properties of the physical world can now quickly and effortlessly make the jump into the digital. As the cost of common sensors drops close to zero, that digital jump is essentially free too. This data—organized and interpreted—is giving us the deep

Digital sensors are enhancing and expanding human perception, broadening our ability to make sense of things.

and broad context needed to make informed decisions about what to design, how to fabricate, and where to operate things more intelligently.

Consider the challenge of recording the location of a person. A low-resolution scanner, with an accuracy of 10 meters, tells you where the person is within a city block or a building. At one-meter resolution, you know where they are in a room. One-centimeter resolution shows the person's posture and, to some degree, what they are doing. At one millimeter, sensors pick up tiny movements, including facial expressions and breathing patterns that can expose the person's physical state. And with a tenth-of-a-millimeter precision, a person's micromovements, heartbeat, and tremors become visible, revealing information about their health and mental state. Today's best sensors can resolve to 1/100th of a millimeter.

As sensors become better, what they tell us about the world changes. With each improvement in resolution, they discern qualities in an object that were previously invisible. (See the amazingly detailed scan of the London Mail Rail by ScanLAB on pages 34–35 for evidence of how far the art has come.)

This superdetailed perception has major implications for the world of making. It accurately gathers data on the characteristics of the objects, environments, and people we need to understand to design for. Indeed, the fidelity of our models is becoming so good—based on the ever-higher resolution of our sensors—that we are entering a mode of working called "reality computing."

Reality computing takes advantage of the broadly available high-performance computers to represent and manipulate ultra-high-fidelity digital models.

These models are becoming more lifelike, more accurate, and more closely approximate reality. The result is an approach that closely integrates digital design and the physical world.

REALITY CAPTURE

For designers, the goal of digital capture tools is to get the best possible model of something physical into a computer as quickly and easily as possible. To understand how sensing is changing the design industries, it is good to start with the basic question: What is a sensor?

Sensors come in two varieties. The most familiar are passive. These work by detecting changes in materials in the sensor—changes that come from the physical world impacting those materials in some way. Digital cameras use sensors called CCDs or CMOS to convert the energy of photons that land on them into tiny electrical signals. Microphones capture the vibrations of a flexible plate as sound waves shake them. In addition to light and sound, passive sensors can record temperature, pressure, orientation, GPS location, altitude, and the presence of chemicals, among hundreds or thousands of other things.

Active sensors, by contrast, gather information by emitting pulses of energy and then recording the reflected signals—they go out and get the data. LiDAR (Light Detection And Ranging), for example, sends bits of light into an environment, measures the time it takes for each bit to bounce back, and constructs a three-dimensional digital model from that information. Other active sensors include X-rays, fMRI, and sonar. At one time, these sensors were very expensive, requiring specialized training. But the tools are becoming more accessible; today, for example, LiDAR is a feature on a few smartphones.

In a large-scale renovation project, a surveyor will typically make 100 measurements that a designer can use as reference points. While that depth of information has provided a good basis for years, new sensing tools give us many orders of magnitude more data. A LiDAR device can record a million points per second. Merging a few of these scans creates a "point cloud," a ghostly three-dimensional image that re-creates the building in amazing detail. That point cloud, in turn, can be converted into 3D and 2D models that can be used by existing design software.

Photogrammetry, another technique for capturing reality, begins not with high-tech scans, but with regular photographs. Sophisticated software can take 20 or so images—taken from a variety of angles—and "stitch" them together into a seamless 3D model.

WHY CAPTURE REALITY?

Reality capture kickstarts design. Beginning with a captured model rather than from scratch allows designers to move directly into the creative work of exploration, analysis, and testing. And high-resolution models mean that work is more accurate—and often more inventive, more efficient, or more fun.

The combination of active and passive sensors has already revolutionized many creative disciplines. Filmmakers routinely use motion capture to re-create the performances of actors, then digitally enhance them into older or younger versions of the actors, into great apes, mythical beings, or blue aliens. Physicians scan our bodies. Geologists use them to pinpoint oil fields. Astrophysicists use them to see the surfaces of remote planets.

As sensors capture more of our world, they will dramatically change the ways we design, make, and use things. Not only will these devices give us a clearer idea of our world, they will also help us make sense of what we might want to create within it.

Sensors are revolutionizing each part of the process of making. They are being used to help establish the real-world context of design, capturing relevant data—of both form and function—and establishing the constraints a design must fit within. They are giving our fabrication tools better perception. And they are being used to monitor the performance of products, making them active, responsive, and, increasingly, actors in their own iteration.

As sensors become better, what they tell us about the world changes. With each improvement in resolution, they discern qualities in an object that were previously invisible.

Modeling Paradise

LiDAR, drones, and other high-tech tools help create the first digital models of the stunning bamboo structures in Bali's Green Village.

Shaan Hurley and Brett Casson awoke in Bali's Green Village not really knowing what to expect. When they'd arrived the previous evening at this community of hand-constructed homes and a connected school, set along Bali's Ayung River, they quickly recognized that they were somewhere unforgettable. Experiencing the breathtaking mansions of Green Village in the first morning light, however, with the audible ripples of the stream outside and the golden October sunrise literally streaming through the bamboo walls, still managed to be a mind-altering experience.

"It was absolutely amazing," says Casson. "Nothing short of incredible."

The homes in Green Village are made almost entirely of bamboo. While this makes Green Village one of the more unique and sustainable communities in the world, it also poses challenges to its builders and architects. Modern architecture software comes loaded with tools that can simulate many different kinds of stressful events—windstorms, earthquakes, water damage, fire, and so on. But the bamboo houses in Green Village are built in such a novel way that testing their stability with standard architectural software is not really an option.

Hurley and Casson, both technologists for Autodesk, were in Green Village to capture comprehensive

Hurley and Casson were in Green Village to capture comprehensive 3D LiDAR scans of two homes. Using the data they captured, they could build simulations of the structures.

3D LiDAR scans of two homes. Using the data they captured, Autodesk would be able to build models and simulations of the structures, which in turn would make Green Village's bamboo architectural designs testable and, eventually, more stable.

That first morning, after the awe of the beauty of their surroundings wore off, Hurley and Casson looked around at the sweeping bamboo curves and wildly complex geometry of the building they had just awoken in, and quickly realized how complicated their work there was going to be.

"Seeing it in real life," says Hurley, "just blew our minds."

Hurley, in particular, was a veteran of extreme field-based 3D scanning projects: unsuccessfully dodging Portuguese man-of-war jellyfish while capturing coral reefs off the coast of Molokai; flying drones over stiflingly dusty Kenyan badlands to capture rapidly disappearing fossil fields; hanging upside down in SCUBA gear to scan the sunken USS *Arizona* in Pearl Harbor; mapping massive Washington mudslides; documenting the natural arches of Utah; and so on. But the Green Village job, set in an environment that many consider paradise, would turn out

to be the most difficult—as well as the most rewarding—scan that Hurley and Casson had ever undertaken.

BAMBOO PALACES

The community of Green Village, in Bali, Indonesia, is curved and nestled into the lush, terraced slopes along the Ayung River, as if it's always been there. Begun in 2010, Green Village now has 12 completed homes, plus 64 additional freestanding structures, some of which constitute the Green School, which is one of the most extraordinary primary schools in the world.

The "green" in Green Village refers to the values held essential by the people who live there, and of those who built the village. The entire community has been master-planned as a model of uncompromising sustainability—and breathtaking beauty.

The buildings in Green Village are designed by a local Balinese company called Ibuku. Ibuku (the name means "Mother Earth") was founded by Elora Hardy, who acts as Ibuku's creative director.

Hardy grew up in Bali but left for high school in California, then art school in New York, and eventually became a print designer for Donna

previous pages: LiDAR captures a point cloud, made up of millions of data points. Autodesk technologist Shaan Hurley likens it to a cloud of mosquitoes.
opposite: A fleet of drones (one is visible at lower left) did LiDAR captures, as well as video and still photography, recording context, texture, and color.

44

They looked around at the sweeping bamboo curves and wildly complex geometry and quickly realized how complicated their work there was going to be. The Green Village job, set in an environment that many consider paradise, would turn out to be the most difficult—as well as the most rewarding—scan that Hurley and Casson had ever undertaken.

Karan. After a few visits back to Bali, however, and seeing what was happening at the Green School that her father, John Hardy, had cofounded, she decided to quit her job and move home. "I recognized that something unique was going on at the Green School," she says, "and I wanted to be a part of it."

The success of the Green School created a demand for similarly sustainable housing nearby. The first two houses in Green Village were already in the planning stage when Elora Hardy arrived. "I had no agenda around being involved in building or construction," she says. "But I was interested in spaces, and making spaces more beautiful." To Hardy,

beauty and sustainability go hand in hand, and Green Village was an opportunity to channel her passions into what would become—at least to date—a game-changing and unforgettable life's work.

THE MAGIC IN THE MODELS

The bamboo varietal Ibuku uses to build Green Village is massive. Called Petung, it is not the bamboo pandas munch on, nor anything like the weedy shoots you might see in your backyard. Mature Petung shafts easily achieve the heft and size of construction-ready lumber, reaching up to four inches in diameter, with a tensile strength equivalent to that of steel. Probably most important to the Green Village community, however, is that bamboo is almost ludicrously sustainable—reaching a building-appropriate size and strength after only a few years of growth. And it grows all over Asia.

But because an Ibuku home is built with bamboo and is essentially hand-constructed on-site by local craftsmen, it doesn't lend itself to the software-based tools used by most modern architects and builders. Ibuku's designs are hardly primitive, however. They are deeply complex, deeply considered, and deeply planned. While Ibuku sometimes uses elements of CAD to

approved, they deconstruct the model piece-by-piece and cut the structure's real-sized bamboo timber to match the scaled-up measurements of every little piece in the model. There are no formal blueprints and no software-generated renderings or plans.

Ewe Jin Low is the lead architect at Ibuku. Trained in England, and having run commercial architectural practices in Malaysia and Australia, he intendend, when he joined a few years ago, to bring more CAD and software into Ibuku's design and building processes. And he still sees the value in testing structural design with software-based

The traditional Ibuku method depends on scale bamboo models rather than CAD drawings. The Autodesk team's scans allowed them to create detailed digital models and drawings of the buildings.

Because an Ibuku home is built with bamboo and is essentially hand-constructed on-site by local craftsmen, it doesn't lend itself to the software-based tools used by most modern architects and builders. Ibuku's designs are hardly primitive, however.

begin their designs, for each structure they design and build, Ibuku ultimately crafts a series of small, handmade bamboo models. To test the strength of a specific design, Ibuku literally applies force to the model, sometimes even standing on it. When a design is

models. At the same time, however, he has been won over by the magic of the little bamboo models. His builders are craftsmen—not trained nor specialized construction professionals. The scale models are easier for them to refer to on-site, and they allow for immediate

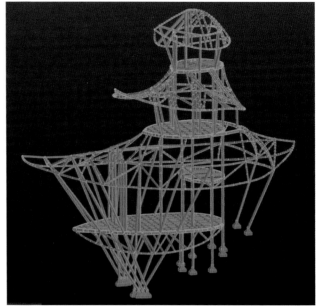

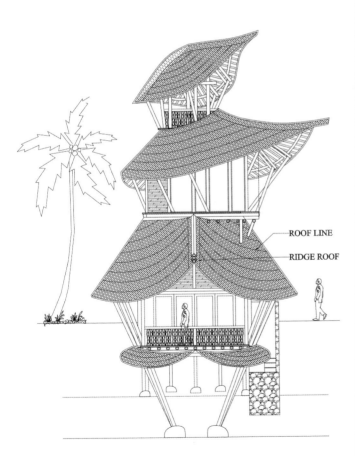

ROOF LINE

RIDGE ROOF

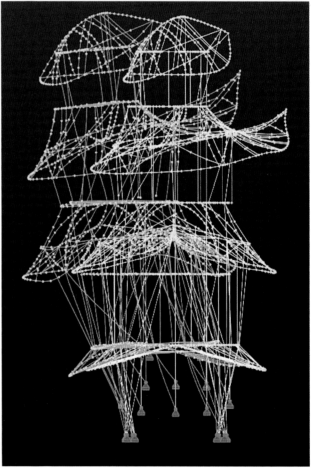

Low's builders are craftsmen—not trained nor specialized construction professionals. The scale models are easier for them to refer to on-site, and they allow for more immediate and tactile communication that can't be achieved through computers.

and tactile communication that can't be achieved through computers.

"The bamboo models, and particularly the studio and site intercourse [they facilitate] between our artisans and architects," Low says, "create the distinctive 'wows' that cannot be produced from CAD, for now."

A CLOUD OF MOSQUITOES

Because the models didn't originate in the computer, the only way to get them there is through scanning—specifically LiDAR.

LiDAR, which stands for Light Detection and Ranging (or it's a portmanteau of "light" and "radar," depending on who you're talking to), is a surveying technology that measures distance similarly to radar. Instead of bouncing radio waves off a target, however, LiDAR bounces light waves. Developed in the 1960s, LiDAR's first practical application was in meteorology, measuring clouds. It gained fleeting global attention when

it was used to scan the surface of the moon during the Apollo missions.

Because light waves have such a higher frequency than radio waves, LiDAR measurements are significantly more precise than radar. And LiDAR projects light thousands of times per second, adding even more precision. Unlike more traditional surveyor's tools, LiDAR is nondiscrete, meaning it measures literally everything it sees, compiling millions of points of data—and therefore extraordinary detail—with every scan.

Casson once helped 3D-capture the Sydney Opera House with LiDAR. "Those sails would be absolutely impossible to do a very accurate capture of without the use of LiDAR," he says. Only LiDAR could accurately extrapolate all the nuanced slopes, angles, and curves of the building, in three dimensions, and much more quickly than the months it would take with manual, discrete measurements. Using LiDAR, Casson and his

Three of the handcrafted bamboo models that are used to test Ibuku structures and guide their construction. There are no formal blueprints, renderings, or plans.

colleagues knocked out that particular project at the Sydney Opera House in just a few days.

Hurley compares the point cloud captured by a LiDAR scan to a giant cloud of mosquitoes. Up close, it's a random-looking mess. "But as you zoom out," he says, "you can begin to make out what it actually is." Stitch a few of those mosquito clouds together, and suddenly you can build 3D renderings of just about anything.

Because Green Village's homes are built from bamboo, they don't have traditional walls, traditional squared corners, or uniform surfaces. The bamboo used to build the structures—which can be up to six stories high—is almost always curved (because bamboo often grows curved, and because the homes in Green Village are purposefully built with curves to best conform to their surroundings). The floors are made of sliced bamboo, creating deeply ridged textures. The interior walls are also made of bamboo, and from the outside, you can literally see clear through huge portions of each home to the forest on the other side.

This makes the LiDAR capturing of Green Village's structures very complex. Some of the light beams will hit curved outer bamboo walls and beams. Others will hit wildly textured furniture and interior structures. Still others will bounce off the beams on the far side of the house. Millions more will pass clear through to the forest beyond. Hurley's cloud of mosquitoes just got much more difficult to stitch together into a coherent 3D model. In fact, the team had to place man-made spheres into the areas they were scanning simply to provide a set of easily identifiable landmarks that the 3D software could reference when compiling the data into usable point clouds.

Due to all this complexity, not only did the team have to choose the angles they scanned from very wisely, they also had to run significantly more scans to ensure they captured everything they needed.

What's more, the structures in Green Village are designed to accommodate the surrounding landscape with minimal imposition. Many of the homes are built on stilts, and all are encroached by heavy foliage. Figuring out all the angles you need to scan is matched in difficulty by finding enough clear views of the structure to capture all those angles.

And that only covers the ground equipment. Getting a drone clear of the foliage—and the glimmering spiderwebs of broken kite strings caught in the trees—was also a stressful challenge.

"When I saw Brett's eyeballs, and the look of terror," says Hurley, "it validated the fear that I was having. We had two weeks on the ground."

The team got to work.

WORKING IN DOUBLE TIME

Hurley and Casson's original task was to scan one house—a house alternatively known as the Ananda House and Dave's House. But they were struck by the grandeur and beauty of the nearby Sharma Springs house, too—a five-story marvel that has been featured on magazine covers and in U.S.-based television shows. They decided there was no way they could leave Green Village, or really do Ibuku justice, without also scanning Sharma Springs.

It was a massive amount of work, far more than they had initially planned. Every piece of equipment had a specific job. The team began at 6 a.m. every day to get the Hovermap LiDAR drone up and down again before the winds picked

The team found themselves perched on steep slopes with a handheld unit, one person operating the scanner and another holding onto him for dear life, to make sure he didn't slip and tumble down the hill.

up by 10 o'clock. They worked through the oppressively hot midday hours, then into the night, using a tripod-mounted Faro Focus X130 3D laser scanner for the interiors, and the Zoller + Fröhlich 5010c Imager laser scanner for exteriors. The Zoller + Fröhlich, in particular, was exhausting to work with, weighing 85 pounds without the tripod. It had to be lugged up and down five sets of spiral stairs every day. The team also found themselves perched on steep slopes with a ZEB-REVO handheld unit, one person operating the scanner and another holding onto him for dear life, to make sure he didn't slip and tumble down the hill. But this smaller piece of equipment provided opportunities to scan from positions the larger scanner and the Hovermap couldn't reach, and thus added significantly to the richness and thoroughness of the data. Finally, the team used two DJI Inspire 1 drones for video and photography to help add context, textures, and color, and help document the project.

Throughout the project, all the equipment worked as advertised, even under the extreme conditions. The project was difficult and exhausting, but it was turning out—slowly but surely—to be a success.

A couple of weeks later, when they were finally finished, the sheer amount of data they had accumulated was staggering.

The Sharma House required 57 internal scans with the Faro Focus X130 3D laser scanner, and 18 external scans using the Zoller + Fröhlich 5010c Imager. The scanning was done in an astonishing 15 hours.

The Ananda House required 58 internal scans using the FaroFocus X130 3D laser scanner and 32 external scans using the Zoller + Fröhlich 5010c Imager.

Several additional terrestrial captures were completed using the ZEB-REVO handheld unit, which was primarily used to capture bridges and paths, and the Hovermap drone.

POTENTIAL AND POSSIBILITIES

The Autodesk team had essentially captured the data needed to create intricately detailed digital 3D versions of the handmade scale models that

Three views from the scanning project, clockwise from top left: A drone photograph; a LiDAR point cloud; and a simulation of wind forces on the building, modeled from the data collected through the team's scans.

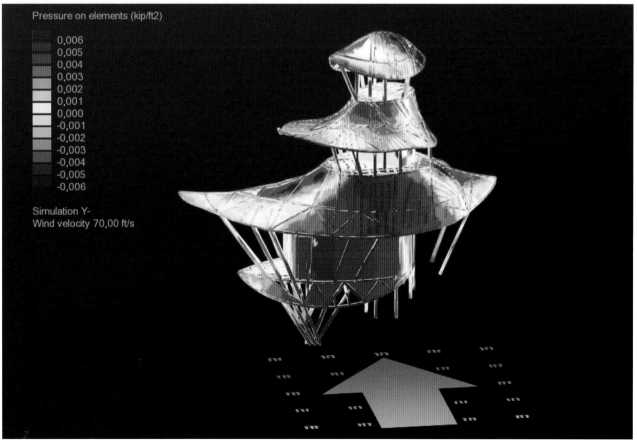

Pressure on elements (kip/ft2)

0,006
0,005
0,004
0,003
0,002
0,001
0,000
-0,001
-0,002
-0,003
-0,004
-0,005
-0,006

Simulation Y-
Wind velocity 70,00 ft/s

Ibuku uses to design their structures. Hurley and his team are now working with those digital models to develop new simulations of the structures to test their resiliency and integrity under various types of natural duress. They've hit the Ananda House with hurricane-force winds, earthquakes, and other load-bearing events—simulations that aren't possible using only the bamboo scale models—and shared their results with Low and the team at Ibuku.

Low is most intrigued by what they can learn from the wind models, and how it might affect their designs in the future. "We can just begin to imagine the potential and possibilities," he says, "looking at structural loading and design and many other technical variables." He imagines the simulations helping them with their design-safety factors and reducing waste on jobs.

But as a true convert to the Ibuku way, Low also cautions against an over-reliance on technology. "How do we harness today's fast-paced technology and not let it overwhelm us, or take over too much of the main role that humans have to play here on Earth?" he asks.

That train of thought has affected how Hurley and Casson think about technology as well. "I do so many presentations to industry, talking about the virtues of the digital world, and I'm a deep believer," Casson says. "But Bali made me really assess what craftsmanship means. It had a profound impact on me."

Hardy, likewise, is excited by what the teams at Ibuku and Autodesk can both gain from the LiDAR project. It's not just "what they will learn from what we've done," she says, "but also that we will be able to be more assured, backed by an understanding of our engineering, to the depth and detail that can be captured." She pauses for a moment, then adds, as though she is surprised by her thoughts all over again: "That's incredible."

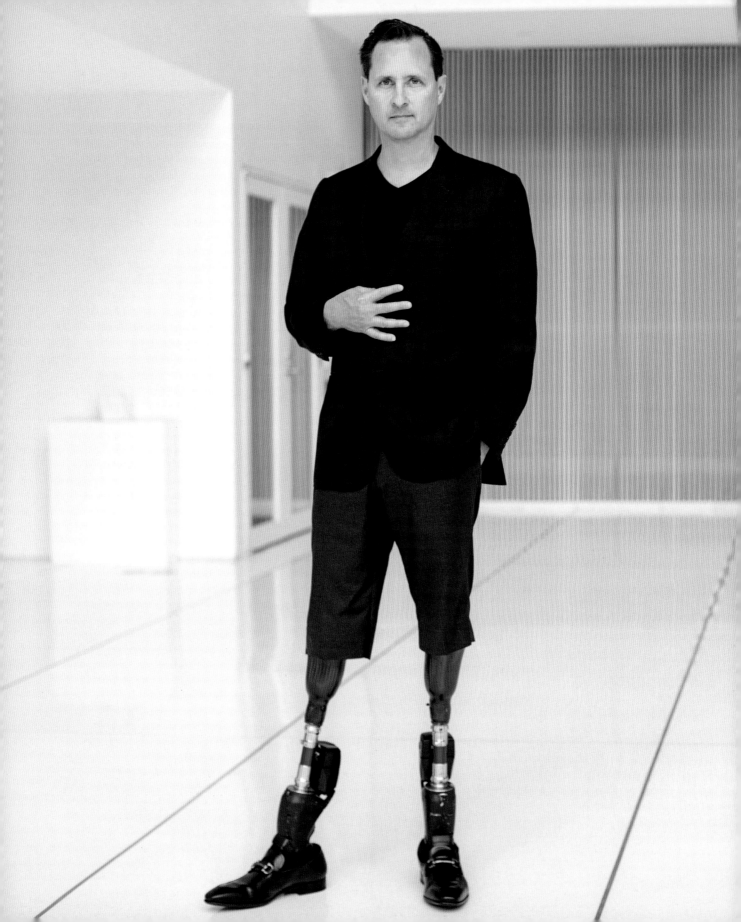

A Bionic Man

Hugh Herr's conviction that he could engineer better legs has produced next-generation, sensor-driven prosthetics.

You'll likely hear Hugh Herr before you see him. The charismatic leader of MIT's biomechatronics research group wears two next-generation prosthetic legs, each barely visible under the cuff of his gray slacks, which produce a faint percussive buzz with each footfall, like the sound of a tiny electric drill. The sound serves almost as a leitmotif—you hear it, faintly, as he ascends the stairs to his office in the glass-and-metal MIT Media Lab, or as he ambles across the stage during a lecture.

Among futurists, Herr's story is the stuff of legend. In the early 1980s, after he lost both legs below the knees to frostbite in a climbing accident in New Hampshire's White Mountains, a doctor told him he would never climb again. Defiant, Herr used a local machine shop to hack together custom prostheses from rubber, metal, and wood. He designed a set of small feet that could find a foothold where his old pair would have slipped, and a spiked set he could use to ascend the steepest walls of ice. He went on to become as confident a climber after his accident as he'd ever been before.

That process of redesigning elements of his own body became an epiphany for Herr. "I viewed the missing biological part of my body as an opportunity, a blank palette for which to create," he told an audience at the 2015 Autodesk University conference. That ethos has paved the way for an exceptional academic and public career that defies easy categorization. He earned degrees at MIT and Harvard and eventually became the head of the former institution's biomechatronics group, which has become a research titan under his leadership; in 2011, the same year that he launched prosthetic maker BionX Medical Technologies—which created the BiOM prosthesis he wears daily—*Time* dubbed him the "leader of the bionic age."

In a sunny room overlooking the airy biomechatronics gait-testing laboratory, Herr doesn't mention those accolades. Instead, he frames his research as a moral imperative to fight against the pain and frustration caused by under-

is," he said, "and the profound human suffering that's caused by bad design."

In a certain light, the central theme of that work could be framed as the notion that effective assistive technology needs to respond intelligently to human activity. However advanced a traditional prosthetic might be, its gross morphology is that of a pirate's peg leg; to adequately bridge a human body and a prosthetic limb, the limb must sense its wearer's intention and respond accordingly.

That's the reasoning that informs the design of the BiOM ankle. Housed in a sleek casing of carbon fiber and chrome is a dense nest of sensors and circuitry

Herr frames his research as a fight against the pain and frustration caused by underwhelming interfaces between humans and machines— a path that will lead to a world in which artificial limbs no longer chafe and bruise.

whelming interfaces between humans and machines—a path, he believes, that will lead to a world in which artificial limbs no longer chafe and bruise, and where quadriplegics might walk again.

"My personal experience underscored for me how poorly designed the world

that control an artificial calf muscle, actuated by a spring and a small electric motor. When the wearer steps down, the spring captures the potential energy; when she steps up, the motor gives a little boost. The device also measures things like walking speed and the angle

CAPTURE / A BIONIC MAN

of the heel strike; the on-board computer calculates what the ankle needs to do for each step.

The result is an elegant hybrid of the biological and mechanical that emulates the function of a flesh-and-bone calf. It is unprecedented in the field of prosthetics: With each step, the BiOM propels the user forward with a natural gait that an old-fashioned, nonautomated prosthetic could never reproduce.

BiOM users speak about the technology in rapturous terms. Former Marine William Gadsby, who lost his right leg in an ambush in Iraq in 2007, started wearing one after prolonged difficulties adapting to a traditional prosthetic. "To me, this guy, Dr. Herr, was an inspiration," Gadsby told *Smithsonian* magazine. "He wasn't sitting around, thinking, 'Gee, I wish they could come up with a better gadget.' He got those degrees so he could fix himself—and fix everyone else."

In Herr's vision, though, prosthetics like the BiOM are only a stepping stone to a broad meshing of man and machine. Though each unit is a sophisticated biomechanical apparatus—"I'm basically a bunch of nuts and bolts from the knees down," Herr said—its intelligence is essentially circumstantial. The BiOM uses sensors to detect a user's stride and react accordingly, but it is still fundamentally disconnected from its wearer's nervous system.

To design a hand more dextrous than any artisan's, or a foot stronger and more nimble than any ballerina's, that gap will need to be bridged, Herr says. New types of sensors will need to connect the human nervous system with the digital.

His team at MIT is looking into a number of strategies to accomplish that. One promising avenue, for example, involves growing nerves through synthetic tubes that use electrodes to pick up impulses directly from the nervous system.

Regardless of the specific tech that brings that bridge about, Herr is bullish on the concept's long-term feasibility. "Basically, if you know how to input and output information to peripheral nerves, you solve a whole long list of disabilities," he said.

Philosophically, it's part of a future Herr imagines in which extremely detailed data about the human body, nervous system, and environment will let us design objects customized for each specific individual. "Better design is going to be informed by a deep, deep understanding of the human being," Herr said. "In the future, every human will have a digital representation of themselves, and there will be quantitative design frameworks that use a digital body to design all kinds of things that humans use."

That's a formidable technical goal, but also an ethical one, since it would free people with nontypical bodies of all types from the irritation and discomfort of using things designed for the average body.

Herr leans back, absentmindedly tipping his chair onto its two rear legs.

One day, he said, he envisions "a seamless integration between the built world and our bodies. A world in which stuff actually works, stuff doesn't cause pain, stuff doesn't cause profound frustration."

The FitSocket uses an array of actuators to sense stiffness and softness in a limb in order to create more comfortable, better-fitting prosthetics.

CAPTURE / THE BIONIC MAN

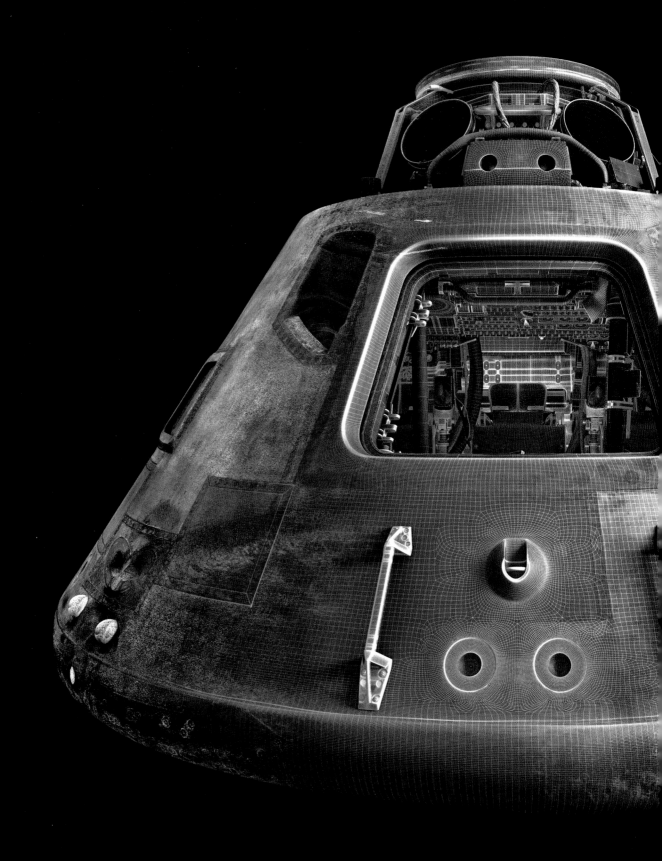

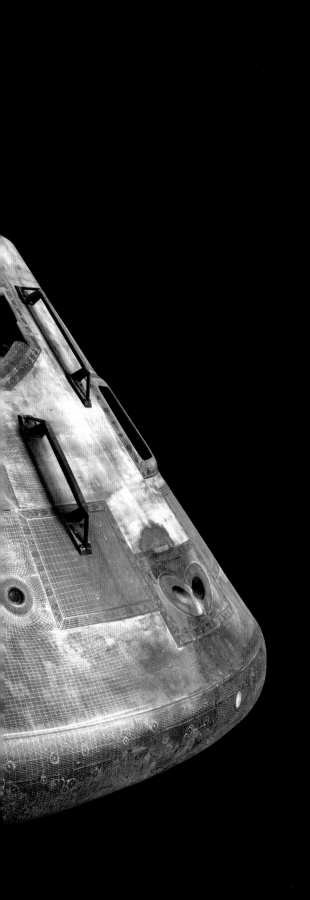

Re-creating Reality

Accessible, scalable 3D scanning is helping designers bridge the gap between the physical and the digital.

Once the domain of a scant few professionals, 3D scanning is about to become a way of life for the masses. Turns out we all have 3D scanners with us at all times, squirreled away in pockets and purses in the form of the cameras built into our smartphones. The sensors on today's handsets are better than those on standalone cameras you would have paid thousands of dollars for just a couple of years ago. Apps and cloud-based software can now stitch images from those cameras into highly detailed 3D scans.

This cheap and accessible scanning is going to revolutionize industries, and it's already happening with a few of them, according to Tatjana Dzambazova, a senior product manager at Autodesk and a "technology whisperer" with an innate understanding of the dramatic possibilities of tech. Dzambazova has seen the future, and that future has all of us making three-dimensional scans.

Photogrammetry—the practice of turning a collection of 2D still photos into a composite, 3D image through clever software—isn't new, she says. "What's new is that it actually works." For years, 3D scanning required nightmarishly complex and prohibitively expensive laser scanning systems. Photo-based scans have been possible for a few years, but resolution was so low that the finished products weren't usable for anything beyond crude digital models, or the equipment required such expertise that it was limited to researchers and a few skilled professionals. Now, says

Dzambazova, "photography is better, and the algorithms are better." Photo-based 3D scans can produce models in much more detail than was ever imaginable before, all at the push of a button.

These new, detailed scans help bridge the divide between the physical and the digital realms—allowing us to create more precise, realistic, and compelling digital experiences and models. And that is true for everyone—millions of users who can now use simple, scalable tools. Scanning is now often the first and most important step in the workflow that defines the future of making things. As a result, she says, "the entire world becomes clay in our hands."

This improved quality combined with simplicity is about to turn us all into scanning fiends. From Dzambazova's vantage point as the leader of the team that developed Autodesk's ReMake, she's watching it happen. Dzambazova's eyes light up and her voice quickens when she starts talking about some of the early and surprising uses of the phone-based 3D scanning tool.

Consider the raven. Thought to be the smartest bird in the world, raven populations have exploded in recent years—fiftyfold in some areas—due to the incredible bounty of food waste in our landfills. But well-fed ravens like to play, and, in deserts like the Mojave, they have found a new favorite plaything: baby tortoises. Specifically, they like to peck holes in the tortoises' shells, which are thin when they're young. As a result, the desert tortoise has become a threatened species.

A potential solution has come from a new company called Hardshell Labs, conservationist Bill Boarman, and 3D scanning. Hardshell Labs made high-res scans of baby tortoise shells, created a detailed digital model, and then 3D printed them in a plaster-like material. The plastic replicas look identical to the real thing, and Boarman took a handful of them as lures to known raven hangouts. He set up a video camera to see if a raven attacked and exactly what happened when it did. The resulting video showed a raven spending 10 minutes trying to peck its way through the dense plaster before giving up. Step two will be to use these lures to teach these intelligent birds to stop hunting tortoises altogether. A test project will use the shells to deliver an irritating liquid, nausea-inducing compound, or shock once a bird does peck through. The goal is to teach the ravens to look for greener pastures.

previous pages: The Smithsonian collaborated with Autodesk to scan the Apollo 11 Command Module; this composite image shows the process progressing from point cloud at left through finished 3D rendering at right. **opposite:** Tatjana Dzambazova, as seen in a portrait made by Factum Arte with its Veronica Chorographic scanner.

Photo-based 3D scans can produce models in much more detail than was ever imaginable before, all at the push of a button.

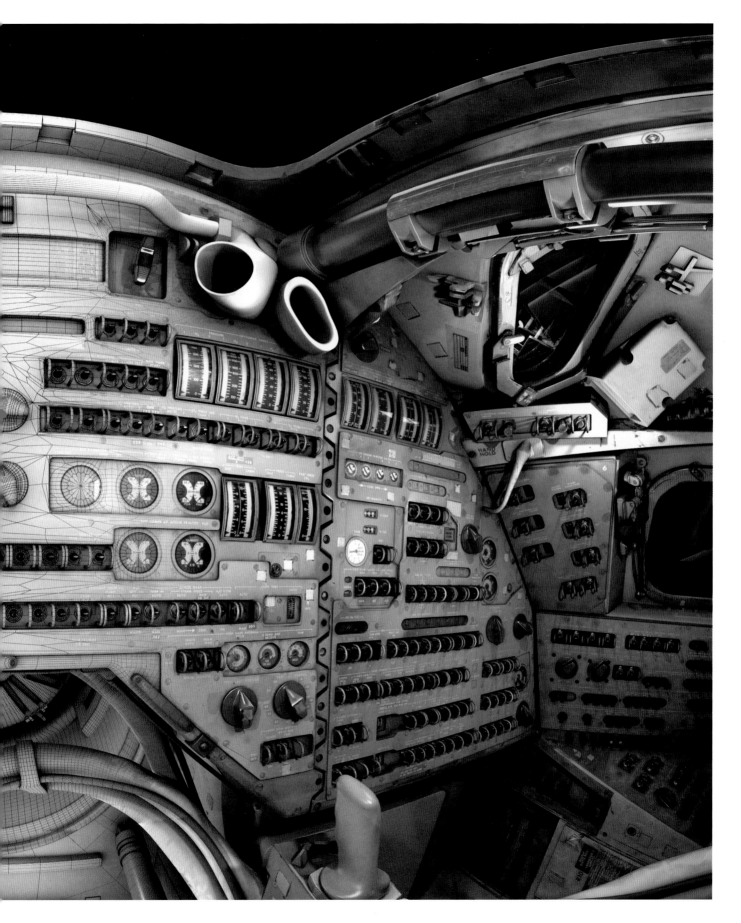

Build, scan, edit, print, and repeat. "Rip, fix, burn," Dzambazova says. "The line between the physical and digital world is starting to disappear."

"This was all incredibly easy," says Dzambazova, "using regular cameras, ReMake software, and a standard 3D printer—and the whole project was crowdfunded." If the broader program, involving dozens of the faux shells, is successful, the ultimate cost of protecting this threatened species will be negligible.

Dzambazova wasn't always a techie. She got her start working in architecture in Vienna, then jumped to Autodesk's London office, working as a product manager for cutting-edge initiatives before helping to found the company's consumer group, which was then a bold new market strategy for the company.

Many of her current customers can be found in the art world. One of them is Cosmo Wenman, an artist who has built a career around using photogrammetry to capture 3D models of existing artworks and make 3D prints from them. A copy of Michelangelo's *Pietà* doesn't have to be made of plastic 3D printing material. It can be finished in real metal or cast entirely in bronze or steel by making a wax mold of the 3D print. Prints can be made at any size and can be altered in software before they return to the analog world. By using Wenman's free online database of 3D scans, artists are able to show

us what famous but damaged artworks might have originally looked like. The *Venus de Milo*, for example, has been given her arms back. Other artists are making money by scanning present-day customers' heads and using software to mesh them onto classical statue bodies, then printing the resulting sculpture for the buyer.

Other artists still work with clay or other physical materials, creating a rough draft that can be scanned and manipulated in software. Once a design looks promising, the object can be printed, edited further, then scanned again until the design is finalized. "This kind of process could be the future of design; instead of starting from zero, you're starting from something," says Dzambazova. Build, scan, edit, print, and repeat. "Rip, fix, burn," she says. "The line between the physical and digital world is starting to disappear."

Scanning is opening up new avenues for museums to explore and expose their collections. Now, kids who cannot take a trip to see art and artifacts can simply fire up a Web browser and visit the Smithsonian Explorer, for instance, where the museum's archives are increasingly being deposited into a searchable database of 3D models. In June 2016, the institution debuted a new collaboration with Autodesk that

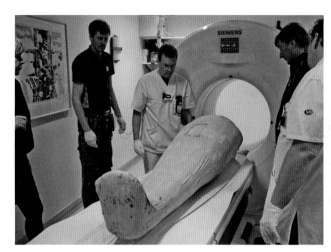

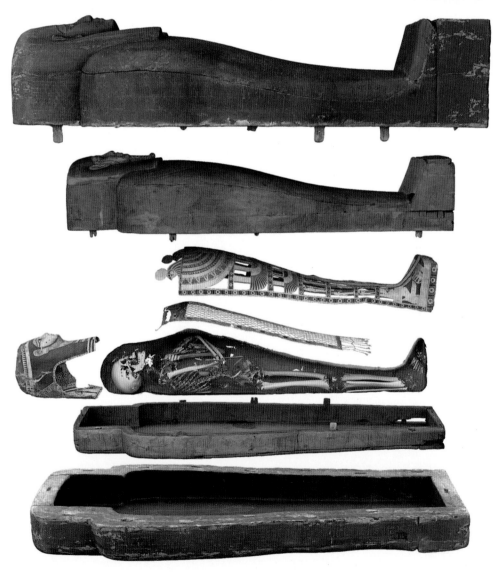

brought this access to a new level: an unprecedented scan of *Columbia*, the Command Module of the Apollo 11 mission to the moon. Some 50 high-resolution scans were converted into an explorable virtual-reality model that has brought the historic spacecraft to life. It also revealed details of the interior of the capsule that museum curators had never seen, such as "graffiti" and a hand-drawn calendar made by the astronauts. (The capsule has been protected behind Plexiglas for decades.)

At the Medelhavsmuseet museum in Stockholm, scanning has helped get around a unique problem in the world of archaeology. When the great Egyptian tombs were first opened and the sarcophagi of the pharaohs were discovered, "unwrapping mummies" quickly became a fascinating spectator sport. The problem is that an unwrapped mummy can't be put back together. Discovering what is inside the wrappings ultimately destroys the artifact.

The Medelhavsmuseet, technology partner Interspectral, and Dzambazova's team used a combination of technologies to preserve the mummy Neswaiu, an Egyptian priest. The exterior was scanned using photogrammetry, while the interior was scanned using medical-grade 3D CT scanning, revealing the layers of wrappings, skeleton, tissue, and various amulets that had been placed around the body during its mummification. A detailed 3D model was created by combining the scans. Now, visitors to the museum can virtually unwrap the mummy and see the various coffins in cross-section.

Here, too, scanning let curators see what had been invisible. More than 100 amulets were discovered wrapped up with the mummy; many of them were then converted to detailed digital models, 3D printed, and put on display.

Dzambazova apologizes in advance for the trite analogy before saying, "With 3D scanning we are building a time machine, able to capture the world in a way that 2D photography simply cannot."

The key is that the software has to be easy to use. Making scanning technology accessible to everyone is a major focus of Dzambazova's work, and she is confident that anyone can master ReMake with 20 minutes of training. "We want to eliminate the 'tech' from the process and make 3D a simple process. We have no excuse anymore to make software that makes you feel stupid," she says.

Scans, of course, are one thing, but Dzambazova also has a thing for the physical world. The ultimate goal of ReMake is to minimize interaction with the software and enable a return to real-world objects through 3D printing or CNC—objects that can be displayed, handled, or further developed through the "rip, fix, burn" flow. This is how history and art come alive. As Dzambazova says, "Life doesn't only happen in the computer."

Stockholm's Medelhavsmuseet and technology partner Interspectral used a CT scanner to explore inside its mummies; among the discoveries were amulets embedded inside. The scans were detailed enough to produce 3D-printed reproductions of the ancient jewelry.

Making Shade in Abu Dhabi

The Al Bahr Towers' adaptive facades reduce energy consumption while invoking architectural tradition.

The subtropical desert climate of the United Arab Emirates makes designing architecture that will keep humans comfortable a particularly daunting task. Temperatures in the summer months regularly top 110°F (44°C), and the sun doesn't quit, even in winter.

Since the Middle Ages, well-heeled Arab homes and palaces were outfitted with window lattices called *mashrabiya*, which let in air and some light while blocking much of the day's heat and protecting the interior from prying eyes. These geometric wooden lattices, sometimes lined with stained glass, are highly decorative as well as functional.

The Al Bahr Towers in Abu Dhabi have achieved high levels of energy efficiency with a high-tech take on the mashrabiya. An intricate network of folding screens suspended from the twin buildings' surfaces opens and closes based on the sun's position, minimizing energy use and maximizing user comfort. The building is smart, but the solution is surprisingly simple.

Architectural firm AHR designed the towers for the Abu Dhabi Investment Council and worked together with the global engineering firm Arup, which developed all of the engineering aspects of the design, including the revolutionary facades. The award-winning construction sits on the north shore of Abu Dhabi Island, overlooking the Eastern Mangroves development. The buildings' design merges environmental efficiency with cultural responsibility.

"It is an adaptive building—the shape and performance react according to the environment," says Giorgio Buffoni, an associate in the London facade engineering team at Arup. He was involved from the beginning of the facade design in 2007 through the building's opening in 2012.

This makes the Al Bahr Towers a high-profile, high-tech, and beautiful example of how buildings are taking advantage of the latest wave of sensors. The facade is operated by sun-tracking software that controls the opening and closing sequence according to the sun's position. Sensors also capture wind speed and solar radiation data to adjust the facade in cases of extreme winds or prolonged overcast conditions.

The towers are not alone in sensing and adapting to their environment.

"Smart buildings" and components have been in use for more than a decade, from the ubiquitous motion sensors that turn lighting on or off to Nest thermostats that learn from residents' heating needs to "people counters" that track how many and when people are using a space. And there are precedents for its big and ambitious adaptive skin. One of the most famous is the Institut du Monde Arabe (Arab World Institute), designed by Jean Nouvel and Architecture-Studio and built in Paris in the 1980s, which has a facade equipped with photosensitive apertures that also reference the intricate patterns of the Arab world.

Clusters of triangular screens on the Al Bahr Towers form the shape of large flowers blossoming across the two 26-story buildings. Precisely 2,098 facade units, each weighing 1.5 tons, are cantilevered 2.8 meters off the building's surface (to allow access for window cleaning and shading system

Al Bahr Towers is a high-profile and beautiful example of how buildings are taking advantage of the latest wave of sensors. The facade is operated by sun-tracking software that controls the opening and closing sequence.

maintenance). The shades are made of polytetrafluoroethylene (PTFE), essentially a Teflon-coated fiberglass fabric. The screens vary slightly in size because the towers are not perfectly cylindrical—the shapes of the towers are based on six tangential arcs taken from three intersecting circles, a traditional geometric pattern in the region.

As the sun rises in the east and sets in the west, a control system follows its path, gradually opening and closing the facade panels in response to its position and strength. An anemometer measuring wind speed and a solar radiation sensor on the top of the buildings can override the preset if there are extreme conditions. But the

"When we prepared our package there was a worry the project might be perceived as too risky by facade contractors," Buffoni says. But the winning contractor, Chinese firm Yuanda, was keenly interested in developing the groundbreaking system with Arup and AHR.

The towers themselves resemble palm tree trunks from afar—all sides of the towers are covered with external shading, with the exception of the north, which doesn't receive direct sunlight, and the very top of the tower, which has glazing with additional ceramic fritting. (One of the towers hosts three skygardens, which are also protected by the external shading.)

The facades were designed to operate in an aggressive environment: In addition to high temperatures and occasional high winds, the air is laden with sand, dust, and salt.

facades were designed to operate in an aggressive environment: In addition to high temperatures and occasional high winds, the air is laden with sand, dust, and salt. During the design phase of the project, Arup developed the specifications to be followed for off-site testing, where a full-scale shading unit was subject to 30,000 opening and closing cycles, equivalent to approximately 40 years of use.

Improving the internal comfort for the occupants—with a consequent reduction in energy use—was perhaps the biggest single challenge facing the design team. Buildings in the region are climate-controlled, and because of the year-round high solar radiation levels, most skyscrapers' glazing is heavily tinted or highly reflective, allowing little natural light into living and work spaces. "If the glass is dark, you have

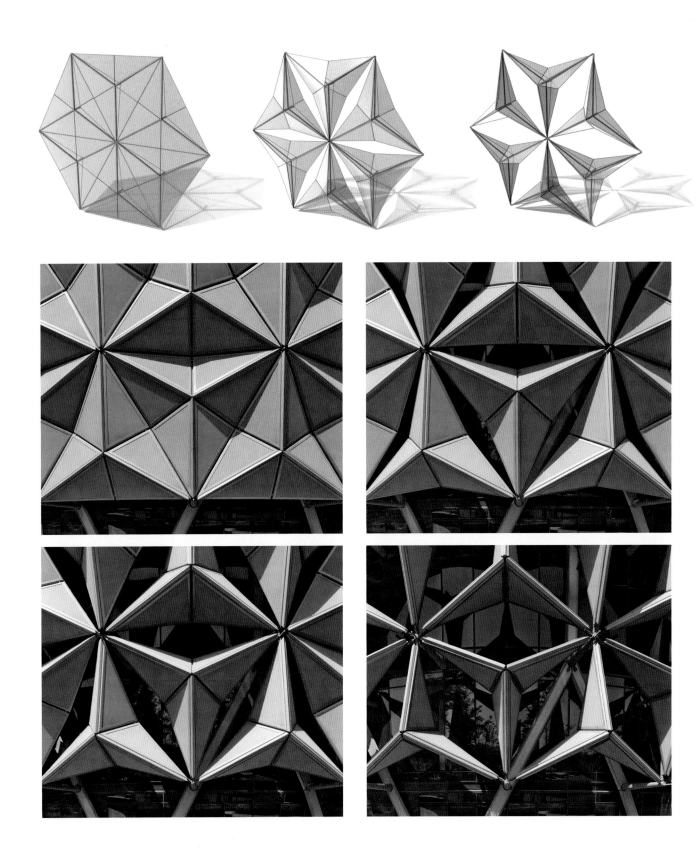

"If the glass is dark, you have to have your lights on all day, defeating the concept of a highly glazed building. A key driver in the design was minimizing the use of artificial light."

The mashrabiya (seen in early sketches at top) operate by sun-tracking software, which determines how much natural light enters the offices over the course of a day.

to have your lights on all day, defeating the concept of a highly glazed building," Buffoni says. "So a key driver in the design was a more natural view from the building and minimizing the use of artificial light."

The facades in the Al Bahr Towers were designed to reduce interior heat gain by 50 percent as compared with buildings of comparable size in the Middle East, and preliminary studies showed cost savings could be made on energy and subsequent reduction in cooling plant size.

The promise of smart buildings has yet to be realized, but perhaps this simpler take is the way to go. The more complex a system is, the more likely it is to break down. And if a building changes hands, manuals to the system can be lost, knowledge and training forgotten. "We know the system is robust and can deliver what we expect. It might not be the most clever, but it is robust," says Tim Casey, project manager at Arup.

"The sensor strategy was to minimize the level of complexity." And that embodies many of industrial designer Dieter Rams' 10 principles for good design: It is innovative, useful, long-lasting, and environmentally friendly; good design is as little design as possible.

The Age of Guessing Is Over

Sensors are already invisibly embedded into the things we make: buildings, cars, consumer electronics, toys, and industrial machinery. They will soon find themselves in furniture, infrastructure, clothing, medicine, food, and even our bodies. These will be upgraded versions of those we use today—smaller, sharper, lighter, and consuming less energy.

What can we expect these sensors to do? What will they record? If they measure our world in exquisite detail, at multiple scales, and record all that information, at costs that approach zero, what will this mean for manufacturing and building?

CAPTURE LEADS TO BETTER DESIGN

Smartphones will have embedded LiDAR capabilities, making it trivial to create accurate three-dimensional models of any object, large or small. Dedicated LiDAR scanners will be commodity items, making the act of digitizing a room, engine parts, or a person's hand as simple as taking a photograph. Sensors placed on moving parts, on doors, and on suspensions will provide ongoing information about the current use of things, informing designers on where improvements are needed.

Sensors will record human physiology, sensing eye movement, facial features, and body position, providing detailed information not only about how the person interacts with an environment, but also assessing how they feel. This data will inform what we should design to help people feel better, a new spin on human-centered design.

Advanced sensing will lead designers, architects, manufacturers, and builders to embrace data-driven techniques—becoming data scientists as well. These data-fluent makers will naturally shift from guessing about design goals to establishing measurable changes; from estimating constraints to knowing specific quantities; from working with approximations to having sampled reality. Intuition will not be replaced, it will be augmented.

CAPTURING FABRICATION LEADS TO EASIER MAKING

With sensors integrated into tools, machines will have accurate feedback to do better jobs and coordinate their operations more seamlessly. Current-generation jigsaws, for example, can project a laser beam to map out a cutting path, making it much easier for the operator to get a clean, smooth cut. Next-generation sensors will grace robots with better vision, hearing, and touch to make them more adaptive, responding to changes in a production line. Sensors are now mixed into poured concrete, initially to provide accurate information about curing, but ultimately to deliver continuous data about a building's stability and performance. While drones are now routinely used to monitor building sites, evaluating progress on a daily basis, construction site–specific sensors will soon record activities of workers and construction in real time.

CAPTURING OPERATION PRODUCES BETTER FEEDBACK CYCLES

Increasingly, sensors are being used not just during design and fabrication, but also embedded into products. These track everything from the health and well-being of users to heating and cooling to lighting and security. LED streetlights will not only illuminate our roads but also have the capability to record sound and video. The augmented and self-driving vehicles that will populate tomorrow's roads will use inexpensive LiDAR, which will feed the world's databases of up-to-date street views.

We can imagine a time when instrumentation will record how hundreds of people actually use a building—informing us how to design a new addition. We can envision a time when traffic routing software like Waze will help improve road designs. We can imagine a time when sensors will be embedded in roads to guide autonomous vehicles.

Perhaps our built environment will become more machine readable, just as standardized bar codes stream-lined the entire retail industry. Can we expect to have sensors built into roads and city infrastructure to guide autonomous navigation? Will clothing continually track our movements, encouraging better posture and healthy habits? Will there be standards of data?

Data exhaust—the information that can be gathered from (and is constantly produced by) an object's presence, state, and behavior—will routinely be used to inform what we have and how we make.

REAL DATA GIVES ACCURATE CONTEXT— BUT FORCES DESIGNERS TO THINK IN NEW WAYS

With increased sensing, designers will need to learn to manage information at scales they are not used to. Immersive and large displays including virtual and augmented reality devices will help us make sense of things. Machines will teach us to see what they see.

Though we can't fully predict the evolution of sensors, we can be sure that immense creativity will be applied to getting accurate, useful information about the world and the people in it. For making, better information means the possibility of better feedback, better designs, better methods of fabricating, and better outcomes.

We will soon live in a world of a trillion sensors. The implications are huge.

For makers at all levels of skill and operating at every range of complexity, sensors will be transformative. They will provide cheap, reliable pathways to bring accurate data about the physical world into the computable digital world. This will create the possibility to rethink and reframe the nature of physical products. Once instrumented, a product's full life cycle can be recorded. Designers have the real chance to shift from making inert things to producing flows of experiences and services, potentially transforming business models from owning products to using products as services to achieve a specific, measured result.

Today, sense-making is a kind of dance between seeing and questioning, feeling and speculating. As digitization continues to evolve, so will our ability to interact with it. Digital capturing will be more than assigning numbers to the world; it will also, quite literally, give us *different senses*, a feeling for the complexity, interconnection, and dynamism of the real world that we can tease apart, slow down, and perceive in ways we never could before.

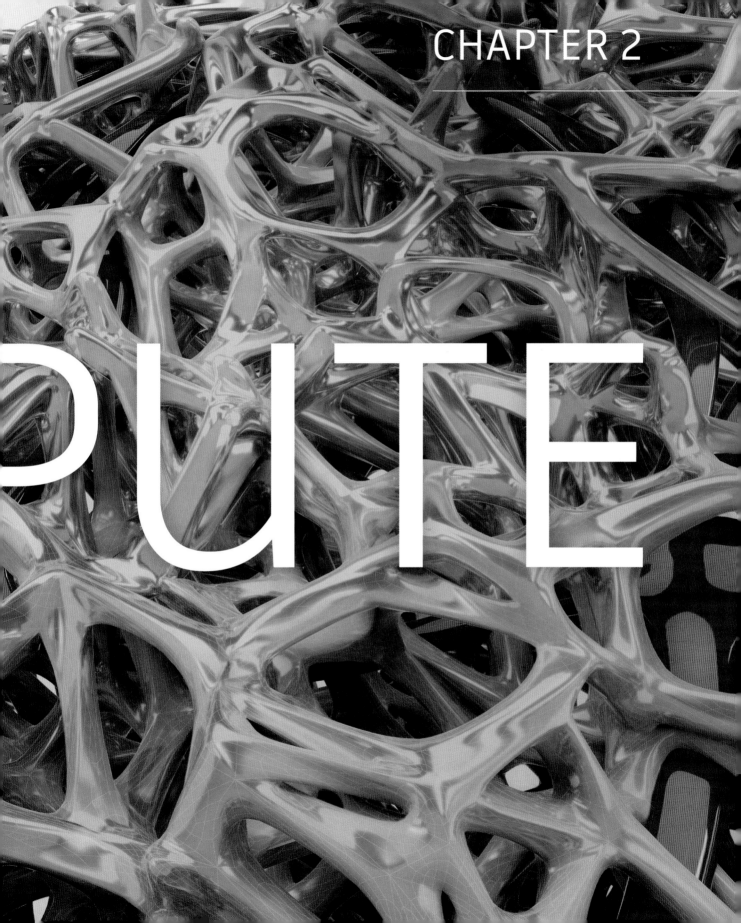

CHAPTER 2

With every surge in their capability, computers take another step from being passive servants to becoming active participants in our lives. Where software once let us document our work, it is now becoming our creative partner in designing, making, and operating what we produce. Computers are freeing us to do what we do best: figuring out *what* to make, while they figure out *how* to make.

Your smartphone contains more computational power than all of NASA had available when it sent astronauts to the moon. The space agency's most powerful mainframes, IBM's System/360 Model 75 computers, boasted one megabyte of memory. But that was enough to plan every step of the mission, run orbital simulations, and, amazingly, design and manage the construction of a 36-story spacecraft. On-board the spacecraft were Apollo Guidance Computers, which controlled navigation, life support, and propulsion systems for the missions. Those did their crucial jobs with just 64K of RAM.

Those computers were designed before the exponential computing growth predicted by Moore's Law really took off. (See "Evolution of Computing," page 90.) Thanks to the constant innovation that has gone into microprocessors since, your phone executes instructions over 100 million times faster than NASA's mainframes back then.

Remarkable as this leap is, the bigger story is what happens when our computers—our smartphones, tablets, laptops, desktops, and the larger systems that power big companies—connect to the vast global network of other computers. Your phone is a portal into a vast world of collaboration and of almost unlimited computation.

What has this produced? Instant global communication. Connections with hundreds or thousands of friends. Global collaboration in real time. Computers that outperform the world's finest human *Jeopardy!* and Go champions. And, now, the ability to design and make just about anything.

THE EVOLUTION OF COMPUTABLE DESIGN

Computers are the most powerful tools ever created because they can mimic virtually any other kind of tool. They are calculators, typewriters, telephones, fax machines, audio and video recorders, paint-brushes, darkrooms, television sets. And they have systematically replaced the traditional tools of design, architecture, engineering, and other creative fields with the digital tools of computer-aided design (CAD).

The act of designing is often the act of creating prototypes, which make ideas visible and help designers figure out the best thing to make—and the best way to make it:

What does it look like? is explored by sketches and models.
How does it feel in the hand? is explored by milled objects made from different materials.
How will we make it? is planned out by producing small manufacturing lines.
Will our customers buy it? is answered by producing small batches and seeding a market.
Will it withstand an earthquake or hurricane? is determined by structural simulation.
How will the plastic flow through a mold and cool? can be answered by complex fluid-dynamics simulations.

Over the past 30 years, each spike in computational power has brought with it new ways to prototype. The first era of CAD mimicked drafting, documenting pen drawings, sketches, and blueprints. The second era duplicated model making: Three-dimensional objects could be constructed, rotated, and disassembled. The third era added physical properties to these models, which could be used in simulations: Change one quantity or quality in a model and the new properties flowed through the entire system.

With each of these tools, computers didn't actually aid design. They aided documentation. The design was, for the most part, still in the imagination of the designer. The computer would need to be instructed to represent the idea from imagination into a machine-readable form.

THE AGE OF LEARNING
The fourth age of CAD has begun—not coincidentally, alongside the dawn of the fourth industrial revolution. It is the era of machine learning, and it marks a major inflection point—for computing, for design, and for humans, as we grapple with how to work with devices that exhibit real intelligence. Machine learning combines a range of algorithms, pattern recognition, neural networks, generative design, artificial intelligence, and distributed computation to change how we make things.

The age of learning is already playing out in several ways. First, digital simulations are becoming exponentially more complex, larger, and more interconnected. Imagine a simulation of a modern car engine. An algorithm can seek to improve efficiencies by starting with one part and making changes to other parts. Start by making a piston lighter. That allows its return spring to be thinner. Which means the connecting shaft can be shorter. Which affects the bearings. And so on. Cumulative improvements cascade through the whole system, leading to the entire engine's weight shrinking by half.

Second, design tools can now come up with creative ideas on their own. In generative design, you tell the computer what you want to achieve—your goals and constraints. The computer then explores the solution space, optimizing for the parameters you think are most valuable, to create thousands or even millions of potential designs (and helps select the most suitable). Human designers could never work in such quantity—and in some cases, the computer discovers ideas that a human might never consider.

Third, algorithms are beginning to understand. They are learning by applying neural networks to learn the qualities of desired outcomes and produce designs that realize that goal. Show a machine-learning algorithm examples of Rembrandt paintings, for example, and it can credibly produce a never-before-seen "Rembrandt" portrait. Show it examples of how to build a Lego structure using a robot, and it will figure out how to direct the robot to make a new Lego structure. Show it ways to make appliances more efficiently, and it will create better manufacturing lines. Show it examples of a product successfully performing in its marketplace, and it will recommend better designs and materials.

This might seem like science fiction. But as Marc Andreessen observed, "software is eating the world." The more computable something is, the more it will be improved and optimized as algorithms seek value.

As algorithms advance, they abstract complexity out of many steps of design and making into simpler actions. Algorithms reduce the number of steps to design something by allowing designers to focus on the bigger picture.

ENERGY

How much power does a process consume? The lower the energy, the more affordable operations are.

CONNECTION

How quickly can one processor connect to another? Faster connections mean better communication.

SPEED

At what rate can information be processed? Faster processing means faster calculations.

Evolution of Computing

As Moore's Law predicted, for more than 40 years we have produced faster, cheaper, and more efficient processors. Now, as we connect them together in vast distributed networks, the computing power we can access continues to grow exponentially. With each step in order of magnitude, the nature of computing has jumped into a new class of cognition.

Combining faster processors (that can help design and build even faster ones), connected computers (that further magnify and distribute computation), and intelligent algorithms (that promote machine learning) sets the stage for computers to enter a new, creative relationship with humans.

INTEL PROCESSOR SPEEDS

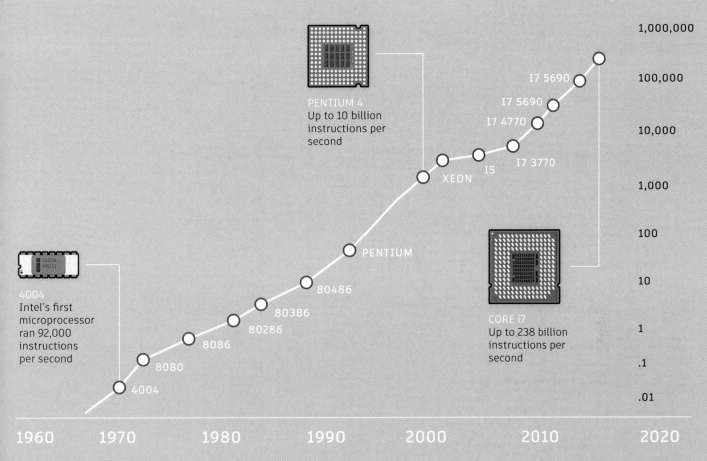

PENTIUM 4
Up to 10 billion
instructions per
second

I7 5690

I7 5690

I7 4770

XEON

I5

I7 3770

PENTIUM

80486

80386

80286

8086

8080

4004

4004
Intel's first
microprocessor
ran 92,000
instructions
per second

CORE i7
Up to 238 billion
instructions per
second

1,000,000

100,000

10,000

1,000

100

10

1

.1

.01

1960   1970   1980   1990   2000   2010   2020

COMPUTING & DESIGN

DRAWING

The first commercial
computer-aided design
system was developed by
French engineer Pierre Bezier
in 1966. It ran on mainframe
computers and could
manipulate simple shapes—
lines, arcs, circles, rectangles,
and a class of curves called
B-splines. When combined,
the pieces became complex
schematic diagrams of
machine parts, assemblies, or
entire vehicles.

MODELING

Two decades and an order of
computing magnitude later, CAD
entered a second age, adding a
third dimension. Machine parts
were represented as fully
realistic, three-dimensional
objects. Now affordable for
professionals and running on
commodity hardware, CAD
infused architecture, engineering,
and construction as well as
manufacturing.

SIMULATION

As computing power reached
a new level, CAD could process
deeper levels of abstraction.
Physical properties such as
weight, stress tolerance, torque,
cost, origin, transparency, or
thermal properties, among
others, could be analyzed and
simulated. New algorithms
figured out how digital objects
interrelated and affected each
other. This concept of a "digital
twin" allowed work such as
crash testing and building
simulation.

LEARNING

The fourth age of CAD is
founded on machine learning,
a blend of pattern recognition,
neural networks, and distributed
computation. Computers are
shifting from being passive
representation tools to creative
partners that help us explore
and make design decisions. With
the help of powerful computing
networks, designers can
optimize not just single designs,
but entire systems.

Making Connections

Computational BIM brings order to design complexity in massive architectural projects.

Building information modeling, or BIM, has been around since the 1980s. The strategy of maintaining a database of all of a structure's components and capabilities lets anyone making decisions about the building know exactly what they're working with. The shared knowledge resource is designed to help from conception to demolition, making replacements, upgrades, and tweaks to a structure more easily achieved.

BIM was made possible by the rise of personal computers, and as computing power has exponentially grown, the practice is evolving. Building information models that were once simple spreadsheets can now be rendered in 3D or even 5D—adding cost and time to the physical dimensions of width, height, and depth. Now, the next generation of the technique, called "computational BIM," is allowing architects and engineers to more easily optimize buildings' design and construction for any number of goals—perhaps calculating cost savings from energy use based on optimizing a design for natural light. Sometimes called "parametric BIM," it's the next step toward generative design, turning the database into a design collaborator.

"You always build models to answer questions of some sort," says Matt Jezyk, senior product line manager for AEC Conceptual Design Products at Autodesk. "How tall or wide is this thing? How long will it take to construct? How much will it cost? But those are static representations, and if you need to change something, you have to start over again." Jezyk is one of the founders of computational BIM tool Revit, which became part of the Autodesk family in 2002.

With tools such as computational BIM, making one change automatically updates the entire system, letting you quickly compare options. You can add behaviors and logic to the components of a building information model, modifying the software to make it do what you want it to. "You're building a system that has a set of things you care about in it," Jezyk says. "It's like a sandbox you've constructed: You can do whatever you want as long as you stay inside the sandbox."

Sometimes computational BIM will answer questions you didn't even know to ask and that previously would have been impossible to ask. The Shanghai Tower, designed by SOM and featured in Autodesk's 2011 book, *Imagine, Design, Create*, twists 120 degrees with a 55 percent taper to reduce wind shear. The architects determined that was the optimal design to reduce wind shear by using computational BIM to test myriad possible options.

"In the past it would have required making a physical model and sticking it in a wind tunnel and evaluating it," Jezyk says. "Now you can have a designer simulate the virtual wind and tell the computer, find me the best option." And that option reduced wind loads by 24 percent and material costs by $58 million.

It's not just about creating a building faster or cheaper; more and more, computational BIM is being used to measure quality, especially for massive projects—such as international airports.

AN AIRPORT FIT FOR A QUEEN

When Foster + Partners started working on the design for the Queen Alia International Airport, in Amman, Jordan, in the early 2000s, computational BIM software didn't yet have the capabilities they needed, so they built custom software to design the groundbreaking roof themselves.

That's not unusual for them: The Applied Research + Development Group (ARD) at London-based Foster + Partners is a crack team of architects,

previous pages: The roof of the Queen Alia International Airport was inspired by the canopies of Bedouin tents. opposite top: The complex roof is made up of more than 80 separate domes. opposite bottom: BIM software helps conceive of a building as data as well as an architectural plan or model.

It's not just about creating a building faster or cheaper; more and more, computational BIM is being used to measure quality, especially for massive projects—such as international airports.

HOW IT WORKS: DYNAMO

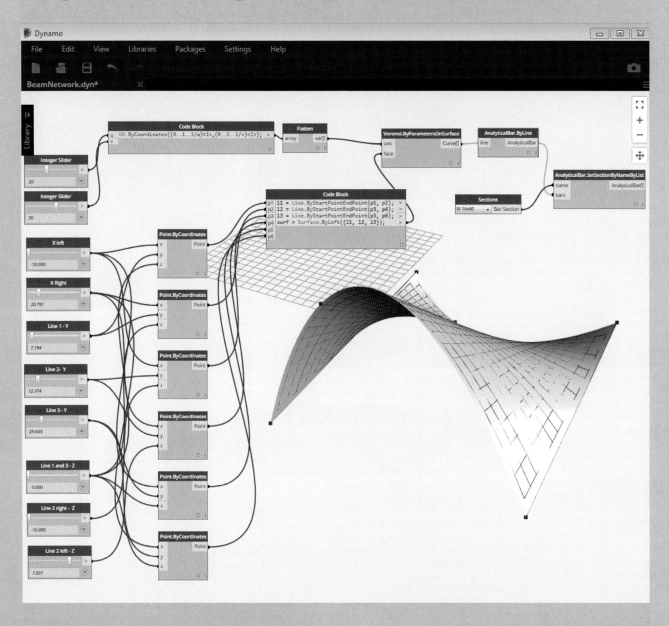

Early computational design began with equations and programming scripts. As 3D models became more complex, and as the desire for real-time interactivity took hold, visual programming languages such as Dynamo, which works with Revit and other software, have made computational design more accessible and more powerful. Designers connect "nodes," which can be simple or complex operations, via "wires" that define relationships. All can be adjusted to quickly create and iterate design solutions in real time, and to explore multiple ideas.

engineers, mathematicians, and computer scientists. Led by Francis Aish, an aeronautical engineer by training, ARD is essentially an in-house consultancy that solves unusual problems for any project that needs help, and their expertise is especially called for when working on groundbreaking projects.

With design inspired by Bedouin tents and traditional Arabic geometry, the tessellated concrete roof of the Queen Alia International Airport is made up of many shallow domes. Open-air courtyards on either side of the main terminal provide respite for travelers, and pools reflect sunlight into the building while naturally cooling the air. From the inside, the broad canopy of domes seems to sprout from palm-like soffits, and split beams let in natural light.

Initially, the concrete domes were each going to be produced in whole, but the team quickly realized the quality-control problems that could arise from casting giant glazed domes, each with a radius of 26.7 meters. So the domes were broken down into their most basic parts: eight component pieces for a dome, plus more pieces for edges, cones, and corners. Every one of these components was built in the system as a parametric design, and as the team worked on the tessellated roof, "any single change on the model would propagate from a single module to the entire airport and be followed by an automatic process to produce directly to the drawing sections," says ARD partner Martha Tsigkari, who was responsible for the modeling and automatic updating of the roof.

The new terminal of Queen Alia International Airport, completed in 2013, and the second expansion, completed in 2016, have raised the traffic capacity from 3.5 million to more than 12 million passengers per year, with the potential for further expansions.

Computational BIM software's high-tech output isn't yet the standard, and the construction industry is slow to adapt. "We work all over the world, and there is a wide range of contractor skills. Not all contractors can work with 3D drawings," Aish says. "One for the Queen Alia airport only worked with 2D drawings."

Associate partner Adam Davis did a lot of the underlying work to transform the information from the Queen Alia airport model to the drawings required by the fabricators. "We weren't just producing sections at right angles, but dozens of radial profiles to ensure the curvature of the domes and arches was properly realized. Our software had to understand how to annotate drawings differently depending on the shape of the profiles," he says.

"The drawing extraction is something people take for granted now," Tsigkari says. "Back then it was a hard exercise to make that happen."

Computational BIM has been a tool in ARD's shed for many years, so the team is acutely aware of its progress. "What's changed is that software can compile them in a more digestible format. And that is very empowering and game-changing in many situations," Tsigkari says. She works closely with software vendors to give feedback and beta-test new products; everyone on the ARD team is also a programmer, capable of tweaking software products to make the tools they need. "BIM is not in its infancy, but it's still a teenager. It can do a lot of things and allows for flexibility, but it has not matured yet to what we would like to see."

Foster + Partners is in a good place to influence the future of computational BIM and parametric design. "There's a huge opportunity to close the loop—the building process doesn't end when you hand over the keys. It has to be designed for reuse. We have to look at the entire lifecycle of a building," Aish says. "At the end of the day, it's all about the experience of the people using the building."

And it's about avoiding obsolescence: "A government building has a lifespan of a quarter of a millennium," Aish says. He says they need long-term software stability and open-data formats to maintain crucial information over long periods of time. Using computational BIM to build a nuclear power plant today is fine, but you have to be certain that future engineers will be able to access the data when the time comes to decommission it.

TAKING OFF FOR THE FUTURE

Around the world, Foster + Partners is working on the new international airport in Mexico City, a 470,000-square-meter structure massive even by aeronautical standards.

Like the Queen Alia International Airport, the idea is to use natural light and cooling methods to cut down on energy costs and integrate with the local environment. The entire terminal will be enclosed in a lightweight glass-and-steel shell that looks as if it could take flight itself. The ARD team is using custom scripts and translating the entire spaceframe and cladding system back into Microstation and Revit via VBA and Dynamo, respectively, with the help of bespoke databases.

The shape of the roof is inspired by the perfect tension of a hanging chain. The roof is supported by 21 funnel-shaped columns, creating a smooth distribution of forces. The finished roof structure will harness rainwater and solar energy to achieve LEED Platinum status.

More than 200 people are working on the Mexico City airport's design, which is complicated by the region's soft soil and propensity for earthquakes. Tsigkari leads a team of four working on the development of the spaceframe, and has worked with the design team since the competition. Construction on what Foster + Partners aims to make the most sustainable airport in the world began in 2016 and is set to be completed by 2020.

Existing computational BIM tools still aren't powerful enough to handle the entire Mexico City airport, Aish reports, so they're using a number of tools. "A lot of BIM tools are designed for standard-sized and -shaped

The domes were broken down to 8 basic parts to facilitate their construction; using BIM meant that any change to any component propagated to the whole airport.

"There's a huge opportunity to close the loop—the building process doesn't end when you hand over the keys. We have to look at the entire lifecycle."

"Sometimes there's an answer that works that you never would have come up with. It's not just a pet; it's an active contributor."

buildings," he says. "But unfortunately a lot of our buildings are more complex or larger or both."

Generative design programs such as computational BIM tools are getting smarter, and people who work with the programs are making them better every day. "When you're working with these computer systems, they come up with answers you wouldn't expect. Sometimes there's an answer that works that you never would have come up with," Jezyk says. "It's not just a pet; it's an active contributor."

Will computational BIM ever replace the expertise of engineers and architects? It's highly unlikely. "Traditionally, in any practice, like engineering or design or architecture, there's the master and the apprentice," Jezyk says. And the time-honored tradition of learning from an expert by working with them is ingrained in those professions. "Sometimes there are so many things that are kind of latent knowledge that you can't really articulate. The guy just knows, if you do it this way, it will work.

Experts know how to solve an optimization problem in their head because they have done it 50 times."

For all of its usefulness, Aish warns against putting too much stock in computational BIM. "We're in the business of producing elegant buildings. And we've delivered great buildings with pen and paper," he says. "These tools can be very transformational. But they shouldn't be overhyped. Tools allow us to do very interesting things, but they're not magically going to solve all the problems for you. You still need to be a good designer."

The Power to Enable Play

At Bjarke Ingels Group, computational power is allowing for more playful designs that push the boundaries of performance.

In our technology-saturated world, the human factor helps to edit, distill, and ultimately choose one path over the other. People still count for something. Will technology always rely on humans in this way? That's the million-dollar question, says Daniel Sundlin, a partner at Copenhagen- and New York-based architecture firm Bjarke Ingels Group, or BIG. But whether humans or machines are making the decisions, Sundlin draws a parallel to biological evolution in BIG's work: It's not the strongest species (or office) that survives; it's the one that's most adaptable.

A portfolio of nimble, diverse solutions to a host of challenges shows just how well BIG can adapt, gaining international recognition by balancing playfulness and performance. The BIG team encompasses 30 different nationalities, and that mix of BIGsters, as they're known internally, ensures no member ever has a default position—each project group represents many different perspectives so that the culture and the ideas never stop evolving. These diverse teams very quickly navigate the divide between a wealth of data and the more important asset of knowledge. "What I love about BIG," says Sundlin, "is we gather a lot of information,

Technology plays a fundamental role at BIG. "Ultimately, the creative solution most likely will depend on creative technology."

but in the end it's the group of people that puts together unexpected things."

The firm's approach is designed to create more questions than answers, at least at first. Bjarke Ingels, the firm's founder and creative partner, has compared this strategy to an architectural game of Twister, in which each new instruction (or performance goal) leads the players to stretch into a new, unconventional shape. But each contortion has its purpose, allowing perceived constraints to instead become creative wellsprings that result in new ideas.

This lighthearted, paradigm-bending approach has become BIG's defining ethos. One example: In 2018, the firm expects to finish work on a power plant designed to transform the idea of what a public utility plant can be. The Amager Resource Center in the center of Copenhagen will turn trash into energy, and the smoke coming from the plant's chimney will be completely nontoxic. The BIG twist: When smoke is released, it will puff into the air in mesmerizing rings each time the center produces a ton of carbon dioxide—a reminder to residents of their responsibility to reduce their environmental footprints. Part civic statement, part art piece, and part public park, the plant's sloping rooftop will double as a ski and hiking slope for topography-seeking Danes.

Other BIG projects, yet unrealized, show promise for transforming not just architecture but whole cities. The firm's team recently won a competition to find solutions for protecting the New York City waterfront from damage like it saw during 2012's Hurricane Sandy disaster, with three flood-prevention zones that would add more than 10 miles of public space while shielding residents from future floodwaters.

Technology plays a fundamental role in allowing the firm to disrupt the status quo. "Ultimately, the creative solution most likely will depend on creative technology to be executed," says Sundlin. Three types of "creative" digital tools come into play at BIG: those that generate designs, those that evaluate those designs, and those that communicate all of the visual parts of a design. By using all three of these in concert, the team can generate solutions at a rapid pace, see if those can meet the performance goals, then discuss the resulting options. This process allows ideas that might have once seemed far-fetched to adapt and evolve into viable solutions faster than ever before.

But an instrument, whether a violin or a parametric modeling system, is only as good as the hand of its musician. While it's easy to be mesmerized by new technologies and software, BIG seeks a healthy balance between how they do things and why they do things. The ultimate goal is a unique solution that rises out of hard-and-fast parameters for performance, budget, and function. The architects establish these criteria first, allowing technology to then become integral to the creative process by producing a wealth of options that can all meet the underlying requirements. "We are incorporating more and more performance-evaluating software earlier on in the design process," says Sundlin. "You could say that the design becomes more informed." In this way, creativity and decision-making become an educated, crowdsourced process—and not just the work of a few leaders. The team works best when it has an abundance of information to analyze, pushing its playful trial-and-error process to its limits, crossbreeding pop culture with history and team experience to generate and then select unexpected solutions.

With a reputation for exceeding its clients' wildest dreams, BIG may have finally met its creative match in Google, for whom they are designing a new campus in Mountain View, California, in partnership with London-based Heatherwick Studio. Ingels credits Google (whose official name changed to Alphabet since the project began) for having a much more far-reaching vision and appetite for creativity than many clients. The two firms' job, he said when the project was unveiled, "rather than trying to stretch everyone's imagination, [is] actually trying to land someone's imagination in a way that would be buildable and doable."

The headquarters will be a redevelopment of four sites, with the goal of creating a community-focused plan that re-creates the Northern California landscape both outside and inside the campus buildings. Google's design brief was essentially a question: How can we create acclimatized transparent structures for thousands of people to work and perhaps live in?

"How will we work five years from now? How will we work 15 or 20 years from now?" asked Google vice president of real estate Dave Radcliffe. "We don't know what it's going to be, but know it just needs to be this incredibly flexible space for it to work."

In models and mockups for the Google headquarters, every piece seems to have an inherent elasticity and modularity—again, imagine a game of Twister, where each new constraint produces a radical, but ultimately practical, form. In renderings, traditional facades have been dissolved into an ultralight transparent membrane, a glass fabric draped over landscapes and villages.

Copenhagen's Amager Resource Center—a waste-to-energy plant—will puff out a giant smoke ring when it produces one ton of carbon dioxide; its angled roof supports a ski slope.

The team works best when it has an abundance of information to analyze, pushing its playful trial-and-error process to its limits.

COMPUTE / THE POWER TO ENABLE PLAY

While adapting a standard brick-and-mortar structure from office space into a new use, like an automotive or biotech facility, would take years, this structure anticipates reconfiguration without the use of new materials—increasingly important as Google moves from the digital realm into the physical world of driverless cars, smart glasses, and balloon-powered Internet.

The BIG team began the design process investigating materials and technologies that could support the domelike structures they envisioned. Modeling showed that the large scale of the dome itself would not mitigate heat gain (the upper floors would have been uninhabitable), so they began to investigate shading systems. With the performance goal of shading a certain amount of the interior, the firm's facade engineers began to explore how

light for people and plants and shade to prevent glare on computer screens.

The building's entire structure will act as a flexible platform, allowing technology to be updated over time. For example, the entire roof canopy will be covered with standardized solar panels mounted like scales, allowing parts or entire segments to be replaced without ripping out the supporting system. The roof structure itself is separate from the interior floors, allowing for true internal flexibility—employees could start new labs, have families on-campus, or launch things into space in the future, and the building's modules would transform to support all of it.

BIG's team has been honing ideas of design-driven performance for years. For the design of a solar panel research facility in South Korea, for example, the building's bulk was restricted to a

BIG's facade engineers began to explore how creative they could be with a shading solution.

creative they could be with a shading solution. What if the shades could be deployed with motors? They developed parametric tools to calculate how many of the shading-system motors might fail, and with what frequency. That modeling made it clear that maintenance would become an overriding concern with an operable system, so BIG began to model a more opaque design with openings and overhangs for daylight and glare control. Currently, they are working to simulate the size of these openings to find a perfect balance between interior

rounded rectangular volume. Since the building was about harnessing solar energy, BIG began to research a design that would maximize solar shading efficiency at any given point on the facade. The team scripted a parametric model that positioned louvers at optimal shading angles, depending on the orientation of the facade. The resulting pattern turned out to look much like a fingerprint. In this way, establishing performance criteria leads to an unconventional form, one for which uniqueness and function are inextricable.

Establishing performance criteria can lead to an unconventional form, one for which uniqueness and function are inextricable.

Out of this kind of project has grown BIG Ideas, a product incubator and technology-simulation lab that will continue to support the firm's work, as only outside consultants could have done in the past. One aspect of the lab's work focuses on designing high-tech tools for environmental analysis, allowing them to speed up the feedback loop between design and analysis for the entire firm. By controlling simulations for everything from daylight to air- and traffic-flow patterns, BIG's projects are increasingly shaped by the forces surrounding them. Other BIG Ideas projects focus on the smallest details, generating designs for products like urban furniture when BIG doesn't find what it wants in off-the-shelf offerings. Currently, the firm is collaborating with the Danish Technical University and the Raket Madsen lab to create the never-before-attempted smoke-ring generator for the Copenhagen power plant.

Sundlin is quick to point out that data supports the firm's approach only as well as it can be interpreted. "Imprecise results and complicated explanations often result in conservative conclusions and missed opportunities," he says. What are the goals for the tools they're developing with BIG Ideas? It's a question the firm is asking every day, he says.

Even with every digital tool at their disposal, Sundlin believes balancing computer-generated models with physical ones is crucial for communicating architecture. With laser cutters and 3D printers, whole cities of ideas can be built and considered in a matter of hours or days. The entire team, and the client, can see the way the light bounces from a model's angles, and perceive scale in a new way. There is still no replacement for the creative spark of gathering together a group, the thing that sets every other calculation in motion.

A rendering of the Google campus shows the roof membranes; the goal was to create a flexible space that can change over the coming decades.

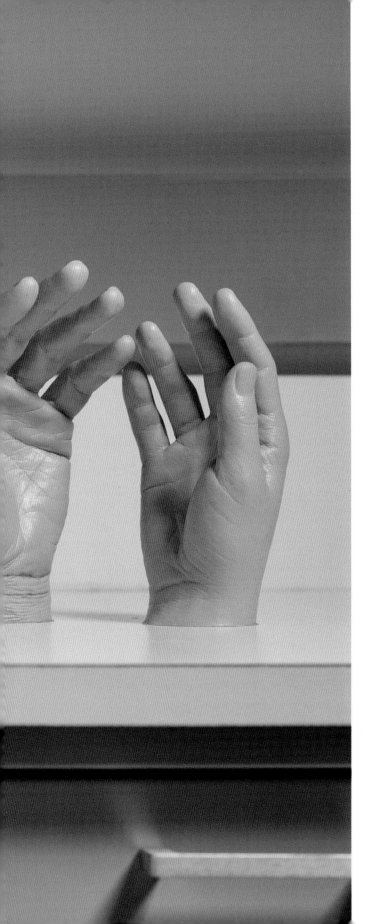

The Upper Hand

Consumer hand simulations are shaping the future of product design at Procter & Gamble.

Designing a product that 1 billion people will touch takes a lot of work. Consider Procter & Gamble, the world leader in consumer packaged goods, which claims an audience of 5 billion people worldwide. People have to use their hands to interact with any product they make, whether it's twisting a cap, squeezing a bottle, or flipping a top. But humans come in all shapes and sizes. Just consider the difference in hand strength between an elderly woman and a young, male rock climber, and all the capabilities in between. How do you ensure that a huge, diverse audience will be able to use what you make?

P&G's first patent was granted in 1841, and the company has continued to pursue innovation in its products as well as their delivery and packaging. In the last decade, though, P&G's rate of innovation in packaging has become exponential. That's because it is now possible to test products virtually on a wide range of hands, turning what used to be years of prototyping and consumer testing into a few days' work.

The new ability to conduct complex simulations of human physiology is also transforming how products are designed. While the human brain can only consider three or four variables at a time, computers can handle dozens of variables simultaneously, consider combinations that most people would never be able to get to, and return insights that would be otherwise impossible to generate. At P&G and other companies embracing simulation as a crucial stage of design, this computing power allows them to consider a huge number of variables and test hundreds or thousands of design iterations in order to find the best solution for consumers.

"It would be impossible to find and engage 1,000 people of different strengths, ages, and weaknesses to test out a bottle," says Mark Meili, research and design director of P&G's Modeling and Simulation Global Capability Organization. The company has been interested in virtual simulations since the 1990s, but it wasn't a practical endeavor until computers became faster and cheaper in the 2000s. Formed about eight years ago, the Modeling and Simulation team now includes about 40 engineers, biomedical experts, computational chemists, and biologists, all making products easier for consumers to interact with.

The hub of P&G's global packaging development force works in the Beckett Ridge building in suburban Cincinnati. And within the modeling and simulation team, says Meili, "Lauren Banzhaf is the hand-modeling and ergonomic expert in all of P&G."

In a two-person office in the heart of the Beckett Ridge building, Banzhaf shares an office with another senior scientist, Gary Gross, and a skeleton wearing a cowboy hat and Mardi Gras beads. On her desk are six latex casts of hands that represent a range of sizes.

The hand, so vital to accessing the products P&G makes, is incredibly complex, with 27 bones and dozens of muscles, tendons, and joints. "In the modeling realm, the hand remains one of the most underrepresented areas for development because it's incredibly hard," Gross says. "There are great models of the human heart, human

joints, spine, foot, but not the hand. Hand modeling is in its infancy compared to where we want to take it."

Banzhaf's title is senior scientist/engineer for virtual consumer biomechanics, and although she spends much of her time at the computer, she also works closely with the consumer testing teams. She's a biomedical engineer by training, with a heavy side of industrial design. The main tool in her belt is SantosHuman's digital human modeling environment, a biomechanics simulator that grew out of the University of Iowa's Virtual Soldier Research program, the gold standard in predictive posture modeling. Banzhaf can drop in a CAD prototype of a product and select a virtual consumer to interact with it, assigning a goal such as pouring or lifting. Then she can watch how the posture changes and measure the joint torque to determine if one product is easier to use than another.

The Modeling and Simulation team wants to eventually have the hand fully modeled in terms of the skin as well as kinetics to determine how a grip changes the surface of the skin and even to predict feelings of softness or texture or discomfort.

Human-product interactions can take many forms: picking it up, flipping a cap, squeezing, pouring, turning a cap, pulling the trigger on a sprayer. The software simulates in real time the interactions of consumers of different sizes, strengths, genders, and other variables. "Rather than having to get the consumers in the building who match the exact hand sizes, we build models to test with," she says. Hand sizes, finger length, muscle strength—all of these variables differ by age, gender, and world region. "We're designing for

previous pages: Six latex models represent various hand sizes of P&G consumers. **opposite:** Using SantosHuman software, P&G can simulate hundreds of hands of different strengths, ages, and sizes.

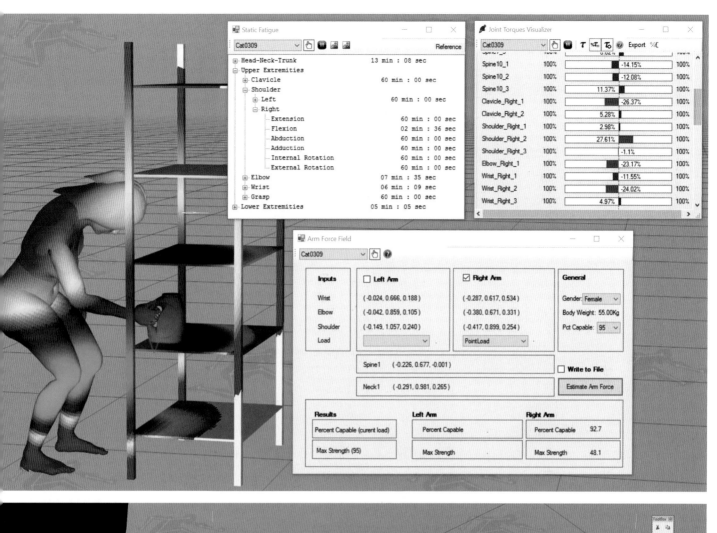

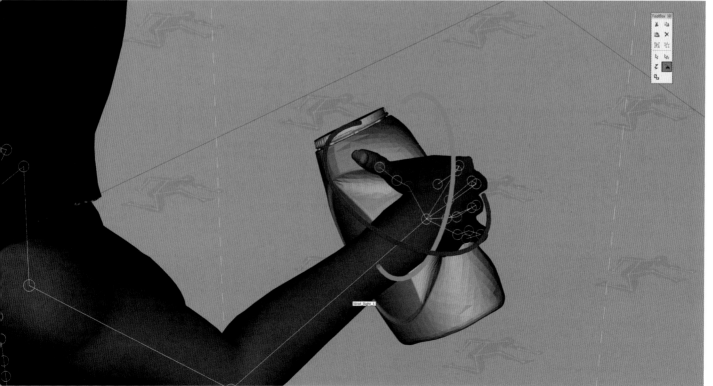

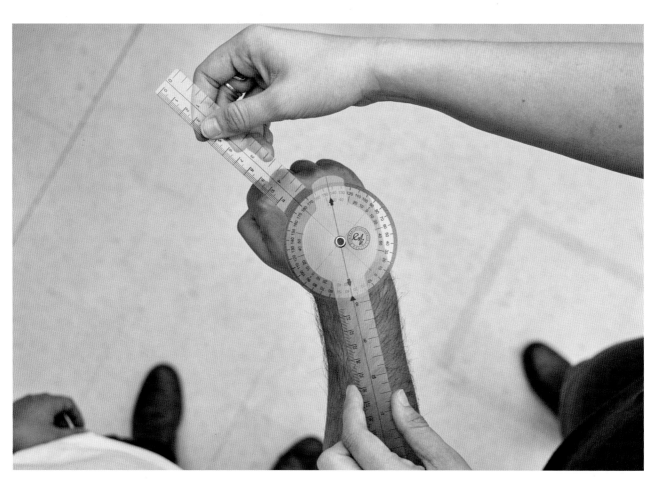

P&G scientist and engineer Lauren Banzhaf combines the live measuring and testing of joints with intensive simulation.

the 5th and 95th percentiles," Banzhaf adds, from the smallest, daintiest hands to the most massive.

When Banzhaf is analyzing consumer motion, she'll watch as the program runs, looking for things like when a consumer reaches a joint limit, which is very fatiguing. "If I raise my hand in class to ask a question, I've reached the joint limit for my shoulder," she gives as an example. "I start to fatigue pretty quickly, and I might use my other hand to support it." She's also watching for weird angles and uncomfortable bends.

When she is measuring joint torque, muscle force, or other metrics in order to compare a product's results with ergonomic standards, she lets the program run and analyzes the data afterward. Then she'll present the most important takeaways to the design and product teams with her recommendations.

Historically, package design focused on ensuring the product didn't leak out. But the performance aspect of the packaging has become equally important—if a cap is difficult to get off, consumers won't want to use the product at all. "Before a consumer even has the chance to use our product, they will create an impression of it simply by picking it up and trying to open it," Gross noted in a talk at the University of Iowa. That initial interaction can be comfortable or uncomfortable, Meili notes, "and that has to do with the force generated in arms and hands necessary to complete the action. Comfort has become a science."

One simulation with one hand and one package generates hundreds of gigabytes of data. In addition to the academic and commercial biometric databases they use, the team is developing vast libraries of their own data from user testing. Though the computer does the data-crunching, human analysis remains vital to creating useful interpretations.

The iteration process at P&G flows both from design to data and from data to design. "People have a fear that computation will replace humans, but that's not at all the way this is happening," Meili says. "It's not a substitute; it's a tool to get better results."

"Before a consumer even has the chance to use our product, they will create an impression of it by picking it up and trying to open it, and that has to do with the force generated in arms and hands."

"You increase your batting average because you can try so many things. We're asking questions that we didn't even know to ask before."

Banzhaf's expertise makes her very in-demand in the organization, but Meili wants to spread the wealth of knowledge. "We have to move from computer simulation being a realm of some nerds in a back room to a way that a large percentage of our scientists do at least a portion of their work," he says. "For answering certain types of questions, you don't need that high level of expertise. In a couple of days you can teach someone to do those basic evaluations."

Sometimes consumers are experiencing unspecified ergonomic problems with a product, and it's Banzhaf's job to figure out exactly what's wrong. Other times, a design group comes to the Modeling and Simulation team early in the process, and it will virtually evaluate 12 or 15 or 20 designs to identify the top two or three iterations to prototype and test with real live consumers. "We can identify consumer tension points early and design around them before taking it to the consumer," Banzhaf says. "It's great if a number [in SantosHuman software]

tells me it's bad, but if a consumer can't confirm with me the number is bad, that's meaningless. Where on the scale of bad is it?"

Many of the improvements P&G is making to packaging are virtually invisible to consumers, but tiny tweaks to caps to improve opening forces, or minute adjustments to the opening force on a trigger or button, can feel like huge improvements. In the liquid laundry detergent space, there's a push for bigger "club-size" packages. But can you pour just one dose out of a 6-liter package rather than a huge glug? Can you even lift the bottle? The simulation will tell—and it will help. "You increase your batting average because you can try so many things," Meili says. "Because of things we can calculate now, we're asking questions that we didn't even know to ask before."

The first thing a consumer may notice about a package is how it feels in their hand, or how easily it can be opened.

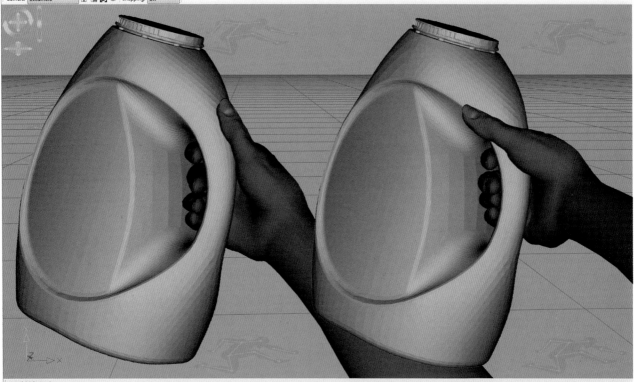

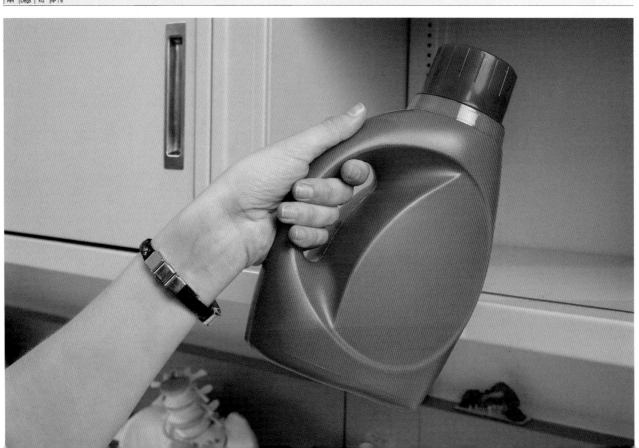

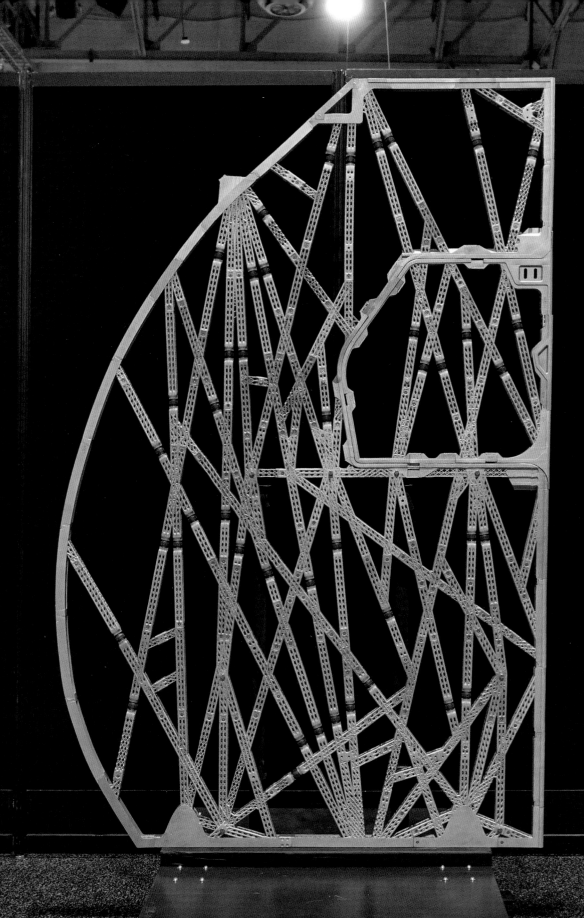

The Alien Skeleton

Generative design allows computers to explore solutions in creative partnership with designers.

When aerospace titan Airbus decided to design a new interior dividing wall for its iconic A320 family of jetliners, it made a peculiar decision. Instead of hiring an outside engineering firm, or delegating the task internally, the company opted to contact a little-known team of researchers in Brooklyn who were studying a nascent field known as generative design.

For the most part, Airbus's goals for the project were straightforward. It wanted the wall to be 3D printable in a proprietary alloy called Scalmalloy, and like every component on a jetliner, it needed to be as light and unobtrusive as possible. Sturdy, as well, since it would be supporting the weight of the chairs where crew members sit during takeoffs and landings.

But as Airbus consulted with David Benjamin, the cofounder of Brooklyn-based design studio The Living, it decided to make a more unusual request as well: Instead of a wall designed by a human being, it wanted one generated by an algorithm.

Benjamin's work has long drawn on the porous borders between computation, nature, and art. He's created fungus-based bricks that can be used for construction and once designed a full-size cave for an installation by the Icelandic singer Björk that was modeled on the sound waves of a song of hers.

For the partition wall, Benjamin turned again to the world of nature. Using experimental Autodesk software known as Project Dreamcatcher, he wrote algorithms based on two natural patterns. One used the growth

"Generative design can allow designers to create, and in some cases discover, designs that would never have occurred to them otherwise."

behavior of single-cell slime mold to generate the geometry of the spokes that brace together the perimeter of the wall, as if it were a growing organism trying to map an efficient path between food sources on the fuselage of the plane. A second used an algorithm that describes mammalian bone structure to arrange the thousands of tiny lattice bars that constitute each spoke, like the spongy tissue on the interior of a bone.

"We'd been fascinated by slime mold for a long time, especially its ability to create an efficient branching network," Benjamin said. "We thought, 'Well, maybe we can use this biological algorithm of the slime mold in a really interesting way.'"

Together, the algorithms generated tens of thousands of wall designs. If you lay them out in a grid, you might be struck by a sense of otherness: They're intricate, spindly, sometimes almost arachnoid, but never in any expected capacity—they're mechanically functional but unbeholden to the mores of any human aesthetic.

And strikingly, they're marvels of engineering. Airbus's initial goal had been to decrease weight, compared to the old partition, by 30 percent. The

design they ultimately selected, created by Benjamin's slime-mold and bone-growth algorithms, decreased the weight by some 55 percent. Airbus estimates that the new design approach could save 465,000 metric tonnes of carbon dioxide emissions per year.

"Generative design can create different results from what a human alone might produce," Benjamin said. "You can use it to create more optimized parts, but what I think is most exciting about generative design is that it can allow designers to create, and in some cases discover, designs that would never have occurred to them otherwise."

To keep all this in perspective, a partition wall is essentially cosmetic, especially compared to an aircraft's landing gear, say, or ailerons. But the project is notable for what it represents: that one of the world's largest aircraft manufacturers is taking seriously the prospect that the future of aerospace engineering will be less about designers using software as a drafting table and more about using it to generate and select from a pool of possibilities. It sounds like science fiction—but Airbus is already performing 16G crash testing as it seeks certification for the wall, so

previous pages: An aircraft partition wall, created for Airbus via generative design and 3D printed using a proprietary alloy.

WHAT IS GENERATIVE DESIGN?

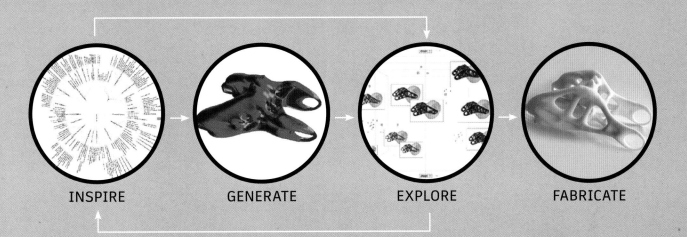

INSPIRE GENERATE EXPLORE FABRICATE

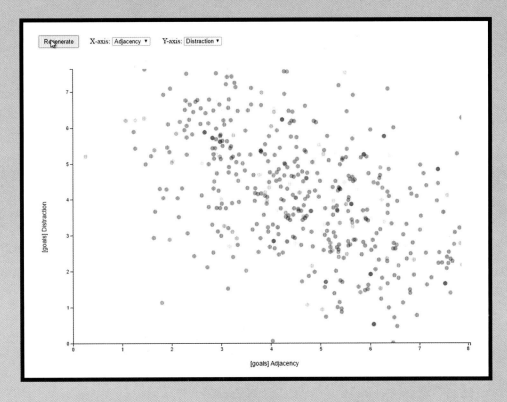

Generative design gives designers a new workflow for ideas and creation, a workflow that supports the capture, compute, create flow essential to the future of making. A designer begins with his or her objectives—the goals and rules that guide the computer's work. The solutions produced can be data (as seen at left) or a design or model. Algorithms help explore the thousands or millions of solutions for the most promising. The digital model can then be fabricated with tools such as 3D printers.

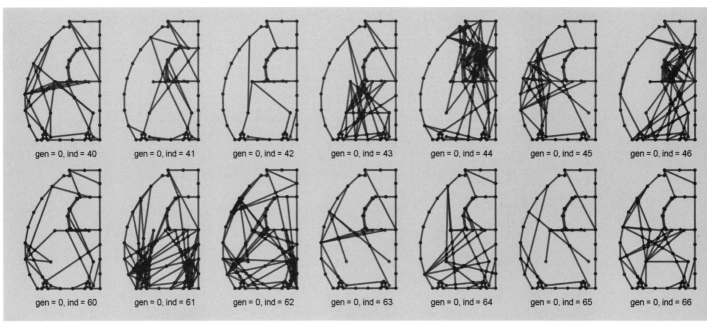

gen = 0, ind = 40 gen = 0, ind = 41 gen = 0, ind = 42 gen = 0, ind = 43 gen = 0, ind = 44 gen = 0, ind = 45 gen = 0, ind = 46

gen = 0, ind = 60 gen = 0, ind = 61 gen = 0, ind = 62 gen = 0, ind = 63 gen = 0, ind = 64 gen = 0, ind = 65 gen = 0, ind = 66

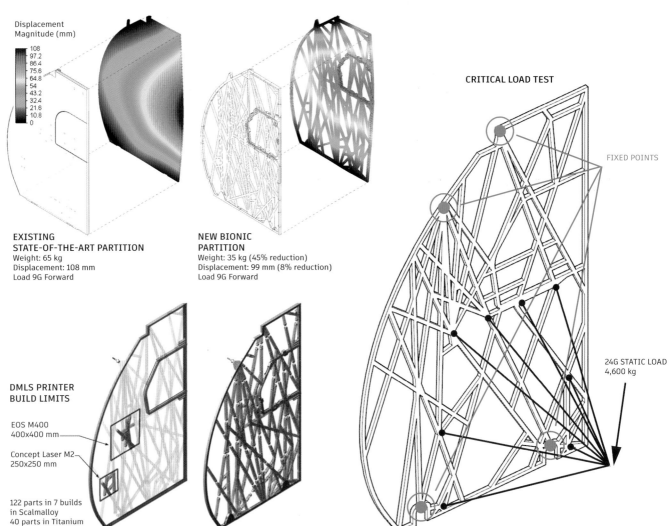

Displacement
Magnitude (mm)

108
97.2
86.4
75.6
64.8
54
43.2
32.4
21.6
10.8
0

**EXISTING
STATE-OF-THE-ART PARTITION**
Weight: 65 kg
Displacement: 108 mm
Load 9G Forward

**NEW BIONIC
PARTITION**
Weight: 35 kg (45% reduction)
Displacement: 99 mm (8% reduction)
Load 9G Forward

CRITICAL LOAD TEST

FIXED POINTS

24G STATIC LOAD
4,600 kg

**DMLS PRINTER
BUILD LIMITS**

EOS M400
400x400 mm

Concept Laser M2
250x250 mm

122 parts in 7 builds
in Scalmalloy
40 parts in Titanium

The Airbus partition wall is one of a growing number of signs that point to a revolutionary trajectory for generative design.

The Living's generative design software evaluated many thousands of arrangements of columns to optimize for strength, weight, displacement, and other attributes.

if you board a plane in about a year's time, you just might turn your head and see one of Benjamin's partitions in the rear of the cabin.

Autodesk's senior director of design research, Mark Davis, sees the partition wall as one of a growing number of signs that point to a revolutionary trajectory for generative design. As he tells it, the wall and similar proofs of concept will soon pave the way for a design revolution akin to the popularization of CAD software in the 1980s and 1990s.

This time, though, designers won't be using a tool to compose and visualize their ideas. Instead, they will be working with these new tools to generate a range of potential models and select their favorite among them, like a hip-hop producer assembling a beat from samples. The human and machine, in a tangible sense, will be collaborators.

"It is a way to design differently," Davis said. "We're not just adding a few capabilities to a tool. This is a whole new approach to design."

It's an approach, he believes, that will come to recast the entire process of designing and fabricating objects. In the corporate world, he points out, design timeframes are notoriously tight—it wouldn't be unusual for a team to be allotted six weeks or less to produce the annual update for a smartphone handset, for example. That means they're

forced to quickly whittle ideas down to a handful, because producing concepts for bolder models would simply be too time-consuming.

Generative design, he believes, could turn that dynamic on its head. "The difference," Davis said, "is that you think of the problem instead of the solution." In such a framework, designers could spend their time carefully formulating the goals and constraints of a project and describing them to a computer. Then they'd use those descriptions to generate untold design permutations and choose the best-performing among them—even if it's as unconventional as Airbus's dividing wall.

Potential applications are as diverse as design itself. In another experiment by The Living, Benjamin used generative design to create a floorplan for a new Autodesk office in Toronto's MaRS Discovery District that minimized distractions while maximizing adjacency preferences, window views, and interconnectivity (see pages 126–127). And sportswear manufacturer Under Armour used generative design to produce and consider many possibilities for its first 3D printed training shoe, the UA Architech.

"You can get a lot of that exploration out front," Davis said. "You can come up with a thousand options, all optimized, and you can choose from them."

GENERATIVE DESIGN FOR ARCHITECTURE

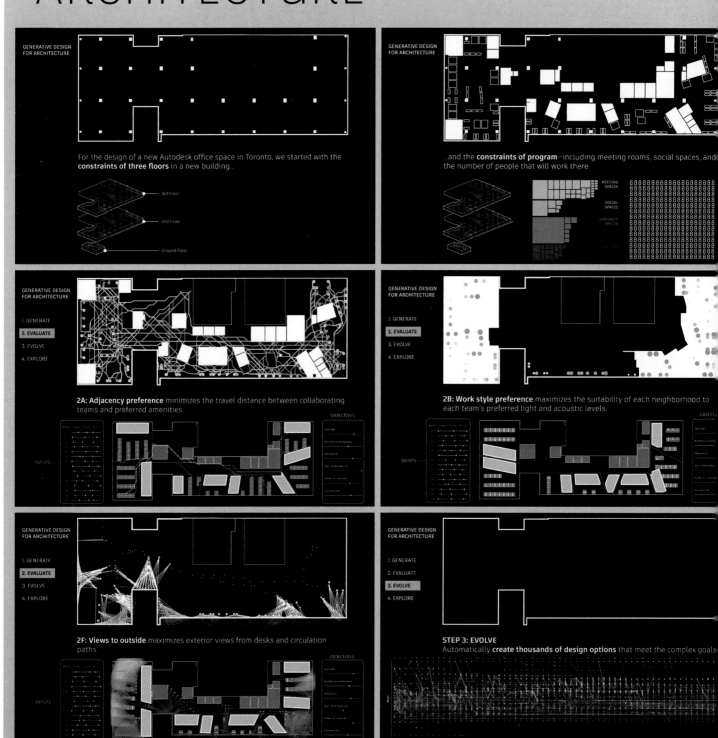

GENERATIVE DESIGN FOR ARCHITECTURE

For the design of a new Autodesk office space in Toronto, we started with the **constraints of three floors** in a new building...

- 3rd Floor
- 2nd Floor
- Ground Floor

...and the **constraints of program**—including meeting rooms, social spaces, and the number of people that will work there.

- MEETING SPACES
- SOCIAL SPACES
- SPECIALTY SPACES

1. GENERATE
2. EVALUATE
3. EVOLVE
4. EXPLORE

2A: Adjacency preference minimizes the travel distance between collaborating teams and preferred amenities.

INPUTS · OBJECTIVES

1. GENERATE
2. EVALUATE
3. EVOLVE
4. EXPLORE

2B: Work style preference maximizes the suitability of each neighborhood to each team's preferred light and acoustic levels.

INPUTS · OBJECT...

1. GENERATE
2. EVALUATE
3. EVOLVE
4. EXPLORE

2F: Views to outside maximizes exterior views from desks and circulation paths.

INPUTS · OBJECTIVES

1. GENERATE
2. EVALUATE
3. EVOLVE
4. EXPLORE

STEP 3: EVOLVE
Automatically **create thousands of design options** that meet the complex goals

For Autodesk's new offices in Toronto, The Living applied generative design techniques to space planning, creating thousands of possible arrangements to balance desires for adjacency, daylight, views, productivity, work style, and "buzz."

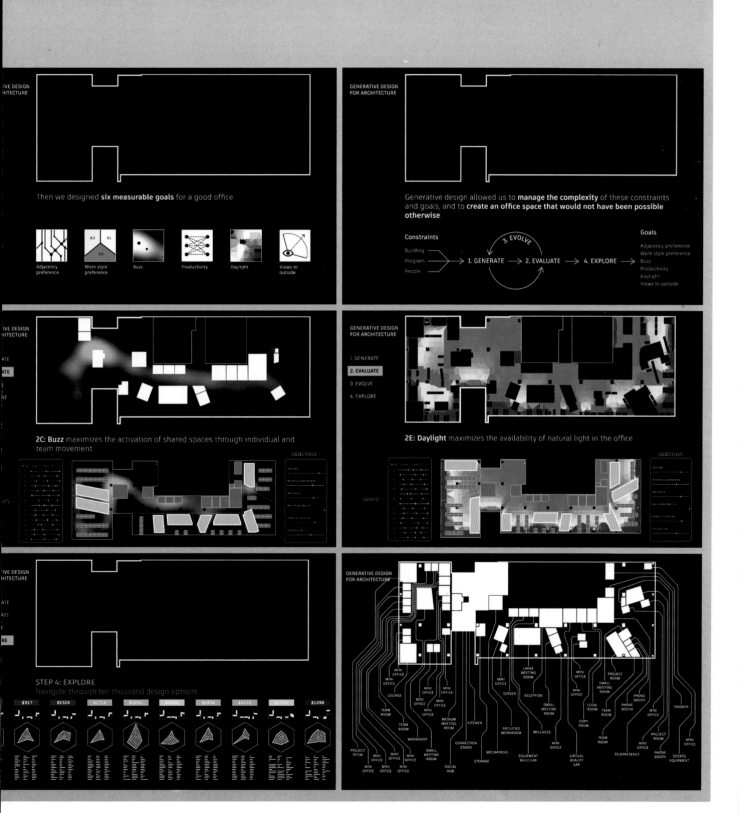

IVE DESIGN
HITECTURE

Then we designed **six measurable goals** for a good office.

Adjacency preference · Work style preference · Buzz · Productivity · Daylight · Views to outside

GENERATIVE DESIGN
FOR ARCHITECTURE

Generative design allowed us to **manage the complexity** of these constraints and goals, and to **create an office space that would not have been possible otherwise.**

Constraints
Building
Program
People

3. EVOLVE
1. GENERATE → 2. EVALUATE → 4. EXPLORE

Goals
Adjacency preference
Work style preference
Buzz
Productivity
Daylight
Views to outside

2C: Buzz maximizes the activation of shared spaces through individual and team movement.

GENERATIVE DESIGN
FOR ARCHITECTURE

1. GENERATE
2. EVALUATE
3. EVOLVE
4. EXPLORE

2E: Daylight maximizes the availability of natural light in the office.

STEP 4: EXPLORE
Navigate through ten thousand design options

#917 #2326 #1718 #3251 #6988 #5934 #4234 #1376 #1098

The implications are astonishing. Davis is particularly excited about the potential for designers to optimize the manufacturing process in unprecedented ways. When optimizing the way a product will be manufactured—its materials, temperature, and other data—is used as one of the goals or constraints in setting up a generative design problem, the algorithms will be able to produce models that are as tailored for the assembly line as for ergonomics or durability.

"What's brand new is that in each one of these designs, we can optimize the way that it's manufactured," Davis said. "With the generative-design method, you can actually put in production constraints, so when it produces an optimized design, it's actually optimized for production."

The ramifications of that concept are profound. When you start to remove design constraints from a generative-design algorithm—by, say, allowing a wider range of fabrication techniques, or materials, or shapes—the variation among the models it produces will become broader and broader, as if you were relaxing the limitations on a search engine query. "If you say, 'Only show me the products that can be produced with injection molding,' that would narrow the field," Davis said, his enthusiasm quickening the cadence of his speech. "If you said ,'Only show me the products that can be done with additive or CNC technology,' it'll only show me that. But if I want to see all designs, for all production methods, it will show me all the diverse and beautiful models, and *then* I can narrow down after that."

Let's take a step back. Projects like Airbus's dividing wall are generated entirely by a computer—they're informed by rules that govern the natural world, like Benjamin's slime mold and bone growth, but they're not governed by data about how the final product will actually perform in the physical world.

It turns out, though, that generative design dovetails elegantly with the budding field of reality capture—using sensors of all types, embedded in objects, to collect data about their real-world use. Combining the two suggests another mechanism by which generative design could be poised to reinvent the way we compose objects. What would happen if you built up a cache of data about an object, then fed that data back into a generative-design algorithm—and then repeated the process, and even repeated it again? Could it create a sort of evolutionary feedback loop in which better data would lead to a more optimized object, ad infinitum?

To explore this intriguing thought experiment in the real world, Autodesk teamed up with Bandito Brothers, a vivacious media and fabrication outfit perhaps best known for constructing a life-size Hot Wheels track back in 2011. Together, the two companies devised a research plan that sounds like a mashup of *The Matrix* and *The Fast and the Furious*.

They called it the Hack Rod. The idea was to design and build a custom automotive chassis, add a souped-up Ducati motorcycle engine that gave it the power-to-weight ratio of a Ferrari, and wire it with a wealth of sensors that would record its vital statistics, from the force exerted on the frame and components to an EEG's biometric data from the driver.

After they constructed the Hack Rod, they took it out to the Mojave Desert and put it through its paces, using Autodesk's ReCap and Memento software to collect a reservoir of

Dreamcatcher helped Autodesk's Arthur Harsuvanakit and Brittany Presten explore variations on "chair," producing an organic shape that was then crafted from wood.

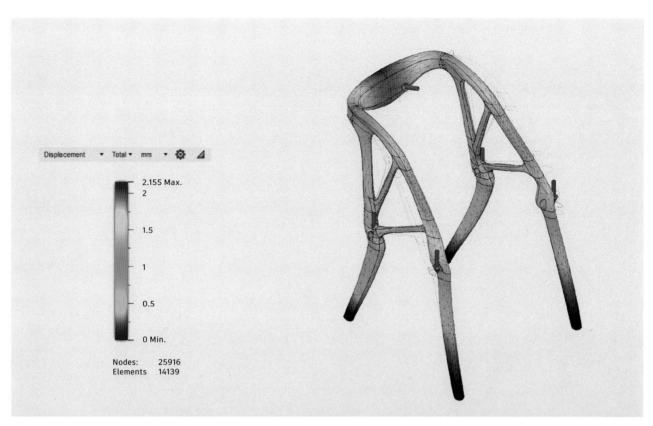

Displacement · Total · mm ·

2.155 Max.
2
1.5
1
0.5
0 Min.

Nodes: 25916
Elements 14139

129   COMPUTE / THE ALIEN SKELETON

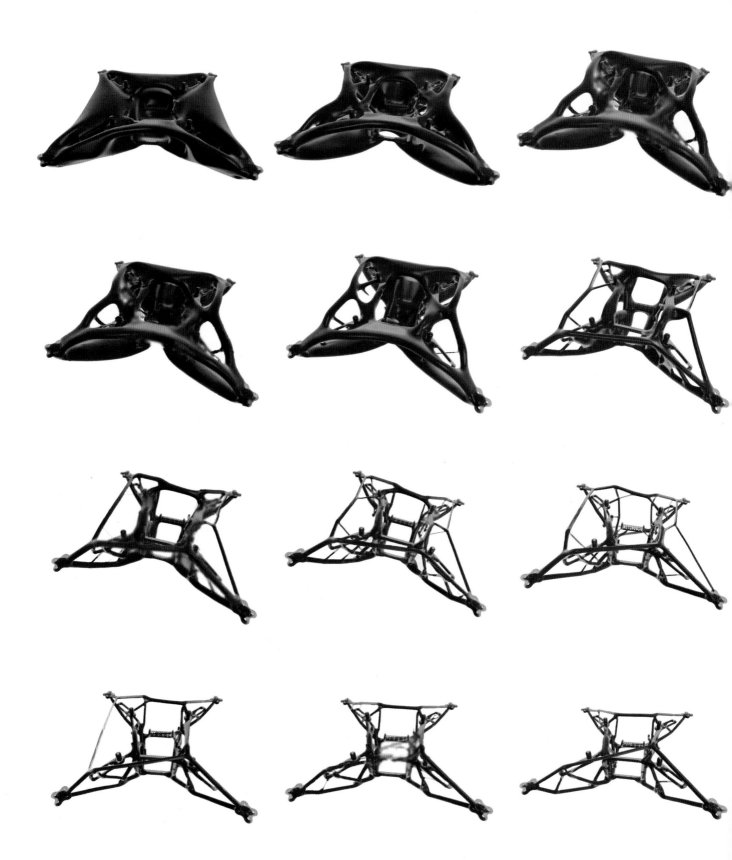

130

This design sequence shows how Dreamcatcher explored the structure of a drone chassis for an optimized (and biomimetic) design.

information that quickly swelled into a dizzying ocean of more than 4 billion individual data points about the stresses on the chassis, the car's speed and acceleration, and the driver's oxygen and airflow levels.

To make sense of all that data, the researchers fed the Mojave data to Dreamcatcher, the software David Benjamin had used to produce Airbus's partition wall. Then they asked it to design a new chassis, informed by the real-world performance of the first iteration.

The result was, to say the least, interesting: One researcher involved with the project likened the generatively designed chassis to an "alien skeleton." Davis estimates that they're about halfway finished welding together the alien skeleton frame, so nothing is certain yet—but if the resulting vehicle is drivable, they intend to take it back to the desert, collect a new stockpile of data, and repeat the process.

If it all works out—the team embraces the uncertainty of the project—it'll be an unprecedented experiment in computer-aided design. But team members tend to frame the project less as a computer science initiative and more in terms of a tool that democratizes invention and entrepreneurship.

"We've seen enough examples of game-changing innovation coming from the technologies and tools on the Web to understand how dramatically the barriers to creativity in that realm have been lowered over the past few years," said Mickey McManus, an Autodesk fellow who has been heavily involved in the Hack Rod project. "But now that revolution—powered by bits, bytes, and Internet packets—has started spreading beyond the digital world to all kinds

of industries, including those that are firmly grounded in the physical world."

Davis frames it more bluntly. "The real vision for Hack Rod is that you or I would be able to put together a car," he said. "Why can't three kids in a dorm room open a car company?"

If the biological sciences constitute Dreamcatcher's theoretical foundation, the allegory about the kids in the dorm room might represent its ideology. Davis calls the notion "design as search"—with the proper software and imagination, he says, the designer of the future might be able to whip up a model as if she were punching keywords into a search engine. (For more on "design as search," see "When Machines Learn," page 138.)

Design as search hinges on two concepts. It holds that all design concepts exist, abstractly, as mathematical possibilities, but also that software made to parse that infinite design-scape—as does Dreamcatcher, in a primordial sense—could be informed by a vast library of historical designs and data. With the proper software, those kids in the dorm room could sketch up a car informed by everything from the blueprints of the Model T to the data collected by the Hack Rod team.

"We think of it as searching for something that hasn't been found yet," Davis said. "A big part of that is machine learning: It can go learn a bunch of stuff, unstructured and unaided by a human, and it'll go and find what it needs. The designer can have this incredible access to information."

That's an acutely democratizing notion, especially in the context of the past decade's explosion in consumer-grade rapid-prototyping technology. As research in generative design starts to mature, though, one of Davis's primary concerns is making sure that the designers whose work could be most enriched by that toolset aren't left behind by the futureshock.

"The biggest challenge in getting generative design adopted is going to be on the social side, not on the technical side," Davis said. "The struggle is to get designers to embrace this new way of designing."

A successful integration will take finesse—not just by educating CAD-centric engineers about the possibilities afforded by generative design, but by weaving a software interface that invites creativity and initiative. A key part of that strategy is that Dreamcatcher is unlikely to ever be released as a standalone product. Instead, Davis expects that successful features will slowly be added to existing tools. That gradual initiation, he hopes, will let creatives adopt the new technologies at a measured pace—and, hopefully, to synergize generative design with older techniques in ways that researchers never anticipated.

In a sense, it's a next-generation angle on a problem that designers have long confronted with tools as traditional as mood boards and focus groups: When you're looking at a hundred possibilities, how do you narrow them down while retaining control of the vision?

"That's the knife edge that we're walking," Davis said. "Let them control the knobs and dials on the music box, but let the music that comes out still be theirs."

If you listen closely, you may already be able to hear that music in the distance. Davis recounts a Dreamcatcher feature the team had been discussing a few years ago that would let the software look at one part in a complex system—the drive chain of a motorcycle, for example—and trigger redesigns of other parts in it to optimize the performance of the entire assembly. Before he knew it, he said, the feature was off the drawing board and incorporated into the code. "It was a concept a couple years ago," he said. "Now it's functional."

The Hack Rod project used data harvested during driving tests to determine the chassis design.

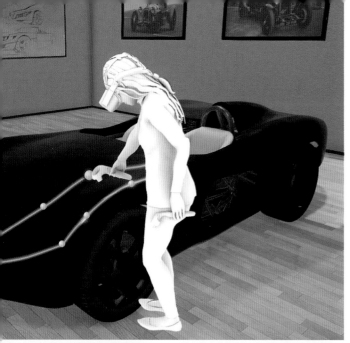

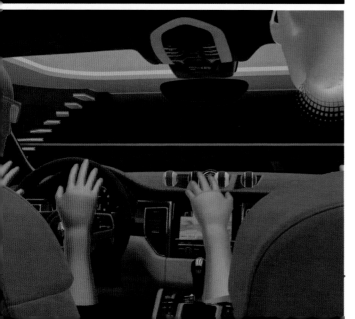

Being There: How VR Transforms Design

Virtual reality is quickly moving from a visualization tool to a full-blown design tool, revealing new details and information to designers in real-time.

In an alcove at Tsoi/Kobus & Associates, an architectural firm overlooking Harvard Square in Cambridge, Massachusetts, you'll find Luis Cetrangolo, the firm's soft-spoken director of design technology and mastermind of its efforts to build VR into the workflow of architectural design. Cetrangolo steeples his fingers thoughtfully as he speaks, seated at a low table covered in VR headsets he's tried out at one time or another: an HTC Vive, an Oculus Rift DK1—there's a DK2 hooked up to a computer directly behind him—a Samsung Gear, and even a humble Google Cardboard.

"Our goal is to have you really *feel* the space experience," Cetrangolo says.

If you've ever tried a VR headset, you probably know what Cetrangolo is talking about. Lower it over your eyes and you'll experience a peculiar type of transcendence that experts often describe as "presence": an acute sensation that your reality has been whisked away and replaced with a convincing stand-in.

In video games, naturally, those substitute realities are often fantastic virtual worlds. Cetrangolo's work is more subtle, but it's still surprisingly effective—in the simulated buildings he conjures up, it's hard not to lean in to inspect the brickwork, or to crane your neck to see over a high balcony.

When Cetrangolo first started exploring uses for VR technology at Tsoi/Kobus two years ago, his assumption was that it would primarily be a tool to help clients understand complex designs in a more intuitive way than blueprints or miniature models. He was correct, in a sense—VR has become an invaluable instrument at the firm for client communication—but its greatest impact has turned out to be as a design tool. Architects at the firm now regularly dive into their creations, often using Revizto, a program that transforms designs in Revit into virtual environments populated with simulated furniture and greenery, rendered complete with shadows as they would appear with the sun in different positions in the virtual sky.

Even more fundamentally, Cetrangolo has found that virtual reality is an indispensable collaborative tool for the firm's designers and particularly when working with Tsoi/Kobus' many off-site consultants. In describing virtual reality's advantages, Cetrangolo often returns to the word *feel* to express a deeper level of mutual understanding afforded by the sensation of presence. "Remotely, you can feel the space and know what you are talking about," he says. "It has huge potential."

Brian Pene, the director of emerging technology at Autodesk, has come to a similar conclusion. He believes that virtual reality is poised to revolutionize the world of design in all three ways that Cetrangolo has seen

it change the workflow at Tsoi/Kobus: by communicating designs to clients with unprecedented clarity, by giving designers a novel perspective on their own work, and by letting both groups collaborate in types of virtual environments that simply didn't exist until the technological breakthroughs that enabled the latest generation of virtual reality headsets.

"What you get out of a true immersive experience is it's a completely intimate process where you almost forget you're looking at something virtual," Pene said. "It's as if you're there. You're truly present with that design in true three dimensions."

At Autodesk University in November 2016, Pene let attendees enter a virtual space to see a Porsche Macan and Ford Mustang in the 3D visualization software VRED. In the virtual environment, they cut the cars in half so that visitors could see the inner mechanics of the engine. Attendees were rapturous, but what gets Pene really excited is the logical next step: building tools that designers can use to craft and modify designs inside a virtual environment, instead of merely visualizing their creations.

The theory is that virtual environments allow us to interact with digital designs in a more natural way than a traditional layout or blueprint. In a sense, Pene believes, virtual reality has the potential to unlock designers' innate cognitive abilities by processing visual information as if they were forming a model by hand.

Of course, it's still a liminal moment for modern virtual reality, so it's difficult to predict what sort of control system will become standard for it in the way that the keyboard and mouse came to characterize interactions with a desktop computer, or multitouch

previous pages: The potential of virtual reality in the design industries is being explored in multiple ways, from 3D visualization to online collaboration to building virtual factories that can reveal new methods and efficiencies.

gestures are now the natural way to communicate with a mobile device. But Pene considers the problem to be a solvable one, and he says inroads are being made to leverage gesture recognition to push and pull surfaces of a CAD model in virtual reality.

In the course of that research, Pene has observed something about virtual co-creation that echoes Cetrangolo: Together, collaborators tend to quickly narrativize virtual projects, working with the design but simultaneously crafting a story about its meaning and origin.

"You're telling a story about it," Pene said. "Not only are you getting this emotional connection, but you're getting this ability to bring all these stakeholders in and just to give them a lot more focus and energy."

Virtual reality can also be a game changer for visualizing complex systems. In an experiment dubbed the Virtual Factory, Pene and his colleagues at Autodesk built new features into the company's Factory Design Suite, which is used to lay out manufacturing facilities. The new features let users dive into a virtual environment, but also used

reality (AR), which uses a headset or mobile device to overlay information or virtual objects onto an actual scene. Using AR, an employer could train workers to operate a dangerous industrial site—or even give builders detailed instructions on how to construct it. "If I have to be on-site and I'm assembling a wall, I need to understand what the fire rating of that is or maybe the material, the cost, the assembly instructions," Pene said. "Today that's all done through paper."

Back at Tsoi/Kobus, Cetrangolo shows me over to the computer terminal connected to a Rift headset. He loads the design for South Street Landing, a multimillion-dollar renovation in the Jewelry District of Providence, Rhode Island, then hands me the headset and an Xbox controller. I struggle for a minute with my glasses, then drop the headset over my eyes.

The sense of teleportation is immediate. It's no longer an overcast morning in Cambridge but a sunny day in Providence, where I find myself in the spacious atrium that the South Street Landing will feature when it's completed in 2017. I thumb the control

VR has the potential to unlock designers' innate cognitive abilities.

industrial physics modeling to understand the virtual factory's performance down to the mechanics of the assembly line and individual pieces of equipment.

One appealing use for the Virtual Factory would be to work inefficiencies out of a new facility before setting mortar to brick. Another compelling application would draw on the closely related technology called augmented

stick to maneuver my way to a pair of glass doors, then turn around—really turn around, that is, in Tsoi/Kobus' virtual reality alcove—and take in the majesty of the lofty virtual space, beams of sunlight streaming through the high windows.

"Oh, that's remarkable," I hear myself say. "It has that intense sense of being there."

WHEN MACHINES LEARN

The biggest wildcard of the fourth industrial revolution is the application of machine learning.

A form of artificial intelligence, machine learning differs from traditional computing because, rather than following explicit procedures set by a programmer, it discovers rules based on observations of and feedback from the real world. Machine learning lets computers identify patterns in vast amounts of data and make predictions based on those findings.

Well-known examples of machine learning include Watson, which defeated human champions at *Jeopardy!*, and DeepMind, which did the same in the ancient and complex game of Go. A more mundane expression of machine learning is the autocomplete feature in Google's search engine. Learning from many billions of searches, it now suggests your search after a couple of words.

Machine learning promises vast and surprising applications. Asking what it will do is like asking what a team of talented and experienced creative thinkers will achieve when they have lots of time and boundless resources. The answer is: anything. We have no idea. But we have some clues.

HOW IT WORKS

"Imagine if I showed you a leaf for the very first time," says Mike Haley, Autodesk's senior director, machine intelligence. "You'd never seen one before. And, say, you walked outside and saw a totally different shape of leaf. You probably wouldn't recognize that other thing as a leaf because you've only seen one example. But if I put 100 different leaves in front of you and told you these are all things called leaves, and we talked about them for a while, once you went out in the world, you would have a sense of 'leaf-ness.' You've learned what a leaf is. That's what machine learning does. The computer has formed a model of what a leaf is.

"What is learning, after all? It is the process of creating a model of the world. A mathematical representation. In our heads, it's a biological, neurological model, a vastly high-dimensional model, and a model that's constantly being updated as we experience more things."

Machine-learning algorithms mimic the ways our own brains operate. A brain is composed of millions of neurons or nerve cells. Each neuron is connected to many input neurons, often hundreds or thousands, as well as many output neurons. When any particular neuron gets sufficient accumulated signals from its input neurons, it fires a signal to its output neurons. The weighting between the connections is all different. Machine learning does something similar, creating millions of digital neurons and connecting them in layers—a neural network.

Machine learning follows three steps: training, analysis, and application. In the training step, weighting among neurons starts in a randomized state. The algorithm is shown a picture of a leaf and it guesses if it's a leaf or not. If it guesses correctly, some of the connections among the neurons are increased, or strengthened. If it guesses wrong, it changes the connections and tries again. Haley explains, "The first time, it's usually wrong. Then it changes the weighting of the synapses. If it's closer that time, it's reinforced. This is what happens biologically when we learn too."

Each layer of neurons creates a layer of understanding. In the first layer, the neurons detect whether there is a dot in the image. A second layer determines lines, corners, and arcs. Subsequent layers recognize stems and veins. And up the cascading level of abstraction it creates an understanding of leaf species and seasons, all without being told. This understanding isn't explicitly programmed; it emerges through massive brute force evaluation. Humans might call this "experience."

In the second step of analysis, the algorithm is allowed to dream or imagine. The model of a leaf is represented by a huge mathematical equation that represents the flow and weighting of neurons and connections. It works through this equation millions of times and gets better and better. In the process, it acquires the sense of leaf-ness.

In the final step, the algorithm is shown new inputs and assigns them values. By this time, it is very good.

WHAT IT MEANS

In the very short history of machine learning, applications are already profound.

One algorithm was taught to play the classic videogame *Breakout*. The only instruction it was given was to maximize the total score. The algorithm started off worse than the worst human player. Within an hour, it had learned the basics. Within a few hours, it had discovered not only how to play the mechanics well but it had also pinpointed winning strategies for high scores. Within a day in "computer time," it had played

world creates data, and data means there is something to learn from," says Haley.

This is the next step after computability. Not only can we now work on any problem within a computer, rather than in the physical world, but our algorithms can too. The disruptive nature of computability will grow exponentially as machine learning evolves and is applied to more industries.

There are several classes of machine learning, but this fundamental one that uses training, analysis, and application can be applied to virtually any situation where there are clear goals, real-world input, and accurate feedback. It is already successful in knowledge creation, image recognition, and

As computation grows more powerful and accessible, algorithms will be trained to participate in every aspect of making.

millions of games in parallel and taught itself to play better than the best human player.

Another algorithm was taught how to play the game Go. With human training over several months, it learned how to defeat the world's best Go player, who dedicated himself to a lifetime of study. During those matches, a remarkable thing happened. The computer made moves that a human never would have. That is: The algorithm had dreamed up a new way to play, and to win.

Machine learning is not limited to videogames, of course. The real breakthrough is that machine learning is able to be generalized. It can discover patterns and correlations in whatever data it has access to. "The

pattern detection, and it is being applied to training autonomous vehicles, insurance fraud, and financial projections, among other fields.

Machine learning will also be used for designing, fabrication, and operations.

LEARNING TO DESIGN

As computation continues to grow more powerful and accessible, machine learning algorithms will be trained to participate in every aspect of making. Show an algorithm examples of efficient, beautiful, sustainably produced furniture, and it will learn the important qualities and produce beautiful, strong, and efficient chairs. Show it examples of products

"Our design tools have no design in them. They're empty vessels."

successful in their marketplace and it will recommend better designs and materials for your project.

With that new understanding, the software can take a 3D object—a generic chair for instance—and apply a specific style to make it more fluid, more Philippe Starck, more Cubist, or more Corbusier.

When an algorithm learned how to play *Breakout*, it had one parameter: a high score. Haley speculates how machine learning can be used for more complex design tasks, with trickier parameters. "Say a client walks into an architect's office and says, 'I need this to be more peaceful,'" he says. "When we think of rooms that are peaceful, there are a whole bunch of characteristics. It's not just the shape of the room. It might be lighting, it might be the smell, the sound—all sorts of factors contribute to peacefulness."

Over time, we can teach an algorithm about those characteristics. It can examine enough buildings and enough human responses to those buildings to discern "peacefulness." Imagine putting a microphone in a room that measures the sentiment of its users. We can pick up all sorts of things—temperature, color, textures, lighting, and hundreds of other qualities—to measure peacefulness. "You could begin to correlate it back to what was unique about that space," Haley continues. "Imagine that done many, many times over. After a while, the system learns what generates various types of peacefulness. It generates a model." With that model, peacefulness becomes computable and can be applied to a design. (David Benjamin's studio explored some of this territory in designing Autodesk's Toronto office; see pages 126–127.)

THE DESIGN GRAPH
Machine learning's capacity for seeing patterns and making connections in huge data sets is being put to use already in a tool called Design Graph. This is an ambitious project that begins to put together an essentially infinite database of parts, assemblies, components, and other elements of your design.

This is not simply a catalog of parts. Rather, the machine learning that underlies Design Graph can understand what you are making and suggest or select the components you need to build it. With the Hack Rod project, for example, a chassis created via generative design was "handed off" to Design Graph, which then specified all of the nuts, bolts, and other parts needed to build it.

The technology uses shape-based machine learning to recognize and understand parts, assemblies, and entire designs. Design Graph learns to identify the relationships between all parts within and across designs. It learns to interpret designs in terms of those parts, and it provides a way to navigate data using simple text search, learned categories of parts, shape similarity, usage patterns, and even smart filters for part numbers, materials, and other properties.

As Design Graph learns more, it can begin to understand the qualities of a design as well as its components. Is it energy efficient? Is it peaceful? And once it knows those qualities, it will remember and transmit them. This represents a huge change in how we design.

"Our design tools actually have no design in them," says Autodesk CTO Jeff Kowalski. "They don't know design. They just know calculations. They're empty vessels."

As Design Graph understands designs more, it becomes less of a library and more of a repository of design knowledge. "Once a computer understands what *aerodynamic* means, it can transmit that learning instantaneously and forever," Kowalski continues. "It's not about showing me every article about aerodynamics. It's the question: Is this thing aerodynamic or not? And the system will know because it will have already done its own experiments to figure this out. In the same way a computer can learn leaf-ness, it can learn aerodynamics."

What makes a Rembrandt a Rembrandt? Can a machine learn those qualities? And what can it create once it does? The Next Rembrandt project explored those questions through training, analysis, and application progression: Learning the qualities of a Rembrandt painting, from geometries to how wrinkles look to the height of the master's brushstrokes, then using that data to "dream" a new portrait in his style, and sending that model to an advanced 3D printer. The "Next Rembrandt" is not fully an original painting by an artificial intelligence—yet it is a remarkable work that creates some of the same sense of beauty and awe as an original.

Thinking Has Been Upgraded

Computation is the only resource that has consistently dropped in price and vaulted in quantity and quality. It offers us enormous opportunities to create new solutions—and presents enormous new challenges.

What might future generations of computers look like? What will they be able to do? Though we find it easy to reflect on how much more powerful today's computers are compared to those a decade before, projecting Moore's Law forward seems to stretch believability. It's safe to say, however, that in 10 years, smartphones will compute a hundred times faster than today's. These improvements will only compound more quickly over the fullness of time. And they will change the landscape of design and making once again.

COMPUTATION WILL ABSTRACT MORE COMPLEXITY

Professional designers and builders will have an increasingly wider and more colorful palette of tools to work with. At one end of the spectrum, they will have better drawing and modeling tools similar to today's technologies. At the other end, their tools will learn and help them think. Design will extend from creating to searching for the best idea in a landscape of possibilities.

As computation accelerates, algorithms will become more sophisticated and pack more intelligence into every action. The one-touch step of hailing a ride-share hides a bewildering digital infrastructure. We can expect certain types of design software to become more "one-click." Digital tools will harness more complexity and simplify work into higher-order activities.

We will, for example, be able to design a home, price and source the materials, project the cost of operating the house over its lifetime, and calculate its carbon footprint, all with a few mouse clicks or voice commands. We will be able to run simulations and have our digital design assistant offer suggestions and alternatives, like an expert advisor, reflecting on our goals. This access to increased complexity will offer a kind of intuition: The digital assistant will have knowledge of vast databases of homes, and will offer its insight as a design partner.

As a result, more people will be able to participate in the act of design and making, no matter what their role is. Computation will increase options but reduce complexity. Computers will have the power and patience to explore and evaluate thousands or millions of options that a human would never have the time to pursue, and explore solutions that a human designer might never think of.

The shift in working with complexity means that designers will spend less time designing forms and shapes and more time establishing goals and constraints, allowing the computer to create forms. They will do less work creating solutions and more time searching through a landscape of viable alternatives and trade-offs. They will begin fewer projects with a blank canvas and more with a data environment gathered from scanners and sensors.

These shifts will also encourage—even force—designers to spend more time thinking about the goals of their work. This may be good news for many, but the new ways of working will not be without costs. Designers and builders will face mounting pressure to be current with rapidly changing tools. They will need to continually educate themselves. They will need to cultivate a new literacy of thinking in systems and identifying the interdependent flows between people, projects, and materials.

COMPUTATION WILL BE MORE NATURAL

With the growth of computing power, digital devices will be able interact in the ways we prefer to communicate, rather than us having to conform to the needs of our machine. Increasingly, we will be able to speak to computers in natural language and have them understand our intentions. Building on the power of abstraction, we will be able to deliver higher-order commands and suggestions.

We will also interact with digital models and simulations in more realistic ways. Whether through virtual reality, augmented reality, large projection surfaces, or through one of the many promising projection and holographic techniques, digital simulations will be more realistic. Our interaction will feel more natural as digital environments more closely resemble the real world.

Computers will develop better human social skills as well. They will increasingly act as guides, posing questions, suggesting avenues of exploration, and challenging our assumptions. Partnership and collaboration mean respecting one another's ways of working.

COMPUTATION WILL SURPASS HUMAN COGNITION

In many ways, it already has. As computers teach themselves to learn, using the compounding growth of neural networks, unsupervised learning, and applying these machine learning algorithms, the changes will be dramatic and spellbinding.

Today, no one person can keep the entirety of a complex design in their mind. A modern car, plane, or building has far too many connected parts—think of Foster + Partners' massive airport in Jordan. But as neural networks grow, they will contain not only entire planes, but all planes. They will know all the steps needed to make them, and how they actually operate over time. The results will be transformative and will help us make things that vastly outperform what we can conceive and make today.

Just as a smartphone has more power than NASA did two generations ago, in two generations from now, your phone and the network it connects to will vastly outperform the state of the art today.

This growth will demand a fundamental rethinking of how we design and work with computers. Increasingly, we will do less of the grunt work and more of what it actually means to design and make—clarifying our intention, focusing on the real problems, and coming up with big outcomes.

Artificial intelligence will spawn a collection of intelligent assistants (IAs)—digital collaborators who bring broad experience and sharp intuition to helping us do our jobs. We will not be replaced with AIs; instead, we will use more IAs in the process of design, making, and operating.

THE IMPLICATIONS ARE VAST

We shape our tools and our tools shape us. As software eats the world—as every aspect of our lives becomes more touched (and governed) by equations and systems that make decisions independent of humans—designers will be more and more responsible for the behavior built in to their designs. This will require a deeper skill to best take advantage of emerging tools, just like every advanced tool that we have developed.

Not every design will need deep computation, but wickedly complex and highly interdependent problems will benefit greatly. Computing power gives designers more time to do what they do best: study the deep nature of complex problems and use the best tools to create genius solutions.

CHAPTER 3

We have always used physical tools to magnify our ability to shape objects. Now, digital fabrication is giving us infinite expressibility. We can shape and place the right materials in the right places at the right times in the right ways, enhancing our craftsmanship.

They are nearing infinite expressibility, placing the right materials in the right places at the right times in the right ways, and in doing so, are changing the nature of craftsmanship.

Every product we make—at least at human scales—is fabricated by applying some combination of just six basic actions: forming, machining, joining, casting, molding, and adding. Coffee cups, cutlery, laptops, jeans, shoes, automobiles, guitars, elevators, cameras, trains—all of them were made using these basic methods.

Robots can now perform all six. By following detailed assembly instructions, robots serve as off-ramps that connect the digital world back to the physical. By translating digital representations into instructions, they can materialize digital models into something real. This ability to mimic human fabrication expands the building capabilities of our hands and has wide-ranging effects on how we make things now and in the future.

WHAT MAKES A ROBOT A ROBOT?

First, it helps to reconsider our idea of *robot*. It's not an android, and it's not necessarily a big industrial robot welding cars together. A robot is any device that satisfies these five criteria: It needs a power source to drive its parts; actuators or motors and hydraulics to convert energy into movement and force; sensors to see and feel what's happening; effectors, which are tools that handle materials and manipulate things; and a control system, the brain that directs the operation. Lose any one of those components and it's not a robot—it's just a machine.

Today's robots service, transport, and, of course, manufacture. They cut and shape fabric, metal, and wood. They machine parts at microscopic tolerances.

Equipped with sensors and a machine learning brain, robots will finally become bright, responsive, strong, fast, and intelligent.

They weld together cars—automotive companies account for half of the world's industrial robots. They cast precious and commodity metals, often operating in toxic environments. They mold plastics of all types. Or they deposit material additively in the form of 3D printers that make prototypes and finished products from materials as diverse as polymers and concrete. All of these robots follow a long set of digital instructions, moving their effectors through a set of discrete choreographed actions to convert a digital model into a physical object.

But with the exception of the automaking robots, we don't often think of these things as robots. "*Robot* is the term you use when something isn't yet useful," quips Autodesk CEO Carl Bass. "When it becomes useful, you call it an airplane. Airplanes take off and land all by themselves; pilots do something when there's a problem. Washing machines, CNC machines, 3D printers—these are all machines that do specific jobs so well that we don't call them robots anymore."

THE RISE OF ROBOTS

For well over 30 years, robots have operated, unthinkingly and automatically, in assembly lines across the world. And in those three decades, robots have grown in productivity, versatility, and especially in numbers. In 2015, roughly two million multipurpose industrial robots were in use. By 2020, another half million will be in service.

Their sophistication and ubiquity have changed how we make things at an industrial scale—allowing fewer workers to make more products, and to do so with higher levels of precision. For example, in the 1980s, a Boeing 767 took more than 1,200 people to make—by hand and by hand-operated machines. Today, a 787 is put together by about 100 people, working with dozens of robots.

Like every digital technology, robots continue to evolve, steadily becoming faster, more precise, stronger, cheaper, and more reliable. Most changes, especially those in hardware—power sources, actuators, and tools—advance more or less incrementally. Actuators and effectors are now so precise that they are trusted to perform microsurgery. But robots' sensors and brains—especially their brains—evolve at the speed of Moore's Law.

NOT THE SHARPEST TOOLS

Saul Griffith, MacArthur Fellow, engineer, and robot builder, says most of today's robots are "blind, stupid, fat, weak, slow, difficult, and unyielding." They are also expensive: An entry-level, single-arm industrial robot starts at $75,000. Add another $100,000 for software, and a full-time salary to program, operate, and maintain the device.

Robots must be placed in special environments, caged in by fences or kept in locked rooms that suit the machines, not people. They can be used for specific tasks, repeating the same set of instructions endlessly. But they usually need some kind of supporting infrastructure that holds together parts to be joined. These fixtures cost as much as the robots themselves—often well over $1 million—and take months to manufacture and set up. When a factory produces a new line, it needs retooling: Fixtures must be rebuilt to keep the new parts fitting perfectly in space.

THE SHAPE OF THINGS TO COME

Now, robots are transforming how we make things at every scale, not just big, expensive products like jets and cars. That's because the idea of what a robot is, what it does, and who it does it for is quickly changing—and this change is bringing all of the ways we make things under digital control at scales that range from the factory to the desktop to the microscopic.

The advancement of robotic creation is closely tied to sensing and computation. Better, cheaper sensors perceive environments at higher resolutions. Faster and deeper computation lets the robot know what or who is nearby and what to do differently. Faster feedback loops driven by better perception, improved spatial accuracy, and sophisticated control allow a robot to adjust its movement intelligently. Sensing and computing are finally making robots perceptive, intelligent, svelte, strong, easy, and flexible.

The future of fabrication is not a story of robot domination. Robots are not coming for *us*. That is, they will not replace all manufacturing jobs or service work. (Though they will disrupt some kinds of jobs in many industries, to be sure.)

Robots will be coming *for* us. They will work with us to do what we don't want to do or cannot do. This will free us to do more creative and valuable work. The future of creation will be played out as stories of how intelligent and versatile tools will shape materials in the ways we want them shaped. This will give us the room to evolve our craftsmanship, extending what we intend to do, but better.

Robots are not coming for *us*.
Robots will be coming *for* us.
They will work with us to do what
we don't want to do or cannot do.

Evolution
of Fabrication

For millennia, humans have manipulated material in six basic ways. We have
designed and used an ever-evolving set of tools to accomplish this and to make
things. As these methods and tools become digitized and, increasingly, applied
via robotics, their accuracy and repeatability grow exponentially.

FORMING

Forming uses mechanical pressure
to shape an object into a new form,
without adding or removing any material.

CUTTING

Removing material to form new shapes is
also known as machining, milling, sawing,
chiseling, and mitering.

CASTING

Casting, a 6,000-year-old process,
involves pouring liquid into a hollow
form and allowing it to become a solid.

Mechanized forming includes rolling,
extruding, eroding, and stretching.

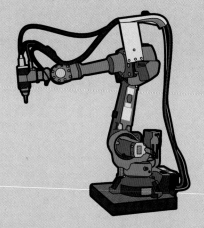

CNC machines perform a computerized
version of cutting.

Computerized casting utilizes precision
injecting and grinding to remove
imperfections.

MOLDING

Molding is the process of shaping a pliable material within a rigid form, called a matrix, to produce a new form.

JOINING

Joining is bringing together two or more forms of similar or different materials by welding, soldering, fastening, taping, riveting, or bolting.

ADDING

Objects are built up by depositing successive layers of materials.

Machine-molded parts have to be carefully designed to allow for flow and cooling patterns.

Robotics easily automate the process of fastening objects.

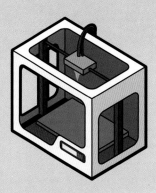

Additive manufacturing, usually known as 3D printing, is essentially a robot precisely depositing layers of a material.

Nike's 3D Sprinter

The global athletic powerhouse isn't out to simply make better gear for athletes—it's accelerating evolution.

"I always feel like I'm fighting the curve." Sprinter and reigning 400m world champion Allyson Felix wasn't satisfied. She knew she could get better, knew that she had to get better.

That inherent dissatisfaction, the relentless drive of the elite athlete to be quicker and stronger, is precisely why Nike exists.

And with those eight little words, Felix launched a two-year odyssey to create the world's most advanced track spike.

If there's one thing that sits atop everything else in the minds of Nike employees, it is this—listen to the athlete. Listen to what they want. Listen to what they need.

"I think this now goes beyond just listening," says Nike's VP of global design, John Hoke. "It's listening, it's looking, and then it's capturing data and going deeper, using the technology for those moments of truth—when it matters between gold or last place. We get to stop and study that moment and ask, What can we do to make that a winning moment?"

I had heard that somewhere before, that idea, and then I remembered. Phil Knight, the creator of Nike, said something similar in his memoir, *Shoe Dog*. "The secret of happiness," he writes, "...the essence of beauty or truth...lay somewhere in that moment when the ball is in midair, when the runners near the finish line, and the crowd rises as one. There's a kind of exuberant clarity in that pulsing half second before winning and losing are decided. I wanted that, whatever that was, to be my life."

Knight's spirit permeates Nike's sprawling campus in Beaverton, Oregon. It's not so much in the place itself as it is in the people. Whether they are talking technology, star athletes, or simply the pure joy of competition, it is the same thing, like they are all quoting from a common holy text. It is a place built on a dream, and they are all, down to a person, true believers.

THE CURVE

Following a triple-gold-medal performance at the 2012 Olympics (200m, 4x100m relay, 4x400m relay) and a heartbreaking hamstring injury at the 2013 World Championships, Felix—and Nike—already had their eyes on Rio in 2016. And now they also had their white whale to chase—the curve.

"That drove the story," says Leslie Barnes, clinical biomechanist at the Nike Sports Research Lab (NSRL). "How do we design a spike for Allyson to optimize running on the curve?"

Enter Isaac Newton. When you're running in a straight line, you're applying vertical forces into the ground, and everything is symmetrical on the right and left sides. There's not a lot happening in the medial-lateral direction. So the shoes you're running in, the right and left, will be virtually the same.

Says the Law of Inertia, once a body is in motion it tends to stay in that same motion, in that same direction, at that same speed, unless another force is acting upon it—the curve. The curve changes everything. Now you have a centrifugal force that's throwing all that beautiful symmetry out of whack. The body wants to keep going straight, but the track, that enemy of inertia, won't let it.

"So the question for us became this unbalanced force," continues Barnes. "How do you design a shoe that optimizes running on the curve but doesn't impact running straight?"

Answer: You go deeper. Deeper into what the data says. Deeper into what the athlete feels. It's what Nike has always done—juggling craftsmanship and technology, playing with proportions, a pinch of science and a hint of art, over and over until they make something altogether new.

Because now, in the curve, you need a left shoe that does one thing and a right shoe that does another. To use a car metaphor, the left shoe is the steering wheel, and the right, the accelerator. But they both have to be equally adept at performing in the straight.

And just to make it fun, these competing interests weren't confined to the plate, the bottom of the shoe. The upper would be dramatically affected as well. In short, what would be required was a complete reimagining of both the upper and the plate, how they would look, how they would feel, how they would perform, and how they would be designed.

Nike would have to capture the critical data, turn that data into models that could be simulated and analyzed to better understand the challenge, and ultimately create an entirely new solution with its arsenal of advanced tools, innovative methods, and newly engineered materials. And it was fortunate that they had such a storehouse of technology and brainpower—because they had only two years to pull it off.

THE UPPER

Listen to the athlete. It's the first commandment, the directive that drives everything, even when, as in this case, the athlete wants something that's never been done.

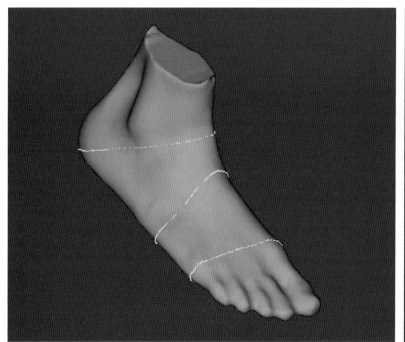
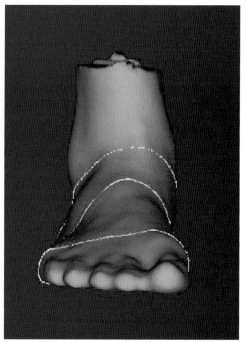

"She wanted it to feel like a sock," says Barnes. "To fit like a glove. She didn't even want to be aware of it." That's really the Holy Grail for a sprinter, when her shoes fit and perform so well that they simply disappear. Because if you're thinking about your shoe, you're not thinking about your race. And sprinters are always thinking about their race. Even for the 11 seconds or so that it takes to complete the 100 meters, the sprinter is thinking and doing something different at every one of those seconds—reacting to the gun, clearing the blocks, accelerating, maintaining maximum velocity, finishing strongly.

That's what Felix wanted, to not think about her shoes. And Nike was determined to give it to her. But first they needed data.

The NSRL's 3D foot scanner uses a number of cameras and lasers to capture 0.1 millimeter microslices of the foot and stitches them all together to create a 3D form that provides key information such as length, width, girth, circumference, and volume. The 3D view highlights Felix's unique morphology, most notably a long, extremely narrow foot. The average female foot is a B width, while Felix comes in at an A, and in terms of volume, at an AA.

"We realized from the start that the upper on our traditional sprint spike wasn't containing her foot. There was too much volume," says Barnes. Employing high-speed video and motion-capture techniques similar to those used in special-effects filmmaking and video games, the team in the lab analyzed Felix's racing stride, displayed on a nearby computer console.

Additional data came from pressure mats measuring pressure and load through the foot, and force plates monitoring the force exerted in multiple directions while running. A human skeleton, rather eerily, raced across the screen. It showed force being put into the ground, what the toes were doing, how the foot was interacting with different shoes, and how that performance was affecting pelvis, head, and arm position.

The bottom line: They needed an upper that could contain Felix's foot better. Seemed straightforward enough. But the forces through a curve are potent. Not just those being applied to the shoe by a world-class sprinter like Felix, which would be challenge enough, but the shear forces she would experience—unaligned forces pushing one part of a body in one direction and another part in the opposite direction—would be doing their very best to spoil her day.

How, Nike designers wondered, could they create an upper that could sufficiently resist those forces, keeping Felix's foot contained, and yet still feel

Felix wanted to not think about her shoes. And Nike was determined to give that to her. But first they needed data.

like a sock that was barely there? Were they worried that perhaps it was an unrealistic goal, simply unattainable?

"No," answers senior design director for footwear innovation Stefan Guest. "It was a performance problem for us to solve. It was a challenge, but it was also something we were excited about." He smiles, and there it is again: the lingering spirit of obsessive inventiveness that saturates the Nike culture.

stitch by stitch to be incredibly light and comfortably foot-conforming. And "stitch by stitch" is no hyperbole. Nike has people called Flyknit Programmers who do exactly that—engineer an upper one stitch at a time to create targeted zones of stretch and support for tuned performance.

But Flyknit had never been used on the track at the highest levels, and the team was giddy at having a new, almost

The lab used in-shoe sensors to see exactly what was going on inside. What was the interaction between the foot and the shoe?

In his memoir, Phil Knight recounts the endless experiments of legendary Oregon track coach and Nike cofounder Bill Bowerman. Like some footwear Dr. Frankenstein, he would sneak into his runners' lockers and steal their shoes, tearing them apart and making countless modifications before stitching them back up. "He always had some new design, some new scheme to make our shoes sleeker, softer, lighter," Knight recalls.

The folks at Nike are still doing exactly that—madly analyzing and exploring, poking and probing, and pushing the envelope of what is possible, looking for that elusive hundredth of a second. The only things that have changed are the tools.

For recreational training, Felix loved Nike Flyknit: an upper made from a combination of ultralight yarn and super-high-strength fibers engineered

antithetical, challenge to attack. It was too intriguing a notion to resist—marrying a sock-like, ultrasoft upper with a high-performance, stiff, and rigid plate.

With the data conclusively identifying the problem of too much volume in the upper resulting in Felix spilling over the plates, the team next set out to analyze her performance on the straights and in the curves, and the different demands on the right foot versus the left in those circumstances.

In addition to 3D motion capture and data from the force plates, the NSRL used in-shoe pressure sensors to see exactly what was going on *inside* the shoe. What was the interaction between the foot and the shoe? How did that differ in the right versus the left? How did that differ in the right versus the left on the straights and then on the curves?

As the data and feedback from Felix came in, Nike pinpointed the different demands of the curve versus the straight on the left and right shoes and could begin to customize the uppers to meet those needs. The goal was to increase performance both inside and when exiting the curve, without impacting straight-line speed.

And here we come back to that holy of holies—*listen to the athlete*. Says Barnes, "We can make a shoe that makes Allyson faster or that contains the foot on the curve, or allows her to generate more force out of the starting block. But if the athlete doesn't believe in the product, it doesn't matter."

Nike takes that very seriously. If the data says, this is the best-performing shoe and that the athlete needs to run in it, but that athlete doesn't *feel* good in it, they scrap it.

But in this case, says senior footwear innovator Troy Lindner, "We were very fortunate. Not always do you get the athlete's voice aligning closely to what the science is telling us. In this case, we pretty much always did."

The result was a design by innovation lead Thomas Bell called the Nike Zoom Superfly Flyknit. A ribbed Flyknit structure wraps over the arch and under the foot, the knit material expanding and contracting as the foot flexes and pressure shifts around the curve. A cable system knitted on a bias into the upper works to contain the foot through the medial and lateral shear experienced on the curve. A three-quarter-height collar—looking like a sock—was added to support a greater portion of the foot and helped to facilitate natural fluidity of motion. It was something never before seen in a sprint spike.

The upper was customized to Felix's foot based on the 3D foot scan, but even with that precise data, it still required about 70 versions before the team

landed on the ideal combination of fit, containment, performance, and comfort.

But there are two interactions for a sprinter: foot to shoe and shoe to track. Once the team was confident in the upper, it was time to tackle the plate. If you thought the process of designing the upper was complex, well, to use an old saying, you ain't seen nothing yet.

THE PLATE

The sole of the shoe—the plate—is where, for sprinters, the rubber meets the road. Pun very much intended. The upper is, of course, extremely important, but it's the plate that helps determine the outcome of those moments of truth Phil Knight and John Hoke talk about. Those are the moments where Nike lives. And now, more than ever, technology is helping to shape them.

"The idea of bringing in new tools and new materials and coupling them with scientific data and putting it all in a place that enables you to quickly iterate and study and explore and experiment and fail—within a matter of seconds versus days or years—is perfect for Nike," says Hoke. "Our objective is to match athletes' ambition with our innovation."

Few Nike athletes heading to the 2016 Olympics in Rio had bigger ambitions than Felix, who wanted nothing less than to become the most decorated female Olympian in track and field history. In order to match such audacious aspiration with an equal amount of invention, Nike had to, once again, create a contradictory product.

The key was stiffness. Sprinters need stiffness. A stiff plate gives you energy return, provides explosiveness. Think about pushing off a brick wall versus a pillow, and you get the idea. But if stiffness were the only requirement, it would be easy, hardly worth all the brainpower Nike brought to muster for this project. Because with stiffness comes weight. And in a world measured in eyeblinks, weight is bad.

"When you think about making a stiffer plate," says Barnes, "things get heavier." And, she adds, "one thing we've learned through the lab and the testing we've done is that ideal stiffness in the plate for a sprinter is very individualized."

For Felix, Nike had to come up with a stiff spike that was conversely light, and, oh yes, very, very comfortable. Because typically, as stiffness goes up, comfort goes down.

The first step was to determine what the ideal stiffness was for Felix—looking at performance and comfort on the straight, on the curve, and out of the blocks. Which stiffness maximized reaction time at the start, allowed her to get around the curve quickest, to transition from the curve to the straight?

For this experiment to succeed, the journey had to be taken on a two-way track. *Listen to the athlete* was carved in stone, but what would make the endeavor a triumph was trust.

Says Barnes, "One of the things we asked Allyson was, 'Where do you get your confidence?' And she said from trusting in the science, and that what we tell her is the best thing for her." Realizing the magnitude of the trust they had been given, the team was bound and determined to earn it.

From there, the norm was constant collaboration. Whether it was Felix and her coach, Bobby Kersee, coming to Nike's campus for testing or the team flying to wherever the two were training to collect data on the track, the two sides were rarely out of contact.

Insights gleaned by the lab's researchers were passed on to Nike's product design team. "We'd come up

with version 2.0, 3.0, 10.0, 12.0 of that shoe," says Barnes, "and then we'd go back to Allyson, put it on her feet, let her try it out, measure performance, get her feedback, and then go back and fine-tune, fine-tune, fine-tune."

Eventually the partnership became more than merely designing a great shoe. The Nike team became almost honorary members of Felix's coaching staff, using the data that informed her shoe's various iterations to also provide streaming performance insight back to her and her coach. Whether it was asymmetry in the straight or lagging forces coming out of the blocks, team Felix was getting usable data to employ during practice.

What about the plate itself? It was one thing to nail down the stiffness. "But how," wondered Guest, "do you reconcile a stiffer shoe with keeping it lightweight?"

It just so happens that nature has quite a few million years of practice doing exactly that, specifically with open polygon lattices. Think beehives, dragonfly wings, and microscopic ocean organisms like diatoms and radiolaria.

Such lattices are light, stiff, strong, resilient, and flexible—in short, an ideal inspiration. This is biomimicry, the emulation of nature's models, systems, and elements for the purpose of solving complex human challenges. But it was also inspiration of a very general sort, and the team needed specifics. What shape should the matrix have, and in what pattern? How many edges? What's the cell size and how thick are its walls?

To answer those questions, Nike's designers needed computational power and tools of a sort that hadn't existed until very recently—a technology called generative design. Using constraints and goals determined by the designer, generative design employs algorithmic

Some of the natural inspiration for the shoe's custom plate included microscopic organisms, dragonfly wings, and beehives.

Plate 12. Legion Spumellaria. Orders Phaeosphaeria et Sphaeroidea.
Families Orosphaerida, Astrosphaerida et Liosphaerida.

The Voyage of H.M.S. 'Challenger'.

Radiolaria. Pl. 12.

E.Haeckel and A.Giltsch del.

E.Giltsch, Jena. Lithogr.

1. OROSPHAERA. 2–4. CONOSPHAERA. 5,6. ETHMOSPHAERA.
7–11. CERIOSPHAERA.

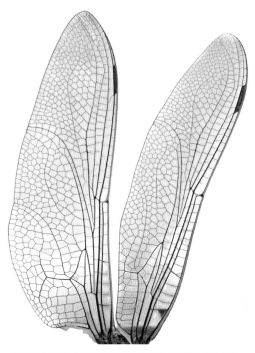

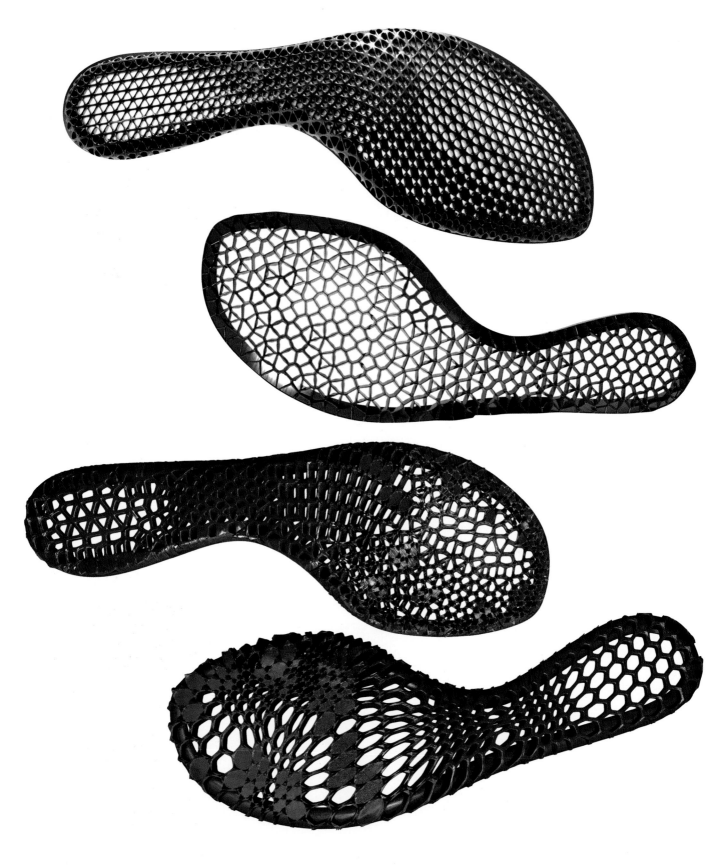

162

scripts to explore all of the possible permutations of a solution to find the best option, quickly cycling through thousands or even millions of design choices, testing configurations and learning from each iteration. The process lets designers generate options beyond what a human alone could create, to arrive at an optimal design. (For more on generative design, see "The Alien Skeleton," page 120 .)

Interestingly, generative design's preferred solutions often resemble nature's. "I think with these tools we're moving from biomimicry to biomastery," says Hoke. "It's not just mimicking and showing. We're extrapolating from that and creating something new." He sees it as a coming together of two worlds, "a unique fusion of the organic and the geometric."

Some people in the design world fear that such technology could render the designer obsolete, but Hoke disagrees. "It's an accelerant of imagination, of creativity," he says. "It's still going to

that just wouldn't cut it. To create a truly great shoe for Felix, Nike needed a stiffness *profile*. "Across the foot, we were looking at different phases of the race," says Lindner, "and really engineering that profile from toe to heel."

The goal was to create an ideal combination of stiffness and flexibility, strength and resilience, that would maximize straight-line speed, provide the loading and release needed for explosiveness, and deliver optimal pace and control through the curves, as the left and right feet were doing different things at different times.

All the numbers collected from Felix, from high-speed video and motion capture to 3D scans and force plate data, were fed into the software, and the algorithms went to work. There were things that were generally known, of course—that the tip of the toe had to be stiff but also flexible. The mid-foot needed to be rigid because of fatigue later in the race, while there had to be more support for the heel to mini-

Nike was able to rapidly produce many prototypes for the shoe plates via 3D printing, which allowed for "fast failure."

Generative design's preferred solutions often resemble nature's.

be this magic of emotion and intellect and intuition. The goal of good design is goosebumps. And the data can't dream."

No, the data can't dream. That was the work of Guest's team, headed by senior computational designer Lysandre Follet. Because as powerful as the technology is, it still comes down to the robustness of the scripts that are written and the inputs provided by the designer to drive the geometry.

The traditional, analog method of creating a plate produces a pretty uniform stiffness front to back, but

mize heel-drop. But it was the nuance they were after. And when it comes to nuance, it's all about iteration.

In Silicon Valley lingo, that means fail fast. Because the quicker you realize that something isn't working, the quicker you'll get to the answer that is.

And in the realm of the physical, the other technology besides generative design that enables fast failure is 3D printing. In fact, because the forms created by generative design are so complex, traditional methods of manufacturing typically can't produce them.

It was the nuance they were after. And when it comes to nuance, it's all about iteration.

So this dream team of generative design and additive manufacturing meant that critical iteration could happen at an unheard-of rate. Showing up at the track with multiple versions of the shoe—all subtly different—the team was able to include targeted learning based on the capture of data from the previous session and see what bubbled up as custom tweaks that might make Felix faster. Then they'd go back and do it again. And again. Says Follett, "It's pretty incredible the speed at which we were able to iterate."

"We knew we wanted a lattice matrix," says Guest, "because it's porous, it's superlightweight, yet incredibly strong." But what shape lattice to leverage from nature? "We ultimately ended up with a more rounded hexagon cellular form." Just like the millions-year-old radiolaria.

During the iterative loop, the team looked at many things, varying for different types of cells and shapes in different formations across the plate, adjusting cell-wall thickness and height, looking for that optimal combination of stiffness and weight that could both mitigate stress and be resilient to it.

They played with the number of edges and cell size, rounded the intersections, and subdivided the grid to create a plate that would perform optimally for both feet, even when each was doing something different.

Another advantage of generative design is that the designer can specify at the outset the material to be used to produce the final product, and the algorithm will adjust the design to optimize the performance for that particular material.

"We just have a much more powerful toolbox now," says Lindner. "With generative design we can tune everything. And we can tune everything to a specific individual."

And that brings up an interesting point. Sports gear has always gotten better—that's nothing new. As technology has evolved, so too has the equipment, and that equipment has enabled athletes to perform at a higher level. But this is light years from that. It's not about a bunch of tennis players, for example, hitting harder because they're all using titanium instead of graphite. This is about maximizing an individual athlete's potential based solely on that individual's unique capabilities—and on a particular venue or event. And that's revolutionary.

There's one more detail about Felix's shoes: They're beautiful. The upper is a gradient of shocking color, a screaming visual Doppler effect, a neon slap in the face meant to echo a body in rapid motion and the pop against the blue of the track.

And then there's the plate. Given that its inspiration is millions of years old, it's ironic that the plate immediately puts one's mind in the world of science fiction. With its organic forms and color-shifting iridescence, it looks like a futuristic beetle.

Felix during her gold medal relay performance at the Olympics in Rio.

CREATE / NIKE'S 3D SPRINTER

THE FUTURE

A few years ago there were people asking, How much better can we really make shoes? We must have reached a plateau where we can no longer do anything else of real substance to a shoe. Now, surely, it's all window dressing.

But the truth is, we're only scratching the surface. Because on some level, the technology is now driving the designer. Not in terms of inspiration, but suddenly the designer is thinking about things he or she never considered before because those capabilities simply didn't exist.

"Now I get to ask questions about chemistry," says Hoke. "I get to ask questions about four-dimensional geometry. Now we can get down to the atoms of the design. You're getting endless exploration. It's magic."

But what does this mean if you're not an elite athlete? Just an average runner hoping for a better 10K?

"We would love for anybody to come into a facility," says Tony Bignell, vice president of footwear innovation, "where they can scan their feet and produce shoes specifically for them, with customized support and comfort, and walk out of the store with their shoes."

Nike can actually already do that. It's what they did for Felix, after all. "That work for elite athletes is a proving ground for the masses," says Guest.

John Hoke sees it this way: "Will companies hold finished goods or will they hold the *capability* to make? And perhaps we'll invite consumers in to finish the process. It's far more personal, more of an extension of who you are, and the consumer is a cocreator."

Beyond the consumer, the product itself will act as cocreator, continues Hoke. Embedded intelligence in a shoe or garment will provide endless improvement opportunities. "How did we do? What worked for the athlete? What didn't?"

Everything's a possibility, everything's on the table, because the core tenet of Nike is to amplify and augment the athlete's body, to change the way it works mechanically—to speed up evolution in a way.

"We're allowed to dream big and have absolutely crazy ideas," says Barnes. "I mean, it's a sprint spike. It has to have a stiff upper, right? But Allyson's spike is like wearing a sock. Whoever thought that someone could sprint in a sock with a plate on the bottom of it?"

WHO INDEED?

"Our role is to invent the future of performance innovation for athletes," says Bignell. And sometimes to get there you need just the right amount of crazy, like an upper that feels like a sock or a plate that's twice as stiff as normal, but more comfortable.

In the end, Felix was measurably better, clocking faster times in practice and greater efficiency through and exiting the curve.

In the summer of 2016, in Rio, Allyson Felix became the most decorated female Olympian in track and field history. Running a punishing anchor leg in the 4x400m relay, she took home her sixth gold medal as the heralded Jamaican team could only marvel from a distance at this once-in-a-generation athlete.

Hoke said it so very eloquently—the data can't dream. And as someone who watched Felix run in Rio, I simply say, thank goodness for that.

The Flyknit upper was also customized for Felix to fit securely and feel like a sock.

Architecture, Assembled

New fabrication methods mean that buildings can be made faster and more efficiently—breathing new life into ideas about design and construction.

Architects, designers, and developers have long struggled to streamline the complex process of building. Now, advances in digital and industrial technology are enabling several companies to integrate best practices in fabrication and assembly to create more efficient and sustainable production methods and more durable and attractive buildings. This is taking place on vastly different scales, from skyscrapers to office buildings to homes in rural England, Scotland, and Canada.

London design firm Facit Homes uses digital tools and modern manufacturing techniques to fabricate building components—many of them on-site in a portable facility housed in a shipping container. The pieces are then assembled on-site.

The D-process, as it is called, begins in the firm's East London studio. Just as with many architects, designers using building information modeling (BIM) software create a 3D digital model of the home according to the customer's budget, site specifications, and design preferences. At Facit, though, the homes are made not from 2x4s and other standard parts, but from a system of precisely designed components that the firm itself makes using the latest fabrication tools.

Construction gets underway after a shipping container with a CNC router—a computer-controlled cutting

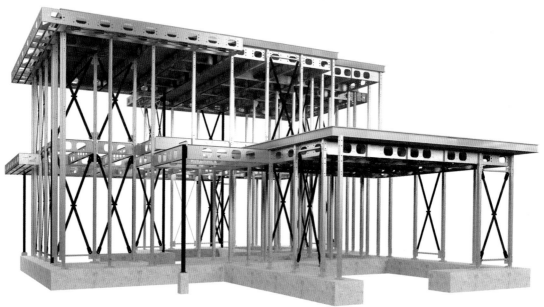

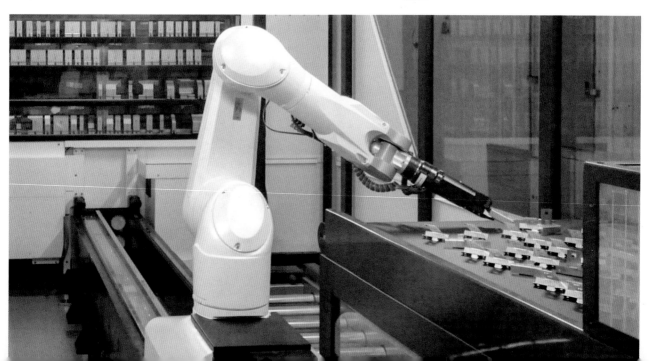

The process resembles a contemporary assembly line.

machine—arrives at the site. The design is downloaded to the router, and the machine mills raw wood panels into modular building blocks for the frame, roof, and other components. (Metal stairs and some other complex pieces are manufactured at Facit and brought to the site.) The router etches a part number into each modular block to guide builders as they assemble the pieces, Lego-like, using large rubber mallets to connect the joints and nail modules into place. In a final step, windows and kitchen and bathroom fixtures are added. Everything fits snugly into place because the router has accurately carved out the right locations for sockets, ducts, light switches, and electric cables.

D-Process resembles the assembly line of a contemporary manufacturing facility in which everything is derived from a single digital model. Like an iPhone, BMW, or jetliner, each Facit home is bolted together in a highly controlled, fluid system. "We believe in manufacturing, and so does the customer because they want the reassurance that every part will be perfect," says Bruce Bell, who cofounded Facit Homes in 2009 and is an industrial designer by training. "That is what contemporary manufacturing does; we applied that to building homes."

The past century has seen many versions of prefab buildings—from the Sears Roebuck and Co. "kit houses" sold between 1908 and 1940, to architect Moshe Safdie's stacked box Habitat '67 at the Montreal World Exposition to the wave of prefab modern homes that *Dwell* magazine and others helped publicize in the early 21st century. These designs prompted public discourse but did not spark a prefab construction boom. By 2008, when the Museum of Modern Art in New York City staged the exhibition "Home Delivery: Fabricating the Modern Dwelling," curator Barry Bergdoll wrote, "The relationship between the drawing board and the finished product has never been more dynamic, but the potential of prefabrication has not yet come to full fruition." Today, companies like Facit reflect growing interest in new types of prefabricated structures that incorporate cutting-edge technologies and more daring and customizable design.

Bell says that efforts to devise an "ultimate building system" using prefabricated or modular units ultimately fail because such designs need to be standardized so they are cost effective. Inevitably, this leads to "boxy, dull, and routine" designs that disappoint customers who want homes with unique features. He considers Facit's D-Process the next stage in the evolution of prefabrication because it is a "digital form of craftsmanship" that combines technology, customization, and traditional building skills. "There's no human interference between the design and the object as it moves from computer model to a physical thing," he explains. "But then tradesmen take over to finish the installation."

At every Facit construction site, electricians, plumbers, and plasterers work with the company's project management staff to oversee construction.

Sometimes even the homeowner pitches in as special features like a laser-cut circular staircase, solar window shade, or front door canopy are lifted into place. But for the most part, Facit does all the fabrication and construction work.

Facit has built 15 homes, ranging in size from around 1,000 square feet to 5,300 square feet, in rural areas and suburbs in Britain and Denmark. Bell says a big attraction is the homes' sustainable features: FSC-certified wood, 100 percent recycled fiber insulation that fills the modular boxes, and built-in mechanical heat-recovery ventilation. And because everything is fabricated on site, there's less waste and lower labor and shipping costs. Yet Facit homes are not a solution for affordable housing: Depending on the configuration and features, the homes cost between $325,000 and $2 million, well above the average $260,000 price of a home in the U.K.

That could change if digital design, fabrication, and assembly methods are more widely adopted across the architecture and construction industries, creating economies of scale. Eventually, Bell says, "What we do will become less uncommon, but only if designers and manufacturing experts work together."

The idea of bringing cutting-edge manufacturing techniques to customized construction methods has captured the imagination of other companies, too, including ConXtech in Pleasanton, California, and BONE Structure in Montreal.

ConXtech, a construction technology company, developed a unique digital design and fabrication process for the small connectors that support a structural steel framing system. The ConX system was conceived around simple, configurable parts that make it easier to assemble the beams and columns that hold up multistory buildings. This allows the company's integration team, architects, and engineers to collaborate at a very early stage of the design process; using BIM, they can create a dimensionally and spatially accurate building framework.

Introducing innovation into established industries like construction engineering can be a challenge. For ConXtech, that meant establishing its own 122,000-square-foot factory in 2003 in Hayward, California, and equipping it with specialized CNC mills to manufacture the connectors, and robots that weld its lower-and-locking mechanism to standard steel beams. Once the materials are on-site, the structure can be put together safely and rapidly, "like an Erector set," says Bob Simmons, ConXtech's cofounder and CEO.

The company also needed to set up a full-scale testing facility in 2008 to prove that its connection technology could withstand seismic events and other stresses. At the time, Simmons recalls, "there was no clear path to accepting our technology because the building code changes so slowly." In 2010, after extensive testing, a chapter was added to the American Institute of Steel Construction (AISC) codebook based on ConXtech's testing results.

In a similar way, BONE Structure has disrupted the design and construction industry with new processes and materials for making homes and commercial buildings. "We really wanted to change the habitation throughout the world," says the company's founder and CEO, Marc Bovet.

Bovet started BONE Structure in 2005 after trying to build his own home, concluding that the way we build today is chaotic and fundamentally broken. "I think the caveman figured it out much better," he said. "Since then we've been literally going backwards." Bovet, who

previously worked in the aerospace and transportation industry, put together a team to consider three critical issues facing the industry: the shortage of specialized labor, including carpenters; endangered supplies of its main natural resource, wood; and the need for greater environmental responsibility, as 60 percent of construction waste now ends up in landfills.

BONE Structure's first home was made of wood, but the pieces were precut by a CNC machine and assembled on-site according to plans that Bovet says were "as precise as an IKEA furniture set." However, this carefully crafted construction strategy was foiled by humidity that caused the wood to expand. So laser-cut galvanized steel—a much more inert material—became the standard for BONE Structure. Not only can steel withstand harsh Canadian weather conditions and seismic shocks (the company is also building in California), but it also resists mold and deterioration. Moreover, a steel-framed structure—which Bovet likens to an airplane fuselage—does not require load-bearing walls, allowing spacious interiors.

For the building process, Bovet insisted on an "idiotproof" construction system based on collaboration, seamless technology, and easy-to-assemble, precision-engineered parts. All team members—architects, engineers, designers, and contractors—are involved from the beginning to avoid any miscommunication and misinterpretation of construction plans and design intent. "I want them to grasp what's at stake here," Bovet explains, "to get a sense of the real responsibility that what they are creating will be here for 150 or 200 years." Each building is custom designed on Revit and Inventor

according to the owner's specifications and run through a series of tests, including an energy-use analysis.

The design is sent to one of BONE Structure's 15 manufacturing plants, where 11-gauge steel beams are cut to size with preset openings for electricity, ventilation, and heating components. The beams are shipped to the site on flatbed trucks with little or no packaging (to reduce waste) and assembled by builders using only battery-powered drills. Every piece of the building clicks together, Bovet says, using Lego blocks as an analogy—85 percent of the parts for every BONE Structure building are identical. Once the steel shell is in place, polystyrene panels and foam insulation are attached for a tight, energy-efficient building envelope that can be designed to meet LEED, Passive House, or Net Zero Energy specifications.

The innovations of all of these new building systems—integrating digital design and manufacturing, durable materials, and environmental benefits—will reshape the industry.

What Lies Beneath the Sequential Roof

The world's largest robotically constructed roof is an impressive feat—but not more so than the robotic architecture experiments that will happen under it.

When the Institute for Technology in Architecture (ITA) needed a new home at the engineering and science university ETH Zurich, the institute approached the challenge as it does most of the work done there: as a life-size research project. Here, the ITA could explore concepts including zero-emissions architecture, the digitization of the construction process, robotic construction, and the creation of a building free of central supporting structures. It would be research done at a scale of 1:1.

The result is the Arch_Tec_Lab, which opened in September 2016. The new building is an impressive feat of architecture and a real-life application of ITA research. Beneath the zero-emission structure's curved wood roof is a workspace—the Robotic Fabrication Laboratory, big enough for four industrial robots to build a two-story building, where the ITA's groundbreaking research continues.

The roof itself is the biggest proof point: It was designed computationally and built by robots, signaling a new generation of construction and a new world of man-machine interaction.

The roof itself is the biggest proof point: It was designed computationally and built by robots, signaling a new generation of construction and a new world of man-machine interaction. The Sequential Roof, as the undulating structure is known, was built by robots working "essentially like a massive 3D printer. It's layer on layer on layer of timber," says Russell Loveridge, the managing director of research at Switzerland's National Centre of Competence in Research (NCCR) Digital Fabrication, a research group housed at ETH Zurich that now resides in the new building. The nationally funded research program is a rigorous multidisciplinary investigation into advanced fabrication, smart materials, and experimental construction techniques.

Also under the new roof, and embedded in the framework of the NCCR, is the research program of professors Fabio Gramazio and Matthias Kohler, NCCR principal investigators. Their research into robotic fabrication helped lead to this innovative roof; their program's past projects (see page 184) indicate the kind of work that the new building's Robotic Fabrication Laboratory will host.

The Sequential Roof is the largest robotically built timber structure in existence. It is essentially a massive timber structure covered in a rubberized polymer membrane, which eliminated the need for interior finishing—there are no drywall or acoustic panels in sight. Rather than a building-wide HVAC system, small heating and cooling units are distributed throughout the building with sensors to fine-tune the climate control. Spaces were left in the roof trusses for installing lights, skylights, ventilation, and wiring, and the roof itself is an acoustical diffuser, creating a quiet space underneath the roof for people to work.

"The choice of materials and the amount of materials you use is by far the biggest input in the ecological costs of construction," Loveridge says. "If we can design something like the roof to serve all these functions and eliminate those other materials, we know that we're building more sustainably than if we do it more cheaply."

The zero-emission build started from the ground up: The structure was constructed on top of an existing parking garage, avoiding the energy and environmental effects of a new foundation. The first level of the building houses

previous pages: The remarkable, curved timber roof of the ETH Zurich's Arch_Tec_Lab. opposite: A robot-based assembly process created the woven trusses, demonstrating the potential of combining digital fabrication techniques with timber.

CREATE / WHAT LIES BENEATH THE SEQUENTIAL ROOF

the Robotic Fabrication Library, which Loveridge describes as an engineering testing hall. Above the testing hall are the offices for NCCR, and above that is an open space under the roof where researchers can work and collaborate.

The testing hall is where the roof was fabricated. During the build, four industrial robots hung from the ceiling of a 60 x 14 x 8 meter space. The robots worked on gantries with six degrees of freedom, all controlled by the same system so they could work in sync. "There's never been a case where four synchronous robots can do things together," Loveridge says. Each robot was capable of holding up to 30 kilograms (66 pounds), so one could hold an object while the other three worked on it with various tools.

Building the structure took a village. ETH Zurich faculty asked ERNE AG Holzbau to realize a parametric roof design for the ITA and employed the robotics manufacturing company Guedal AG, which had created a small robotic woodworking system. Zurich-based ROB Technologies was tapped to provide control and operation software.

The Sequential Roof is made up of 48,624 individual timber slats, assembled into 168 roof trusses and truss girders that are interwoven into a 2,308-square-meter (24,843-square-foot) free-form roof. Fabricating the complex roof geometry was dependent on an integrated digital planning process that mixed together elements of structural analysis, design, and fabrication data generation.

Architects at the institute built a 3D model of the Sequential Roof, which they sent to structural engineering consultants who used a nail image generator to place each of the 800,000 nails necessary in the model. (Nails were a better choice than glue for the roof, but also involved intense calculations related to the material and the complex geometry of the roof.) Then ERNE checked the data and prepped it for robotic machining.

During production, the gantry robot also functioned as a quality analyst. A photogrammetric system compared each node and nail image with the target plan, creating a QA feedback loop that ensured everything was being built

A ceiling-mounted gantry allows for large-scale implementation of robotic fabrication projects by means of four cooperating industrial robots.

"If we can design something like the roof to serve all these functions and eliminate those other materials, we know that we're building more sustainably than if we do it more cheaply."

correctly. After the system checked all the nails, the trusses were brought to the site.

Despite the success of this project, Loveridge doesn't believe that robots will ever entirely replace construction workers. Instead, the backbreaking work of construction will evolve into a job that has a symbiotic relationship with the machines, and it will no longer be a young man's realm. Computational analysis has improved in the past decade to give machines enhanced spatial awareness and precision. But you still need someone to make sure the computers are making the right decisions and completing tasks in the correct order. Even now, you see workers becoming more intellectually engaged in construction and less physically engaged, and that will accelerate with the rise of robotic fabrication.

"A lot of the jobs being done in the construction industry rely on the human's ability to look, process, and judge things, and rely on experience, and then do the physical work in reaction to that," Loveridge adds. "There's an inherent tacit knowledge that comes from working on a construction site that is not programmable. The way things come together is never perfect, no matter how much you do. There's always going to be a need to have people who know how things go together."

The Unbearable Freedom of Manufacturing

New technologies take flight at GE's most advanced factories.

Engineers find inspiration in the strangest places. A few years ago, Charlie Hu was browsing through a diamond industry catalog. He was thinking not about designing the perfect engagement ring, but gas turbines. Hu is an industrial manufacturing engineer at GE Power, the GE division that makes equipment for power plants, and he spotted a diamond-cutting laser machine that could perfectly solve a problem he was facing at work.

That problem involved another project from the industrial frontier. Scientists in GE labs spent the last two decades inventing a special kind of ceramic material as tough as metal, but only one-third as heavy. Called ceramic matrix composite, or CMC, it can operate at 2,400°F—500° higher than the most advanced alloys, which makes it perfect for the hot sections of advanced gas turbines and jet engines. But it is also very difficult to shape.

Hu convinced his boss to purchase the diamond-cutting machine, built by the Swiss company Synova, and reengineered it so that it can shoot a powerful laser beam through a hair-thin jet of water that envelops and focuses it like an optic fiber. The water also cools the surface of the target part and flushes out debris. "I thought it was a good idea," Hu says about the machine, called a Laser MicroJet. "I am very proud that the concept went into the real machine."

So was Kurt Goodwin, one of GE's technology mavens and the leader of GE Power's Advanced Manufacturing Works in Greenville, South Carolina. "The

MicroJet slices through CMCs like a hot knife through butter," he says.

Hu's epiphany is just one example of how GE engineers are remaking manufacturing. Goodwin's works is stocked with 3D printers churning out intricate turbine blades and fuel nozzles with little more than just a powerful laser and a bed of fine metal power. Elsewhere in this factory of the future, there are ovens with argon atmospheres that cure CMC parts. There is also a robot nicknamed Autonomous Prime—after the *Transformers* character Optimus Prime—that scans its work area with LiDAR eyes and services a computer-controlled milling machine. In fact, much of the technology here comes embedded with sensors that stream data over secure Industrial Internet links into the cloud for analysis and insights that can optimize production on the go. "This facility is the bridge between the lab and reality," Goodwin says. "It's an incubator. We collaborate with engineers to allow them to realize their big ideas and help turn them into a process that you can do reliably over again at the right price."

The Advanced Manufacturing Works isn't GE's sole such site. Just a few weeks before it launched in April 2016, GE opened a gleaming Center for Additive Technology Advancement (CATA) in Pittsburgh. The place looks a lot like a futuristic set for a Stanley Kubrick movie. Everything seems to be white: the walls, the gleaming floors, even the noise coming from various forms of 3D printers sprinkled throughout the hangar-like space.

3D printing is the poster child for additive manufacturing—a production method that adds material rather than cutting it away. "Normally when you want to produce a part, you start with a big piece of metal and machine it down," says Jennifer Cipolla, who runs CATA. "But you also create a lot of waste. Additive allows you to grow something from the ground up from a bed of metal powder, sand, or other material. There's hardly any waste because you can reclaim pretty much everything. It also allows you to create much more complex internal geometries that would be otherwise very difficult or expensive to achieve, creating parts with improved performance."

previous pages: A sand binder jetting machine prints casting molds in a single day—a huge breakthrough. opposite: A diamond-cutting laser inspired GE's Laser Micro-Jet, which was developed to cut ceramic matrix composite.

"This facility is the bridge between the lab and reality. It's an incubator. We collaborate with engineers to allow them to realize their big ideas and help turn them into a process that you can do reliably over again."

CREATE / THE UNBEARABLE FREEDOM OF MANUFACTURING

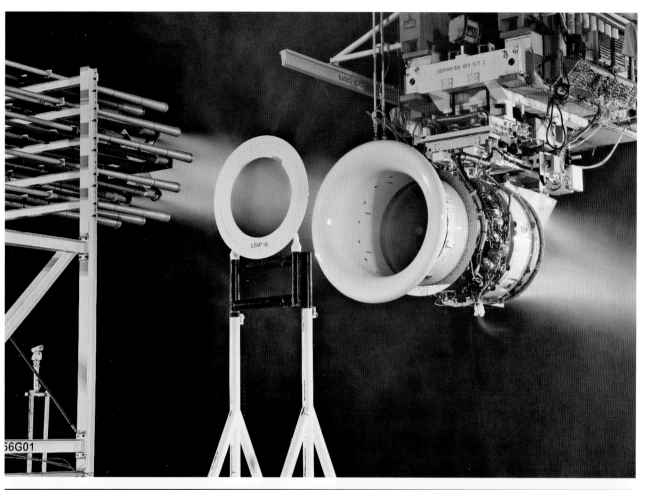

GE is exploring three main areas in additive: rapid prototyping, full-scale industrial production, and "spares on demand."

The LEAP-1A jet engine (top), produced by CFM International and now used in some Airbus aircraft, includes the world's first production 3D printed jet component: a complex fuel nozzle (bottom).

GE is exploring three main areas in additive: rapid prototyping, which allows designers to quickly come up and test new designs; full-scale industrial production; and "spares on demand," which could one day allow astronauts to print a replacement part in space, rather than hauling it with them or waiting for a delivery.

At CATA, there is a huge rapid-prototyping device called "sand binder jetting machine." It prints castings molds from layers of fine sand, each 280 microns thick, infused with a special chemical called the activator. When the two mix, they start an exothermic reaction that hardens the sand into the desired shape. "We are making the Jell-O mold for the jelly," says Dave Miller, the engineer working with the machine. "The sand mold gets stronger as it ages. It's like concrete."

Miller can print one complex mold in a day and have the casting back from the foundry the next day. "This is a huge breakthrough for rapid prototyping," Miller says. "You'd normally spend many thousands of dollars and many weeks to achieve the same results. With this 3D printer you are cutting down costs and also your lead time."

Like Greenville, CATA has rows of direct metal laser melting (DMLM) machines that use lasers—sometimes several beams at once—to fuse one fine layer of metal powder after another in the right design pattern directly from a CAD file. Each layer is between 20 and 80 microns thick, and there are as many as 1,250 layers per inch—each less than the thickness of a human hair. The laser power ranges from 400 watts to 1 kilowatt, enough to burn a hole in a wall. It's just like welding, but on a microscopic scale.

GE Aviation is already using DMLM machines to produce fuel nozzles for jet engines powering aircraft like the next-generation Boeing 737 MAX and Airbus A320neo, which entered commercial passenger service in 2016. (The same engines also use CMC components for the first time.) Other GE businesses like GE Oil & Gas and GE Power are also printing valves and other parts. "The immense appeal of additive manufacturing in the design community is breathtaking," says Prabhjot Singh, senior principal engineer for additive manufacturing at GE Global Research. "You will be able to make things that are completely unrealizable today. At GE, additive started with aviation, but it spread like wildfire to other businesses."

Singh says that GE first started experimenting with additive manufacturing in 1997, and he got to play with his first 3D printer five years later. But it took more than 15 years for core technologies like lasers and powdered

"If you're a designer who has always designed for conventional manufacturing, you need to unlearn some of what you know."

materials to mature and key patents to expire. "That's why you are starting to see the boom now," he says.

Another thing that needs to expire along with the patents is the old way of design thinking. "If you are a designer who has always designed for conventional manufacturing, you need to unlearn some of what you know," Singh says. "The paintbrush with which you are building parts now is a speck of metal dust smaller than the width of the human hair. You have to learn to work with that amount of freedom. The possibilities are immense."

So immense that his team is using supercomputers to not only design better parts but also figure out the best ways to make them. They feed the computers with algorithms that can optimize design and also manufacturing rules. "When you have something as complex as the fuel nozzle for a jet engine, you can optimize its design and production to such a degree that would be very hard for a human to comprehend," Singh says.

Despite his optimism, there are things that keep Singh up at night. One of them is quality. It takes weeks to print large metal parts, and each cubic inch includes many miles of tiny welds.

They all have to be perfect. When something goes wrong in additive printing, it usually can't be fixed. "I would love to have an erase button," he says.

He and his team are working with Cipolla at CATA to put sensors on machines and use machine vision and other tools to pick up defects as soon as they occur. "Most additive machines are still not production-ready," Cipolla says. But she and her colleagues are determined to change that.

opposite top: An engineer inspects 3D printed test bars at GE's Advanced Manufacturing Works.
opposite bottom: The Laser MicroJet created the precision holes in this component using thin streams of water.

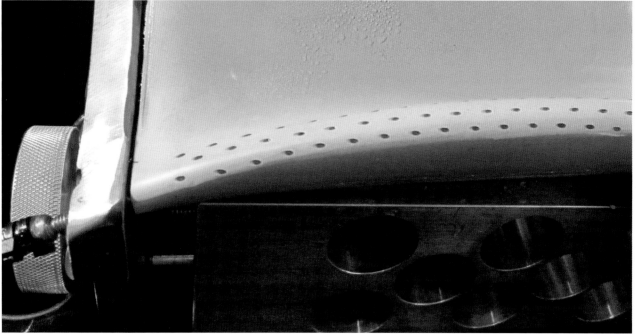

Robot
Be Nimble

The latest breed of robots remain untiring workers— but now they are bringing deft, adaptable, and smart behavior to their tasks.

A dinosaur hides in a block of foam. How do you get it out? At Garner Holt's eponymous animatronics company, this used to take a team of carvers a week or more of work, toiling in a dust-filled room, "whacking away with chisels," Holt says. The company had always used robotics, but that had come later in the process, to animate the lifeless foam once human hands had given it shape. Robots were precise but repetitive. Powered by robotic servos, the dino's tail would sway the same way every time. Humans were the clever ones: The dinosaur's likeness—and the client's satisfaction—rested on their variable skills with a chisel.

That power balance is shifting. As the fourth industrial revolution accelerates—bringing smart machines and robots they control into the mix—more creative manufacturers like Holt are handing their tools over to machines. But today's robots aren't replacements—they're partners, ushering in a new kind of collaborative manufacturing driven by very human creativity.

With limited memory and cumbersome software, teaching robots used to be a laborious, hands-on affair, says Steve Hobbs, vice president of CAM and hybrid manufacturing at Autodesk. "When I got involved with robots 30 years ago, to teach them a series of positions—go from here to there, open and close a gripper, lift something up—you had to literally move the robot around by hand, with your head stuck in the works to see where it was going."

This kept tasks simple. Picture the classic, car-factory drone slapping in rivet after endless rivet, doing that same job until it dies. And often, that's exactly what would happen: A robot facing an unplanned event or overly complicated movement would freeze, or break, or worse. "Robots aren't rigid like a machine tool," Hobbs explains. "They move a little bit under loads, and that introduces risk. Plus, a robot can tangle itself up if you just give it a series of positions and say, 'Go for it,'" he says, miming a phenomenon called gimbal lock, or "wrist flip," in which a robotic arm gets stuck along an axis while trying to act out convoluted or conflicting moves (picture that same drone on a mid-rivet coffee break, trying to check its watch without spilling its mug). Reprogramming a robot meant taking it offline to walk through the entire cumbersome teaching process again.

With nimbler mechanics and cheaper, smaller memory systems, today's robots can be trained on the fly, keeping multiple movement paths in storage and learning new ones with a simple software upload. And the software has improved too, incorporating more accurate kinometric simulations to predict things like gimbal lock and keep robots moving smoothly—and coffee safely in mugs.

All of which brings Garner Holt's dinosaurs to life faster, more cheaply, and more accurately. In the chisel-wielding days past, Holt's carvers were usually working from drawings and artist sketches; today's characters, though, are digital. "Many of the characters we do now, for movies like *Ice Age* or *Planes*, are already on a computer," Holt says. "They're a CGI model, not a drawing. And we can upload that model right into the carving robot, so a client can look at it on the screen and know that's what they're going to get."

That precise, complicated carving ability was what originally drew architectural fabrication firm Kreysler to the work of Delcam, a U.K.-based CAM software company Autodesk acquired in 2014. CNC machines are giant, room-sized contraptions. A software-driven robotic arm—usually an orange machine made by Kuka—is light, portable, and endlessly maneuverable. "Machine tools are huge, heavy structures that cost a lot of money, but robots are cheaper and lighter," Hobbs says. "If you're cutting lightweight material like expanded polystyrene, you can put it on your extremely expensive machine tool, capable of cutting hard metal at high speed, or you can save money and use a robot." And that's what Kreysler did, hanging their Kuka arm upside down above foam blocks to carve hard-to-reach areas and stay out of the way of falling debris. Their Kuka makes a great foam-mason, but it's so much more.

previous pages: The San Francisco Museum of Modern Art's expansion, which features an undulating facade. opposite: Kreysler & Associates used precisely controlled robots to carve molds for the undulations.

A software-driven robot—usually a machine made by Kuka—is light, portable, and maneuverable.

"We didn't want to limit it—it's much more versatile," says Kreysler's Joshua Zabel. They can snap in a new attachment—a hot-wire cutter, say, or a spray nozzle—upload a new program, and it's an entirely different machine. Kreysler used that same Kuka to help build the molds for the undulating fiberglass panels that clad SFMOMA's new facade. Each of the 700 panels is unique, but every one is roughly the same size, requiring 700 different molds to be lined with ever-so-slightly different configurations of gel so the finished fiberglass panels can be removed once they set.

"It's a mass customization problem," Zabel explains. "If all 700 panels were the same size, we could just write a straightforward automation to fill them with gel. But we can't use the same program for each one." Without a robot up to the task, they'd have workers with backpacks and respirators spraying each mold. Now, a robot can do it.

And what else can they do? "We have a laundry list of ideas," Zabel says. "Mostly heavy lifting jobs we've normally had to do ourselves. If a guy can walk around the shop carrying a fiberglass mold, why can't a robot?"

Well, sensory perception, for one reason. "But it's a solvable problem," Hobbs says. "We're working on having sensors built into the robotics so they're more situationally aware and can detect if they hit something they're not expecting to and figure out what to do."

Some day soon, Kreysler might have one less worker huffing under heavy loads around the shop; Garner Holt already has fewer human carvers whacking away at foam—but that doesn't necessarily mean fewer creative brains at work. "If you're carving by

hand, you have to have someone with artistic skills," Hobbs says. "But if you can upload the original computer-based geometry or 3D scan to a robot, what was an artistic process becomes a machining problem." But must you take away an artist to gain a more perfect dinosaur? No, Hobbs says. "Some people say it's like photography versus painting: You take the art out. But we're past that now. It doesn't remove creativity, it just changes the balance of creativity. When robotics make the grunt work easier, like shaping big forms of foam, people can invest more in other creative aspects of it, like the initial design or the finishing process."

"The creative element is upfront now, in the design," Holt agrees. "Now we have one really good artist designing the characters instead of a room of sculptors carving them out."

These new robots are unmistakable descendants of that assembly line drone: They won't get sick, they won't get tired, they won't get hurt. But in other ways, they're remarkably different. They can learn faster, work smoother, and most importantly, they can adapt. But far from making human heads and hands obsolete, they liberate them. With robot collaborators helping out, human workers can think bigger and take more design risks. They can be more, well, human.

The Gap between Idea and Object Is Vanishing

There was a time when a powerful computer cost as much as a house. Someday soon, we will look back in wonder why powerful, versatile robots were so expensive. As robots follow the exponential growth curve—becoming smarter, more powerful, and more connected—and transform into general-purpose machines, they will do things that will seem unlikely today. More and more things will be built with the assistance of other robots. Things that we consider too delicate or in need of human craftsmanship will eventually be modeled by robots. The growth will happen slowly—then suddenly—as breakthroughs in machine learning are made and that knowledge is shared.

What will future generations of robots look like? They will have better sensors and better computation. Sensors let them feel what they are doing, rather than blindly following instructions; better brains give them more nuanced learning. That is, capture and compute combine with create to create adaptable, generalized making. The robots that come out of this process will be more nuanced, more like skilled craftsmen.

EFFICIENT CREATION WILL TRANFORM BUSINESS

Robots will make things better. Eventually, virtually everything will be made by robotic devices; the only separation will be the *roboconomics*: Once the hardware capital programming cost is less than labor, robots will take over production.

The results will cascade through business models. As the number of steps to produce an object decreases, and as machines become smarter, production will become faster and less wasteful. And as devices become more flexible—as with multiheaded devices that can cut, grind, weld, staple, and polish or do what several people or several machines would previously—retooling disappears, saving time.

Shorter lead times from design to production will mean a deeper capacity to meet ever-changing customer needs. Makers will produce what's needed, when needed, leading to lower inventory, less waste, and reduced transportation costs. Robots will tighten the loop between demand, design, fabrication, and purchase.

We will see more examples of mass-market customization and product personalization. Since manufacturing lines will be nimble, able to change in hours rather than months, we will see more organizations producing made-to-order products, whether jewelry or furniture or cars or houses.

DIGITAL CREATION WILL BE MORE CONNECTED

Once one machine figures out how to make something, every machine that is connected on its network will know how to do the same. The knowledge and insight gained through machine learning of one robotic system will be able to be shared to other similar systems.

The steps in fabrication are ideal candidates for machine learning. A robot that learns to paint a Rembrandt will be able to share its new skill with other similarly equipped robots. A robot that learns to assemble a collection of bamboo sticks into a hut will be able to share that with other devices globally, and those devices will be able to make the translation from bamboo to pine to bricks. This will be a fast transition because of the compounding nature of network effects. Connected robotic devices will be smarter, safer, and more precise, building a collective understanding of how to make things as they complement the skills of human craftspeople.

ROBOTIC CREATION WILL COMPLEMENT HUMAN CREATION

A growing trend in manufacturing is the shift from developing *automation*, where robots replace humans, to *autonomation*, where robots are designed to work with humans. The goal in autonomation is to make human work more interesting, creative and rewarding.

This will continue to change the nature of craftsmanship. It will expand to take advantage of technology and integrate digital skills with physical skills. We will see general robots on more job sites. Some will service a single purpose, like cutting holes in walls for plumbing, electrical and HVAC. Others will have general capabilities from sweeping floors to keeping track of progress.

Baxter, a robot produced by ReThink Robotics, is among the first intended to operate around people. It is meant to be trained, not programmed, and to work outside of a cage performing low-level repetitive tasks, like boxing, packaging, loading and unloading, and moving materials around.

AS CREATION EVOLVES

With advanced robotics, designers will have the opportunity to rethink not only what to make, but how to make things using process simulation. Computable manufacturing and building opens new possibilities, bespoke solutions, and custom creations. Designers and makers will need to learn how to take advantage of these capabilities to fully realize their potential. Many techniques, especially those that combine additive and subtractive manufacturing, will seem nonintuitive. Yet they can make products and parts that are simpler, with fewer joints and seams.

The democratization and increased application of robotics will affect jobs, the cost of labor, and transform factories. We will see the growth of new microfactories, populated with more skilled people, that serve specific niche markets and geographic locations. We will also see robotic fabrication continue to expand at the largest scale, leading to so-called "lights out" factories, which can be run in the dark because their robots don't need human intervention. The joke goes, this factory of the future will be staffed by a man and a dog. The man is there to feed the dog. And the dog is there to make sure the man doesn't touch anything in the factory.

The tools of capture, compute, and create complete a cycle of digitization and materialization, linking the computable virtual world with the physical. Capture is the on-ramp to make digital sense of the world. Compute is the engine to analyze, explore, simulate, learn, and design optimal solutions. Create is the off-ramp to make those designs real, bits back into atoms, placing the right materials in the right places in the right ways.

This virtuous loop between the physical world of fabrication and the digital world of abstraction is playing out in countless ways, at many time and spatial scales, with variations in every industry that makes things.

COM

CHAPTER 4

POSE

What something is made from can be far more important than the form it takes. The great breakthroughs that have changed our world—skyscrapers, cars, computers, smartphones—happened not just because we could envision new forms. They all depended on new materials that allowed them to be made.

As we apply digital tools to the materials we select, engineer, and make, tomorrow's materials will have qualities that seem simply magical today—and that will allow for far-reaching innovations.

The properties we desire in the objects we use emerge from a combination of their form and their materials. A stainless steel knife cuts because it has a sharp machined edge and because it is made of a metal that doesn't easily dull. A coffee mug contains your hot latte without burning your hands because the ceramic insulates and keeps the outside cool to your touch. Your smartphone display has sharp, vivid color not only because of well-written software, but also because it incorporates rare-earth metals like scandium and yttrium.

In 1980, designers could choose from about 60,000 different materials to work with. Today, the number is well over 300,000. That will likely double within a decade. And it's not just new variations on traditional materials. Highly engineered materials, biological materials, and nanomaterials have expanded the range of what designers can use. This unprecedented choice gives designers the opportunity to rethink how they make things—and the chance to explore entirely new processes and forms that can work only with new materials.

EVERYTHING IS MADE FROM SOMETHING

The materials designers select have impacts not only on the form their work takes, but also on its performance, its effect on the planet, and even its soul.

In building, for example, we desire materials with specific performance properties. They need to be strong, yet light. Flexible, but not too flexible. They need to conduct heat and electricity, or block light. They need to not wear out. They need to not scratch nor succumb to rust.

The fundamental qualities of materials—performance, aesthetics, and impact, intuitively understood and applied by makers—are now becoming computable.

Material proliferation directly impacts the challenges and opportunities in manufacturing and construction in at least three ways. First, it allows us to address the performance properties needed for a particular project. With greater choices, designers have more options to balance trade-offs with desired properties.

Second, materials are valued for their aesthetic qualities. Materials imbue objects with soul: They give things tactile qualities that we respond to emotionally. Though a polyester suit jacket may fit and function well, it will never evoke the feeling of cashmere wool. Materials speak to us at a gut level. We know this when we settle into a luxury vehicle. It just feels really good.

Finally, materials have a profound impact on our planet. Every material takes energy and skill to harvest, process, create, transport, and manipulate. The grand challenges facing the world will be tackled in part by making things with revolutionary materials—those that need less energy for manufacturing and cause less disruption to the ecosystem.

CAPTURE, COMPUTE, AND CREATE MATERIALS

As we understand how to capture the vast range of properties of materials, compute the ways they will perform under various conditions, and create them with precision, we remove more of the guesswork from making. This is good news.

This understanding emerges by studying materials at various levels of magnification. A material's properties emerge from a combination of the composition (the constituent elements and compounds that make it up) and the structure (how the compounds are organized at various levels of hierarchy). For example, most metals are made up of a few elements organized in relatively simple regular structures that don't vary much across different scales. This combination imbues them with familiar physical properties. Composite materials, on the other hand, are made up from a greater number of elements in more complex arrangements, and have more complex behaviors.

These combinations are staggeringly complex and give rise to the fantastic materials we encounter in our lives. The qualities of every substance we encounter—from the shade of paint to the knap of fabric to the color of a hot light bulb filament to the smoothness of your smartphone screen—emerge from the combination of material and its hierarchical structure.

Capture technology allows us to understand why materials have the properties they do. For example, the most prized swords from the Middle Ages were made from Damascus steel. They were light, flexible, and kept their sharpness even when cutting through a lesser blade. The specific recipe to make the metal was closely guarded, but was known to combine alloys from Sri Lanka with mixtures of bark and leaves. Modern capture analysis reveals that these blades are infused with nanotubes and nanoparticles. These impurities, from the carbon added by the organic material, was exactly what gave the swords such valued qualities.

Materials scientists are rapidly building databases

to deepen their understanding of how composition and structure produce specific properties. These will augment what makers know intuitively. Woods are useful for making housing framing or a fine tabletop. Metals are strong and electrically conductive. Ceramics are brittle. Composites, combining two or more materials, create new properties; for instance, concrete and rebar together make walls stronger and resilient. Material databases will provide better, more informed options for building.

This data is also paving the way to design materials from scratch. If we know the complex chording of properties we'd like to have in a material, shouldn't we be able to select the molecules and organize them into structures that give us these properties?

It is a very complicated discipline—and nature is more nuanced than our best computer models. However, the work is promising.

Designers now consider the impact of the materials they select not only on the form their work takes, but also its performance, its effect on the planet, and even its soul. This is leading to a better sense of how to use woods, glasses, ceramics, and composites with greater precision.

The qualities of every substance we encounter—from the shade of paint to the smoothness of your smartphone screen—emerge from the combination of material and its hierarchical structure.

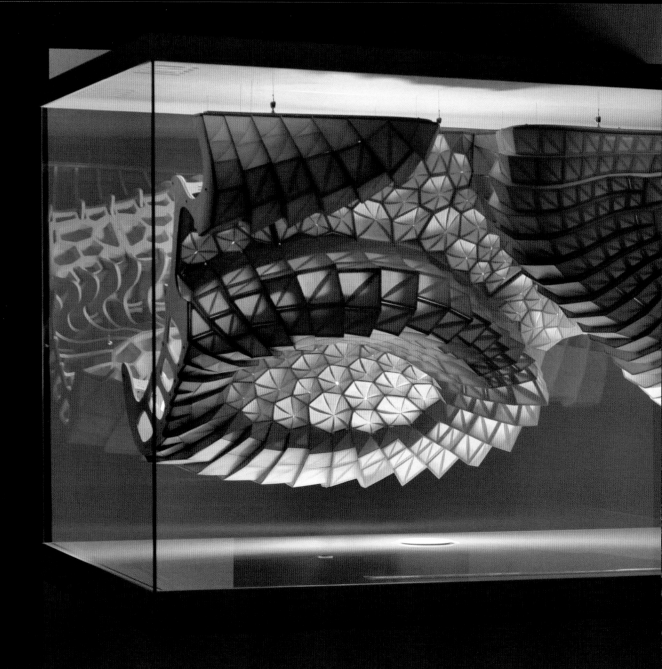

Design by Design: The New Generations of Materials Science

At labs around the globe, researchers are charting the future of advanced materials.

Designers are used to making trade-offs. The possibilities for making something are often limited by the materials available. A very large structure needs to be stable and strong, but the material it's made of can't be so heavy that the construction collapses under its own weight. Or an object might need to be extremely lightweight but still withstand a certain amount of pressure.

New materials are making new ways of making possible, adding functionality to objects through the structure of the materials themselves, and designers are learning to work backward, starting with the process of making and working forward with the aid of high-powered computation.

Around the world from each other, two institutes are building never-before-seen structures and pushing the limits of design: One fabricates microarchitectures that form all-new materials to meet custom specifications, the other creates life-size architecture inspired by microstructures in nature. Researchers at California's Lawrence Livermore National Laboratory and the University of Stuttgart's Institute for Computational Design are designing new materials and methods in addition to forms, with the potential to change the shape of the world.

CALIFORNIA'S LAWRENCE LIVERMORE NATIONAL LABORATORY

When it comes to working with "normal" materials, scientists often use what are commonly called Ashby charts to help decide which is best for the task at hand. All known materials are plotted on two axes determined by the requirements, say, strength vs. density, stiffness vs. cost, wear rate vs. hardness, or thermal conductivity vs. electrical conductivity. Based on your project's needs, you select a material that will behave in the way you want it to.

But what if you need something that doesn't fall in the right place on the chart? Lawrence Livermore National Laboratory's Additive Manufacturing team is starting to create materials with physical characteristics that don't exist in nature by designing backward. Using any of a number of proprietary 3D printing techniques, they create microscopic unit cells that are designed to have a specific functionality they need, like high levels of strength as compared to weight. Those tiny printed cells, made of a polymer, resin, or metal, form a material that maintains the desired characteristics.

"We can design material behavior to satisfy any requirement, and we don't have to mix materials or have rigid boundaries between materials," explains Erin Bradner, a research scientist and Autodesk's liaison with Livermore. "We couldn't do that without software." Computational analysis determines the form and geometry of the unit cells and how to join the cells into trusses to distribute the desired property. "Up until now, designers were designing an object knowing what material they wanted to use," she says. "Now we can make the material satisfy the properties we give the system." And they can test tens of thousands of cell designs, rapidly speeding up the research process.

previous pages: Achim Menges's hygroscope explored a kind of responsive architecture that exploits the characteristics of wood. opposite top: Autodesk and Lawrence Livermore National Laboratory (LLNL) are working on a novel kind of helmet that uses stiff, low-density materials— materials that fit into the unpopulated "stretch-dominated lattices" area of this chart. opposite bottom: This varying density lattice is intelligently distributed across a cantilever shape to maximize stiffness while minimizing weight.

"Up until now, designers were designing an object knowing what material they wanted to use. Now we can make the material satisfy the properties we give the system."

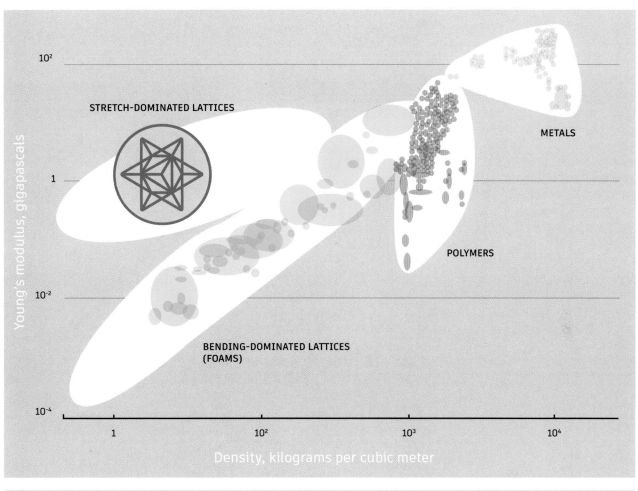

STRETCH-DOMINATED LATTICES

METALS

POLYMERS

BENDING-DOMINATED LATTICES
(FOAMS)

Young's modulus, gigapascals

10^2

1

10^{-2}

10^{-4}

1

10^2

10^3

10^4

Density, kilograms per cubic meter

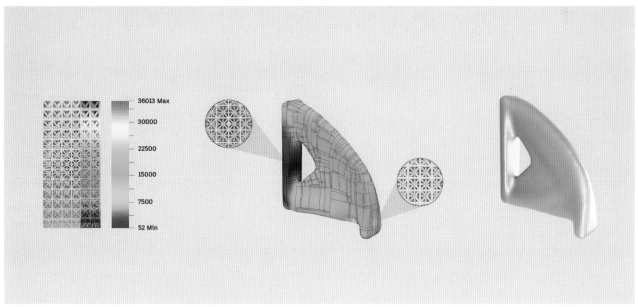

36013 Max
30000
22500
15000
7500
52 Min

COMPOSE

214

"It's also about nailing the property you want rather than creating something completely unusual," says Chris Spadaccini, head of the additive manufacturing program at Livermore. "You might want 4.1 microstrain per Kelvin, where every existing material has 3 or 5. Negative properties are really exciting, but it's equally achievable to get the exact property you want."

In the research process, the Livermore team is creating dozens of new materials every year, many of which are still in the early phases of development. The bespoke additive manufacturing processes Livermore uses to create these new materials are working in scales of nanometers and micrometers.

Livermore, located east of the San Francisco Bay Area, is one of 17 national laboratories funded by the Department of Energy. Autodesk's relationship with Livermore, solidified by an 18-month collaborative research agreement, had to have a focus. The helmet project was selected as a test case more for its complexity than for potential commercialization. New algorithms have been developed to grade the helmet material in a way that responds to various forces across its surface. Currently, those calculations have to be done by hand, and materials combined to make a helmet have margins between them.

"When you're designing a helmet, you have to be able to anticipate a wide array of conditions and strain rates based on the incident or sport," explains Eric Duoss, a Livermore engineer who is leading the Autodesk collaboration. Many cushioning materials are highly nonlinear in their behavior, so doing the analysis for those dynamic events is challenging.

In a helmet, the shell material is rigid, designed to distribute impact loads across a larger area, and the cushioning material further dampens the blow, protecting the wearer's head. Setting up the simulation capacity was essential to be able to predict the effects of multidirectional impact on a helmet. Livermore gave Autodesk a number of potential unit cells to evaluate, to see how changing the strut diameter in the lattice affects stiffness and distribution.

Initial tests are showing 3D printed foams outperform traditional foams. Livermore researchers found 3D printed foam aged more slowly, retaining mechanical and structural characteristics, than traditional foam, which experienced more extreme stress in their tests.

Livermore has developed eight custom additive manufacturing processes so far, with a few in fairly advanced (but still precommercial) states. For the helmet project, they're mostly using microstereolithography (MSL), a process that can be used to create complex 3D structures, and direct-ink writing (DIW), which Livermore has been using to print rubbery, energy-dissipating materials. DIW uses nozzles as small as 200 nanometers to print highly flexible material that flows at room temperature. Livermore has built printers that can travel up to 10 centimeters per second while maintaining submicrometer resolution. MSL is capable of producing very small features over large areas and creating materials that are very stiff for their weight. As opposed to mechanical 3D printing techniques, MSL employs ultraviolet light and photomasks to cure photopolymer liquid resins.

Livermore is also developing new feedstock materials—what you use in the additive manufacturing process—which are often polymers, but also metals and ceramics. Although they are composed of microarchitectures,

LLNL engineer Chris Spadaccini (left) and material scientist Eric Duoss (right) use an additive manufacturing system; both are involved in the investigation of a new helmet material.

the materials are printed at such high resolutions that the naked eye wouldn't see the individual cells. Using microarchitectures in additive manufacturing is harnessing the power of nature. "So much of nature is cellular structures, repeated like a honeycomb," says Bradner. "Computational design is letting us move between scales and really perform biomimicry."

As Livermore and Autodesk rounded into the final third of their joint research agreement, production of helmet prototypes was on the horizon. Custom-fit 3D printed helmets are still a few years away. Because Livermore gets Department of Energy funding, the project possibilities are tackled more like an educational institution than a corporation that has monetization and commercialization to worry about.

"Ultimately, when we set up the helmet project, it wasn't about helmets. It was always about how you revolutionize design and manufacturing," Duoss says. The goal is to start with high-level objectives, like functional problems, cost requirements, or manufacturing constraints, and have the computer design for you. In some cases, the complexity of the objectives is impossible for a human to parse, with tens or thousands of variables. "You don't have to have intuition about what the final design should look like before you start. And then in the future the computer will design it for you."

STUTTGART'S INSTITUTE FOR COMPUTATIONAL DESIGN

In the Swabian city of Stuttgart, the many hills seem to hold just as many construction sites. While the city is undergoing a traditional transformation, a cloister of experimental architects is investigating techniques for the future.

"We try to investigate new technologies not just to make them better but to investigate the very properties of these technologies to discover what we can build," says Achim Menges, founding director of the Institute for Computational Design in Stuttgart. Menges, an architect who has held professorships across Europe and the United States, is known for his experimental projects. "Usually new technology is used to make old products better. But we want to construct entirely different designs, processes, and constructions by embracing new technologies."

In creating new processes, his team often looks to very old source material: nature itself. And nature doesn't inspire just the designs of ICD projects but the methods with which they're made. Simpler is often better: Complex mechanical systems that rely on networks of sensors and power sources tend to degrade over time, but simple material systems with embedded functionality will last longer.

One of the projects Menges's team is working on is making wood smart. By coating a thin slice of wood in laminates, one responsive to moisture and the other less responsive to moisture, you can create a controlled curvature that responds to the environment. "This laminate is both the sensor and the actuator," Menges says. One example, inspired by the structures of the spruce cone, is the HygroSkin pavilion, which has apertures made of thin pieces of plywood that close when humidity reaches a tipping point and open when the weather is dry.

Since 2010, first-year master's students at ICD have produced a pavilion, an exercise Menges describes as a "pedagogical playground." Going from research to final product within a year, "it introduces students to the future of

opposite top: Achim Menges's 3D printed hygroscopic material can sense, actuate, and respond to climatic changes; here it is opening in response to lower relative humidity. opposite bottom: One-millimeter-thick test samples of the material are programmed to respond differently to increases and decreases in humidity. It is "both the sensor and the actuator," Menges says.

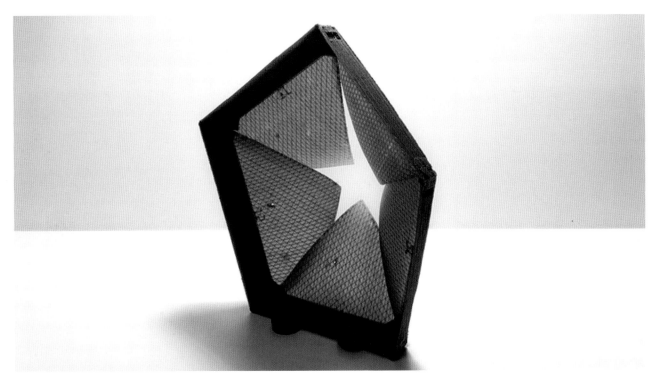

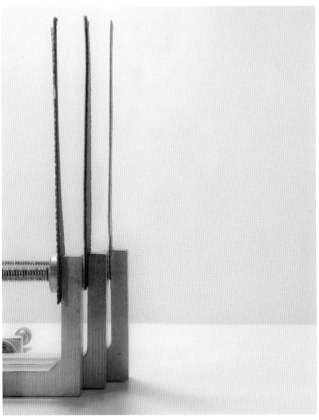

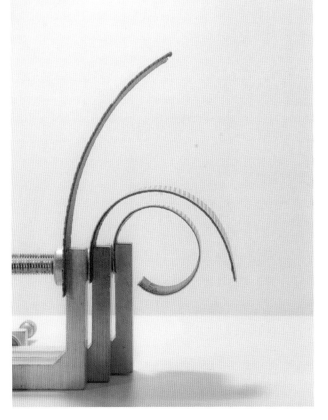

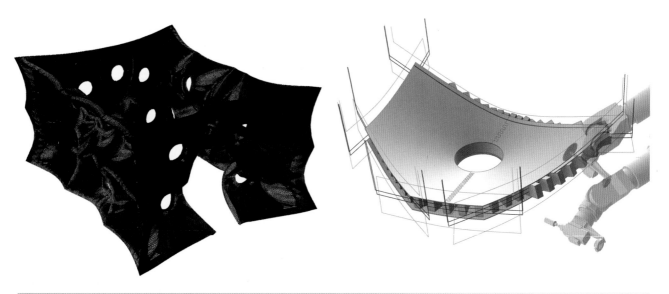

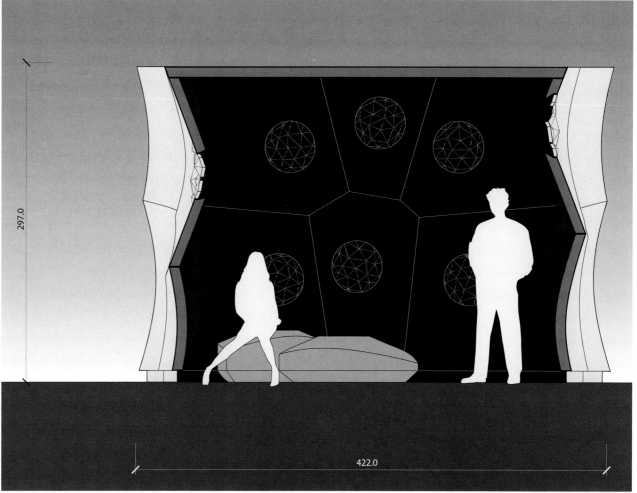

297.0

422.0

Rather than looking to nature to solve a particular problem, Menges's team screens nature for interesting things.

making by getting them to think around what exists," he says. "You're not only designing an object but the processes of making. Design these days is not limited to shape, but it can mean a really comprehensive activity: Tools, structure, concepts, everything is designed and everything has an incredible importance for the building."

Stuttgart's history with hands-on pedagogy and experimental architecture goes back to the 1960s, when Frei Otto founded the university's Institute for Lightweight Structures. The architect's organic Olympic stadium roof, completed in Munich in 1972, was praised for its lightweight strength and is an obvious ancestor to ICD's current work.

Though they are only allowed to stay on the Stuttgart campus for six months, the pavilions are important as a proof of concept and as architectural exercises. Menges cites as inspiration the Barcelona Pavilion built by Ludwig Mies van der Rohe in 1929, a modernist, minimalist structure that blurred the boundaries between inside and outside. Though it was torn down a year later, it's had more impact than many "permanent" buildings, he says.

Organic shapes are a never-ending well of inspiration: Menges's team has a partnership with biology researchers who feed them ideas, identifying

principles of process, structure, and methods that could be translated into architecture. The biology team presents 20 to 30 options, which Menges's team narrows down to five or six items to carefully consider before selecting one to run with. Rather than looking to nature to solve a particular problem, they more often screen nature for interesting things. "There's a lucky moment when those two things align," Menges says.

"Compartmentalization of disciplines is so bad for innovation," says Lauren Vasey, a doctoral candidate at ICD who teaches master's students. But computation is allowing various fields to more easily sync up with one another, making quantification of performance possible to a degree never before achievable.

One concept currently being pecked at is the nest-building habits of birds. Menges's team is fascinated by the behaviors a bird embodies to resolve a complex task: The bird picks up random objects to build a nest—the plants available for building materials are different every time, as is the environment, but the bird manages to build a nest that meets its architectural requirements. So rather than program a robot to build a structure based on your requirements, could you program a robot to make something from the materials it has at its disposal, to react and learn as it goes?

COMPOSE / DESIGN BY DESIGN: THE NEW GENERATIONS OF MATERIALS SCIENCE

COMPOSE / DESIGN BY DESIGN: THE NEW GENERATIONS OF MATERIALS SCIENCE

That was part of the inspiration for the team's pavilion at the Victoria and Albert Museum in London. The roof of the pavilion is made of carbon glass composite fibers that were wound on sprockets by an on-site robot. But the design of the pavilion changed based on how people used it, with live robot construction events throughout 2016. Small thermal-imaging cameras tracked traffic, and fiber-optic sensors used in the construction itself measured temperature within the structure. The robot is gathering data and using it to inform its own actions. Menges could see the techniques used in the V&A pavilion eventually being used to create a stadium roof—the larger a structure is, the lighter weight the materials have to be.

By thinking about manufacturing from Day 1, jumping from vision to construction isn't "as great a leap as traditional architecture, where you have a great idea and you think, 'How the hell am I going to build that?'" Menges says. "We don't have a preconceived idea of how things should look." The pavilion on the plaza below looks a bit like a spaceship. The hull looks substantial but is very lightweight, made with thin sheets of plywood that are bent into shells, inspired by the plates of a sand dollar, and sewn together with laces by robots. Invisible to the naked eye, the surfaces of living sand dollars are actually made of plates sewn together with microfibers, giving their hulls flexibility.

Getting these innovations out into the real world is often challenging. The building sector is conservative, and insurance risks are high for unconventional materials and manufacturing methods, so the timeline for techniques to show up in practical applications is uncertain. "We see automation really affecting the automotive industry, but it's been slow to affect the building industry," Vasey says. So far, 3D-printed houses tend to just be replications of existing designs rather than real innovation. "Building systems have been derived by a human-centric logic of construction."

Traditionally, architecture was a cerebral activity, with the duties of the designer and the builder starkly separated. But for Menges, "We try to engage the material world and its complexity right from the beginning as an accomplice or agent in the design process." Computational design only used to make existing architectures better is boring. Menges wants to know, "What kinds of architectures are only possible with these technologies? You could make a robot lay roof tiles in a faster way, but what kind of roof would a robot want to build?"

previous page: The hygroscope, a sculptural use of Menges's novel wood, on display at the Centre Pompidou in Paris. opposite top: The ICD/ITKE research pavilion for 2013–2014 investigated the fabrication of fiber-reinforced polymer structures via synced robots winding glass and carbon fibers. opposite bottom: The pavilion's design was adapted from the structural principles of a beetle.

The Self-Assembly Line

Skylar Tibbits is exploring "Active Matter"—a new kind of material that we can program.

Skylar Tibbits's passion, originally, was architecture, and his career in the field looked bright. He'd already earned a degree from Philadelphia University, interned at the firm of famed neofuturist designer Zaha Hadid, and worked for the prestigious studios at Asymptote Architecture and Point B Design.

Increasingly, though, he found himself drawn to architectures grander than any skyscraper—and smaller, too, by many orders of magnitude. His mind wandered to structures as bafflingly vast and dynamic as planets and stars, and as minuscule as individual cells and proteins. In DNA that replicates millions of base pairs in an hour, or in the astrophysical forces that shape celestial bodies with the force of untold millennia, he saw levels of sophistication that human technology had yet to reproduce. He became convinced that those stars and proteins had something fundamental in common: Each could assemble itself, or replicate itself, or even repair or restructure itself.

"Everything at the smallest of scales works on the principles of self-assembly, but also at the largest of scales," Tibbits says, clad in a black Calvin Klein T-shirt, with a light beard and studs in his earlobes. "If you think about astrophysics and other domains where there are no top-down machines, no planetary printers, no sledgehammers and screwdrivers making very large-scale or very small-scale systems, the only way for those things to assemble is with components that interact with one another and respond to the environment and the energy around them."

He wondered whether self-assembly could be translated to a human scale—to the realm of vehicles, clothing, firmament, or furniture. The question drew him to MIT, where he obtained master's degrees in design computation and computer science. Afterward he stayed on as a research scientist, and in 2013 he founded the institution's Self-Assembly Lab, a bustling workshop on Massachusetts Avenue where some of Cambridge's brightest designers now hunch over drafting tables, iMacs, and 3D printers to wrestle with the future of matter itself.

in precisely engineered patterns that, when released, sprang into the shape of a wearable shoe.

Then there are the high-profile collaborations. Tibbits politely declines to comment on a rumor that he's working with Ikea on furniture that can assemble itself straight out of a flat pack, but his work with other A-list companies is well-documented. He used a carbon-fiber composite to develop a concept for Airbus that flexes in response to heat changes in order to regulate the airflow into a jet engine. He worked with Briggs Automotive to develop a smart spoiler for race cars that changes shape to maximize traction in slick road conditions. He partnered with Stratasys and Autodesk to devise a technique to

"If you think about astrophysics and other domains…the only way for things to assemble is with components that interact with one another and respond to the environment."

In Tibbits's cluttered office, he ticks off the lab's flagship projects with a practiced rhythm. There's the series of Tetris-like solids that, if left in turbulent water overnight, will hook together to form a chair. There's the process they invented to print wood composite into flat sheets that, when exposed to moisture, warp into lovely origami-like figurines, or even functional furniture. There's the time they extruded plastic onto sheets of tightly stretched textiles,

print lengthy strands of filament that, when dropped into a tank of water, fold themselves into complex shapes, much like the proteins that called to him as an architecture student.

But Tibbits downplays the individual importance of those projects. Collectively, however, they can become something significant. He wants to see them converge into a novel field of study, tentatively termed "Active Matter," that would encompass not

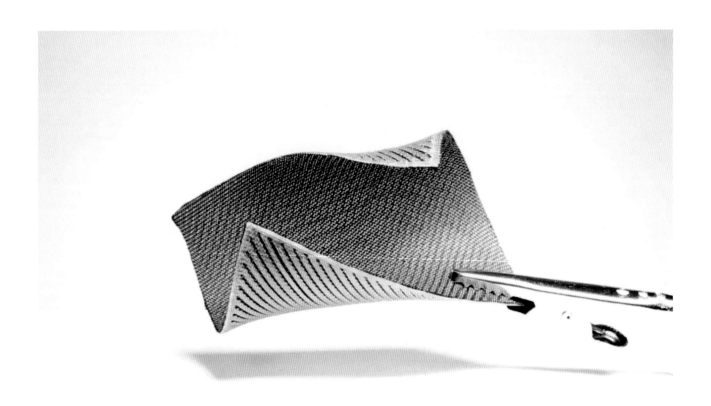

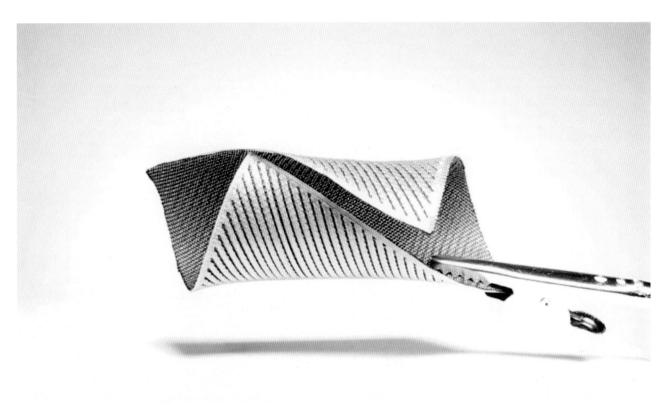

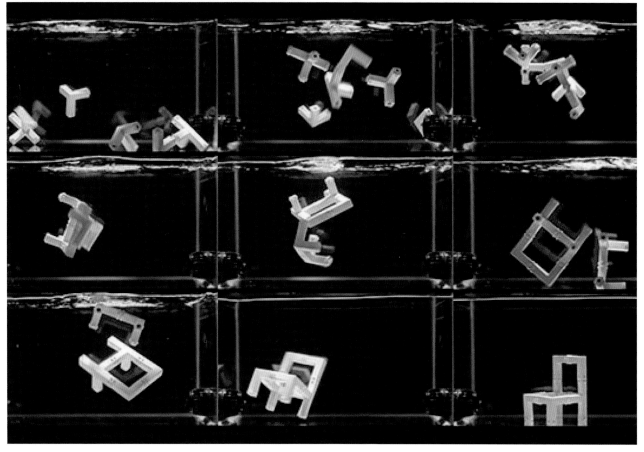

"Tomorrow we will program matter itself."

page 228: One focus of the Self-Assembly Lab is programmable textiles; these fabrics change depending on temperature. **page 229:** Components buffeted in turbulent water assemble themselves into a cube (top) and the first ever self-assembling chair (bottom). **opposite:** The lab is packed with projects that explore how to program intelligence into the materials we use to make things.

only self-assembly but also materials science, synthetic biology, nanotech, robotics, and more. Those fields will converge, he hopes, into a design Zeitgeist that could supersede the breakthroughs in software and hardware over the past several decades, bringing a shift away from automating systems with actuators or microcontrollers and toward programming intelligence into materials themselves.

Tibbits is the first to admit that it's not clear what that might look like in practice. The most important work coming out of the lab, he says, is still purely theoretical; even the flashiest projects the lab has developed for Airbus and Briggs offer little more than a glimpse at a future where clothing could adapt to the temperature or build of its wearer, where buildings might capture the energy of the wind and rain to repair themselves, and other applications too far-fetched to even imagine.

The next step is for researchers in diverse fields representing academia, industry, and government to start teaming up and sharing knowledge about work that could contribute to Active Matter as a creative and scientific movement. "What we're trying to demonstrate is that these principles—of assembly, of programmable materials and phase change—are things that many researchers are working on across all the spectrums to get to this kind of Holy Grail of Active Matter," he said.

To get the ball rolling, in 2015 the Self-Assembly Lab organized the Active Matter Summit, which drew luminary speakers including John Main, DARPA's defense sciences office program manager, and Neil Gershenfeld, the founder of MIT's seminal Center for Bits and Atoms. ("I want to give you a progress report on making the Terminator," Gershenfeld quipped, pulling up a slide of the liquid metal villain of the 1991 action film *Terminator 2: Judgment Day* on the projector behind him, to laughter.)

When Tibbits took the stage on the first day of the conference, he laid out a challenge for attendees: to start thinking, in broad terms, about what sort of tools the designers of the future might use not just to shape matter into traditional mechanical systems, but also to program intelligence into it directly.

As he spoke, he pulled up a black-and-white clip of Ivan Sutherland's 1963 Sketchpad software, which is viewed by historians as the earliest predecessor to contemporary CAD systems.

"I think this event is specifically looking at the lineage of technologies from the past, and then how that propels us into the future," he said, addressing the auditorium. "If today we can program computers and machines, tomorrow we will program matter itself."

Gone Viral

The next frontier of design is biological.

The advent of rapid-prototyping technology has softened the border between matter and data. It's now a simple task to transform information into a material object using a 3D printer or CNC machine, or even to digitize a physical artifact using a 3D scanner.

Andrew Hessel, a research scientist at Autodesk's Bio/Nano Research group, wants to blur the distinction further by printing functional organisms—an objective that repositions living matter as yet another material in the designer's repertoire and that may, potentially, be poised to remake medicine as well.

Fundamentally, Hessel argues, living cells are tiny computers that carry out the instructions contained in biological software. "Living things do compute," he says. "That's how they stay alive. It's chemical and biochemical computing." And like the software that runs a digital computer, he adds, that code can be hacked.

As Hessel and his team see it, the biological sciences are poised for a paradigm shift. Researchers are sequencing the DNA of great swathes of life and collecting bulk biometric data at the individual level. There's unprecedented access to scientific publications, and the Internet has made it easy to share raw data. And, crucially, genetic engineering is starting to mature.

We've already become accustomed to the notion of genetically engineered foods (even if we have not made peace with it). Hessel, whose background is in cell and genetic biology, believes we'll soon see the same science revolutionize many other industries—manufacturing, for example, or the energy sector, not to mention health care.

Soon it will be difficult for manufacturers to ignore the advantages of using microorganisms to produce rare or expensive compounds. Biological building blocks like carbon and nitrogen are plentiful in the natural environment, and the everyday temperatures and pressures that facilitate life sidestep the safety concerns and energy consumption associated with foundries and chemical plants.

"Life is fantastically diverse in what it can produce," Hessel continues. "All you have to do is look around at the creatures in nature to kind of get a sense of that. But by learning how to code it better, it's opening up the diversity of living things to human creation or modification. So, it's a really vast, creative space."

As evidence, look at ventures that are already leveraging genetic engineering into the manufacturing sector. A Raleigh, North Carolina, start-up called bioMASON, for example, is using a bacterial slurry that excretes a binding compound to emulate the properties of cement; mix the slurry with sand, and it can be used to make concrete or bricks. Boston's Ginkgo Bioworks is manipulating yeast DNA to produce valuable fragrances. And Emeryville, California, biotech outfit Zymergen closed a $42 million funding round last year to develop similar technologies for industrial manufacturing.

Yeast and bacteria, of course, are relatively complex microorganisms. When Hessel started to investigate synthetic biology about a decade ago, he was swiftly drawn to the idea of engineering something far simpler, in biological terms: viruses.

What drew him in was the virus's distinctive life cycle. In nature, a virus reproduces by injecting a living cell with genetic material that manipulates the cell into creating copies of the virus. In cases like HIV or smallpox, the consequences for the host organism can be grave—but in principle, he learned, the entire process could be hijacked: If you rewrite the code that a virus uses to infect a cell, you can manipulate the cell to do almost anything.

The virus, then, becomes a sort of biological USB drive you can use to deliver a software payload to a cell. It's like the meta version of bioMASON or Ginkgo: Instead of engineering a novel bacteria or yeast, you could create a virus loaded with the instruction set to modify an existing organism.

Those hacked viruses could even be used to modify how entire existing organisms function. The implications, as Hessel describes them, could be ripped from the pages of a superhero comic.

"If you wanted to change a microorganism to produce a material, you might simply create a virus that has the instruction set for that material and infect the bacterium with that instruction set," Hessel said. "If you want to add a new function to an animal, all you really have to do is encode that new function into the program that can be delivered by a virus, because the viruses are so surgically accurate in their ability to deliver software."

At the Bio/Nano Group's offices at Pier 9 in San Francisco, Hessel's team has developed a number of next-generation tools to facilitate that work. With a program called Genetic Constructor,

"Life is fantastically diverse in what it can produce…. It's a really vast creative space."

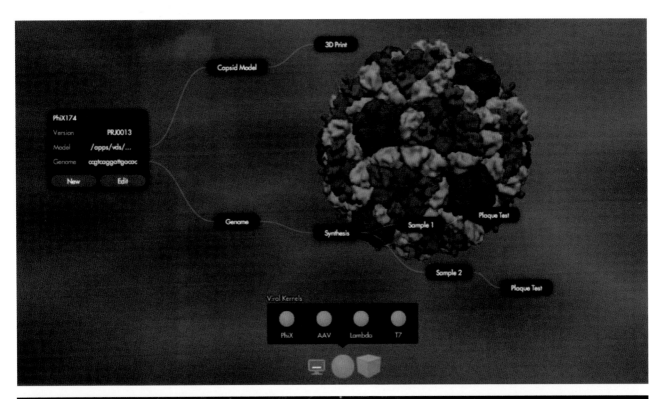

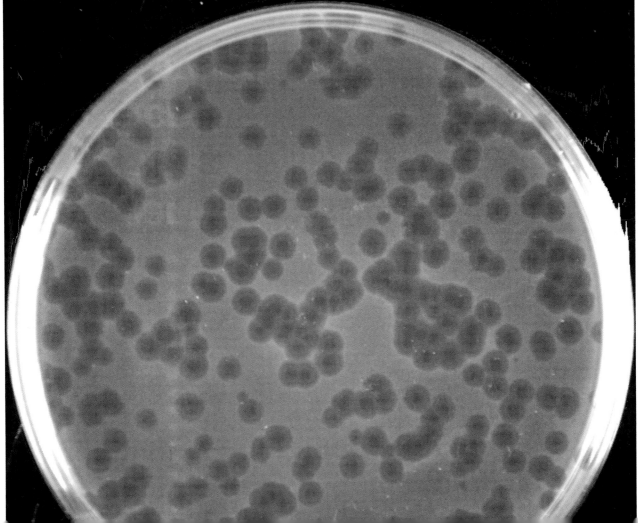

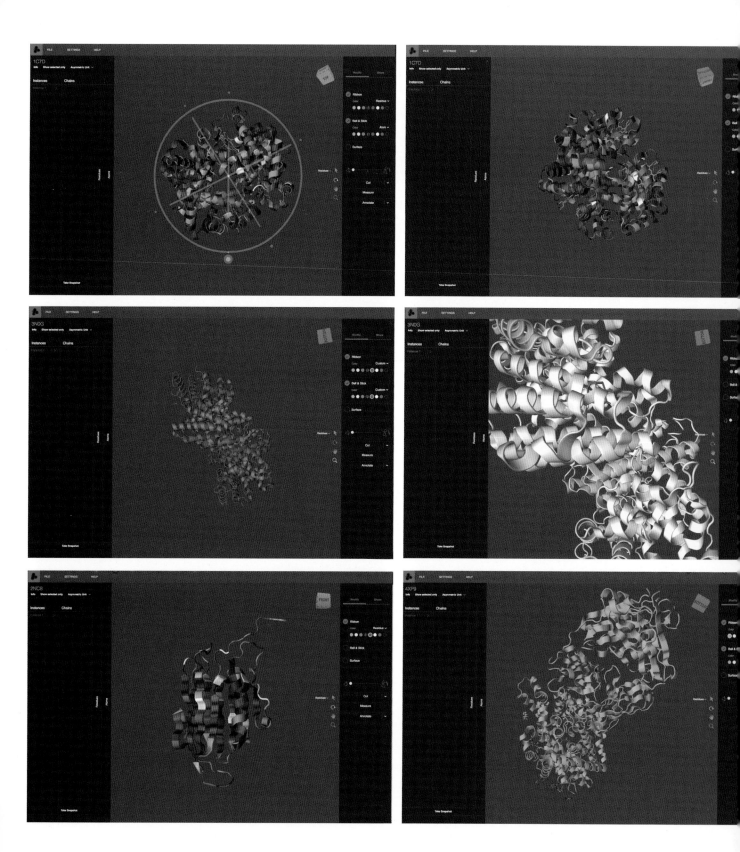

they're working to create a genome sequencer with the rich features of academic software and the usability of proprietary biotech tools. A Web-based application called Molecule Viewer, which they've made free to the public, explores and edits proteins and DNA. Another tool they're working on, called Verian, is a massive database of virus species and components that will link into the same viewer technology.

Another important project is called Wet Lab Accelerator, an open-source tool that lets researchers code drag-and-drop instructions for a new type of genetic laboratory that uses robotic systems, instead of human scientists, to create organisms.

much like on-demand fabrication services like Shapeways have done for the prototyping industry. "Every feature, every base pair of code, is designed on the computer," Hessel says, "and then you hit 'print' and you synthesize the entire virus genome from base elements."

Hessel is humble about Bio/Nano's accomplishments, but the group's strides toward a comprehensive suite of software tools for manipulating, composing, and fabricating microorganisms are starting to look formidable. "We essentially have a tremendously powerful digital pipeline for doing a lot of this bio design and construction work that simply wasn't available even a few years ago," he said.

"If you want to add a new function to an animal, all you really have to do is encode that new function into the program that can be delivered by a virus."

A key partner in that project has been Transcriptic, an automated biological facility in San Francisco that describes itself as a "robotic cloud laboratory." Using Wet Lab Accelerator, Bio/Nano last year successfully designed, built, activated, and tested a virus using no human hands.

That's not just a cool tech demo—it's also a proof of concept for a far more economical school of genetic hacking, and one that could bring on board researchers with more modest funding,

The most profound long-term implications of that pipeline are likely to be in therapeutics. This is the topic that gets Hessel really animated: He imagines a future in which doctors could craft a virus that would target only a particular patient's leukemia cells, perhaps, or lymphoma cells—reductively, a cure for cancer. It sounds like science fiction, but there's already intense interest in the medical research community. Last year, the Food and Drug Administration approved an Amgen treatment, marketed as Imlygic, that uses a modified herpes virus to target skin cancer cells.

Building on the foundation of its growing software suite and work with automated laboratories, Bio/Nano recently partnered with veterinary scientists at Alabama's Auburn University to study canine cancer. Researchers at Auburn had already been working on a viral therapy to fight cancer in dogs using naturally occurring viruses, and last year Hessel reached out to ask if Bio/Nano could help by using its new tools to tailor the virus to each dog in the trial.

"Andrew told me he wanted to customize the virus to every single patient, based on understanding that patient's tumor," said Bruce Smith, the director of Auburn's Research Initiative in Cancer, of the collaboration. "I thought he was crazy!"

The experiment is ongoing, but the viruses Bio/Nano synthesized for the research have since been validated in a lab setting, and Hessel expects the project to move into the clinic in coming months. Most important, it lays the groundwork to use the group's toolset for future cancer research.

"This is significant for us because it is demonstrating that we have the capability of making synthetic viruses for a therapeutic clinical application," Hessel said. "We understand the cost and the timelines and the process now. It's very low-cost to do this work."

The exhilarating promise of the Auburn collaboration is that dogs and humans aren't terribly different, biologically speaking. Though there are significant logistical obstacles to organizing human clinical trials, the canine cancer research suggests that, when the time comes, the software framework Bio/Nano has created to synthesize viruses will be applicable.

"You could essentially use the same process to treat a human or an elephant or a cat," Hessel said. "It doesn't matter. It's the process that's important because you're essentially making a single-use therapeutic for cancer."

That outlook is emblematic of the vision of the research group. Looking at today's tools, they imagine a future in which genetic information will be as adaptable and ubiquitous as smartphone apps are today.

In two decades, Hessel predicts, "our kids will be sitting down and designing microbes as school projects. Hopefully our tools will make it faster, easier, and safer to explore those spaces as well as start to produce really valuable outputs."

opposite: Virtual reality combines easily with tools to edit molecules; the results can be 3D printed so they can be explored in large, physical form.

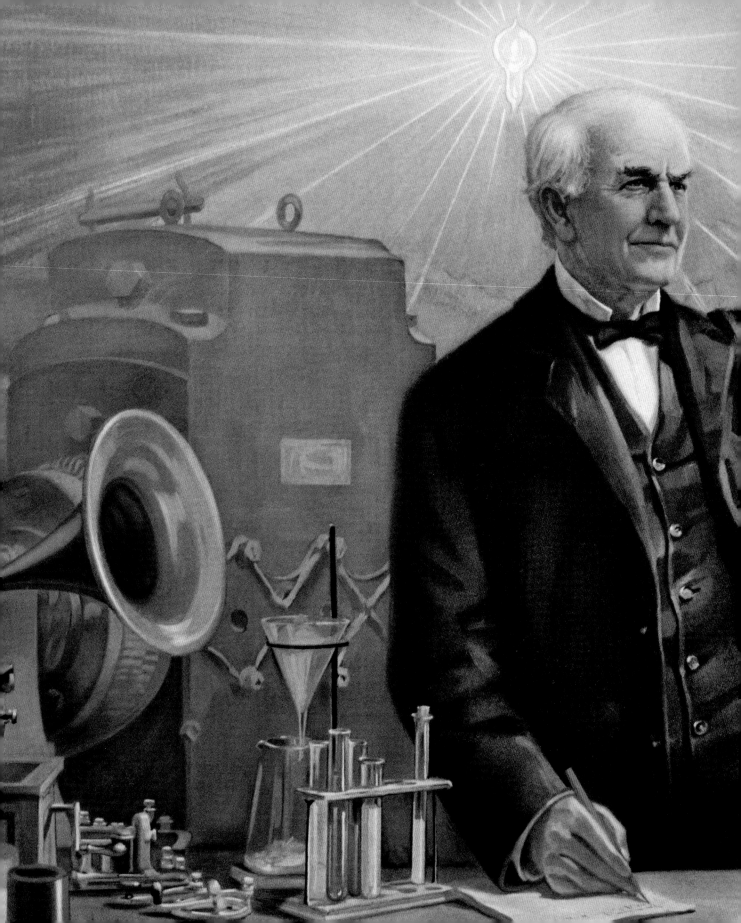

The Material Genome

Will the convergence of digital and physical technology drive a revolution in advanced materials?

The story of Thomas Edison inventing the light bulb is a story of the process of materials selection. In an approach now known as "Edisonian," he and his lab conducted thousands of experiments with different materials, guided by a very limited theoretical understanding of what made one material a better filament over another. But Edison and his lab had the capacity to try many, many different variations and have most of them fail completely, until an acceptable solution was found.

This approach led to one of the most important inventions in history, which helped usher in the 20th century—but it has also resulted in many technologies taking far too long to reach commercial success. Given the ever-increasing demand for innovation in transportation, energy, food, housing, and health and wellness to support a global population that is growing in both number and prosperity, this hit-or-miss process cannot be relied on to bring new, materials-enabled solutions to the market.

Gerbrand Ceder, a materials scientist then at MIT, was grappling with exactly this problem in the early 2000s. Ceder understood that the advances we need in technologies like renewable energy, electric and hybrid vehicles, and sustainable building will all require continual breakthroughs in new advanced materials. The Edisonian approach would not be sufficient. Ceder brought a different approach to the problem of materials selection and discovery called "first-principles prediction." This approach starts with the idea that the laws of physics, and in particular quantum mechanics, are sufficient to predict the properties of any material. If researchers can accurately model the behavior of all of the atoms in a material, they should be able to predict its properties—without actually making the physical material.

Given the complexities of quantum mechanics theory, though, and the very large number of atoms involved, the challenge has been having enough computing power to make useful predictions. Ceder's approach taps directly into the exponentially growing capabilities in high-performance computing enabled by Moore's Law. (It's interesting to note that the relentless improvement in price and performance that Moore's Law represents is itself driven by physical technologies such as materials science, chemical engineering, and physics. These enable the semiconductor industry to improve manufacturing and drive this core technology forward.)

Ceder recognized that the need was for more than just one-off predictions of material properties, and, together with Kristin Persson from Lawrence Berkeley National Laboratory,

envisioned a comprehensive repository of information on advanced materials and their fundamental properties. The Materials Project is accessible to everyone (at materialsproject.org), so that it can accelerate the discovery, development, and commercialization of new materials.

To achieve Persson and Ceder's vision, existing datasets of experiments on the tens of thousands of known materials would need to be augmented by first-principles predictions of tens of thousands of additional materials that had never been discovered, synthesized, or studied, but could be predicted from the periodic table and the laws of physics.

In 2011, the U.S. government decided to build on this vision of the Materials Project. It recognized that the major challenge we face with advanced materials is the time and resources it takes for a new material to go all the way from discovery to market—typically measured in decades, not years. The Materials Genome Initiative (MGI) was launched with the ambition of cutting that time in half. Building on the original vision of Ceder and Persson, the MGI brought together dozens of laboratories from across the United States to establish a comprehensive knowledge base of advanced

If researchers can accurately model the behavior of all of the atoms in a material, they should be able to predict its properties.

THE POWER OF DATA AND THE MATERIALS PROJECT

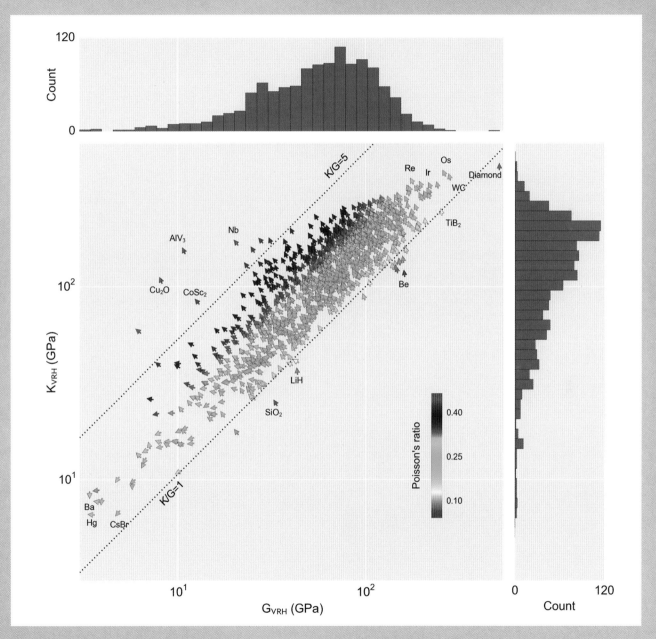

To conceive novel materials, a materials scientist needs a lot of data. Lawrence Berkeley National Laboratory published the largest set of data on the elastic properties of inorganic compounds. Above, the graphical representation of the dataset shows volume per atom (arrow direction), shear modulus (x-axis), bulk modulus (y-axis), and Poisson's ratio (color). The data is essential for the Materials Project, which is aimed at accelerating materials innovation.

MATERIAL
Li₄Ti₅O₁₂

ID:
mp-685194

DOI:
10.17188/1284125 📋

⚙ Show Help Guides

Electronic Structure   X-Ray Diffraction   Substrates   Elasticity   Calculation Summary   Provenance/Citation

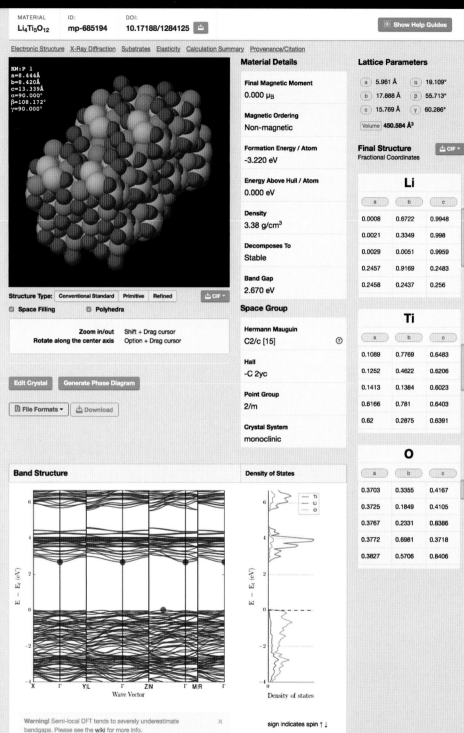

HM: P 1
a=8.444Å
b=8.420Å
c=13.339Å
α=90.000°
β=108.172°
γ=90.000°

Structure Type: | Conventional Standard | Primitive | Refined | ⬇ CIF ▾

☑ Space Filling   ☑ Polyhedra

| Zoom in/out | Shift + Drag cursor |
| Rotate along the center axis | Option + Drag cursor |

Edit Crystal   Generate Phase Diagram

📄 File Formats ▾   ⬇ Download

Material Details

Final Magnetic Moment
0.000 μ_B

Magnetic Ordering
Non-magnetic

Formation Energy / Atom
-3.220 eV

Energy Above Hull / Atom
0.000 eV

Density
3.38 g/cm³

Decomposes To
Stable

Band Gap
2.670 eV

Space Group

Hermann Mauguin
C2/c [15]   ⑦

Hall
-C 2yc

Point Group
2/m

Crystal System
monoclinic

Lattice Parameters

a	5.961 Å	α	19.109°
b	17.888 Å	β	55.713°
c	15.769 Å	γ	60.286°

| Volume | 450.584 Å³ |

Final Structure   ⬇ CIF ▾
Fractional Coordinates

Li

a	b	c
0.0008	0.6722	0.9948
0.0021	0.3349	0.998
0.0029	0.0051	0.9959
0.2457	0.9169	0.2483
0.2458	0.2437	0.256

Ti

a	b	c
0.1089	0.7769	0.6483
0.1252	0.4622	0.6206
0.1413	0.1384	0.6023
0.6166	0.781	0.6403
0.62	0.2875	0.6391

O

a	b	c
0.3703	0.3355	0.4167
0.3725	0.1849	0.4105
0.3767	0.2331	0.8386
0.3772	0.6981	0.3718
0.3827	0.5706	0.8406

Band Structure

Density of States

— Ti
— Li
— O

Warning! Semi-local DFT tends to severely underestimate bandgaps. Please see the **wiki** for more info.   ✕

sign indicates spin ↑ ↓

Interactive plots

⚛ Cu Ag Mo Fe   ⚠   ⬇ XRD JSON

Calculated X-Ray Diffraction Patterns
Click and drag to zoom

☰

125

100

materials. The name and the mission of the MGI mirror those of the Human Genome Project, which first mapped the complete human genome and then provided that data in a comprehensive repository of information. It is openly accessible as it accelerates our knowledge of disease, and more important, it accelerates the discovery and development of new therapies.

A year after the launch of the Materials Project, the database included more than 20,000 inorganic materials. By late 2016, the database included more than 67,000 inorganic materials, 21,000 organic molecules, and 530,000 nonporous materials. The Materials Project allows anyone to explore these materials—their structure as well as dozens of physical qualities. Users can even invent new structures by combining elements. Since launching the Materials Project, Ceder has moved to the University of California, Berkeley, where he and his team continue to collaborate with Persson to develop more efficient and accurate algorithms for first principles predictions of materials properties. His group is also focusing on particular areas of prediction and discovery such as new materials critical for next-generation batteries.

The breakthrough of the MGI is not just the cataloging of new materials, but also the use of machine learning and artificial intelligence to discover new materials with optimal properties. In one example, Citrine Informatics used a large database of experimental and calculated properties, together with a machine-learning-based recommendation engine, to identify new materials with enhanced thermoelectric properties—the ability to convert heat into electricity—that were then verified experimentally.

In another example, Alexander Norquist and his colleagues at Haverford College and Purdue University used a database of chemical reactions and a machine-learning algorithm to discover new hybrid metal-organic materials. What was unique about Norquist and his team's approach is that they included information on many failed reactions in their database. Typically, only successful reactions are published and therefore available; the authors used data from old, archived lab notebooks that contained the data on failed reactions. The information in those failed reactions was essential in predicting with high success the discovery of new materials.

The broader impact of the MGI will be to accelerate the entire cycle of materials innovation, manufacturing, and commercialization. To achieve this goal will require the integration of theory, experiment, data, data analytics, and artificial intelligence into a unified approach to accelerate materials discovery. This will extend beyond the process of materials selection to the optimization of materials for particular applications and for sustainable and economical manufacturing. Doing so will make the return on investment in new materials discovery and deployment much higher and dramatically expand the availability of new solutions essential for human welfare.

The Materials Project, conceived to aid in designing better batteries, allows anyone to explore the properties of more than 500,000 materials.

Stuff Matters

As our understanding of materials continues to advance exponentially, and as material databases connect design, fabrication, and operation more tightly, we will manage entire life cycles of products like never before. Computable materials will be treated increasingly as flows of energy and substances. Digitization also promises to make using traditional materials far more efficient by shortening supply chains and allowing us to select better combinations or alternatives. And, of course, it allows us to create entirely new materials, which can lead to breakthrough solutions.

The development of future materials will be a meandering path. Though material scientists know the properties of many complex materials—ultralight foams, perfectly conductive fibers, or carbon-gathering surfaces—the process of commercializing them is slow, expensive, and fraught with enormous technical challenges. Nonetheless, we can envision material breakthroughs in several ways.

COMPOSITIONS WILL BE MORE PRECISE AND PREDICTABLE

The digitization of material properties will improve the qualities of the things we make. Combined with robotic tools, new compounds will go into buildings that are lighter and sturdier, and where needed taller and more expansive. Cars will weigh less, becoming nimbler and more responsive. The continued advances of metallic alloys, composites, plastics, and ceramics will mean that everything from bicycles to computers, furniture to industrial machinery, and dental implants to camera equipment will perform better.

Today, many buildings are over-engineered. In some cases, twice as much concrete is poured into the building than is needed to keep the structure safe and sound. The reason: The cost of analyzing, simulating, and engineering optimal solutions is greater than the cost of concrete. It's just easier and cheaper to pour in a lot of concrete, rather than do a detailed analysis of where the concrete needs to go. But with access to infinite computing, the analysis becomes faster, easier, cheaper, and more accurate. The result: We will over-engineer less.

Material databases will offer designers the information they need on qualities—such as embedded energy, toxicity, and the detailed steps within supply chains—to select substances that reduce the overall environmental impact of the things they make.

With increased transparency, more consumers will select products based on the entire cost—and impact—of what goes into them.

NEW COMPOSITIONS WILL PRODUCE NEW SOLUTIONS AS WELL AS NEW CLASSES OF PRODUCTS

Borrowing from nature, we will produce products that display and change color based on their physical makeup. Rather than using pigments, we can borrow the structure of insect shells, flowers, or mollusks to change hues. The color emerges from the pattern of molecules, not from dyes. Imagine clothing, furnishings, and buildings that respond to the environment.

We will also make products that can maintain themselves. Already we see examples of self-cleaning paint and concrete. Surface molecules cut up organic molecules, preventing them from sticking. Soot, dust, and dirt simply fall or wash away. Infrastructure will be cleaner, longer.

We are also seeing products that have self-healing properties. Experimental airplane wings are made from composites that have been coated with a thin layer of nanosensors. This coating serves as a nervous system, allowing the component to sense pressure and temperature. When the wing's nervous system feels a tear, it sends a signal to the microspheres, releasing uncured material to the damaged area—like putting glue on a crack. The material cures and fixes the crack.

New materials may even provide solutions that seem nonintuitive. We think of joints and hinges as parts that bring together two mechanical objects. What if the interface between them was on a kind of material that had qualities of "bending" and "joining," which could adapt under various environmental conditions? This would change the very concept of what it means to have a joint.

COMPOSITIONS WILL BECOME BIOLOGICAL

The line between our digital and physical worlds is smearing. Routinely, surgeons combine biological material with nonbiological substances in medical procedures. Hip and knee replacements are already commonplace; now, meshes between bone and tissue are emerging, as well as the capability to print complex organs such as tracheas, kidneys, and livers and tissues for the skin, stomach, and heart.

The combination of biological and chemical is finding its way into the building industry to create self-healing concrete. Bacteria called *B. pasteurii* are found at the bottom of very alkaline volcanic lakes. They are extremely tough and can survive dormant, encased in rock. When mixed into concrete with traces of starch, the bacteria's preferred food, the combination develops self-healing properties. Should a crack form, allowing water to seep into the bacteria, they wake up and consume the starch, allowing them to grow and replicate. In the process, they excrete the mineral calcite, a form of calcium carbonate that bonds to the concrete. As it builds up, the crack is filled and sealed.

Biological programming may become the most powerful and dramatic tool in our ability to compose materials. Will we be able to manufacture silk artificially? Already this is occurring by programming yeast. Could we make better building materials? Fungi and algae are being used to create carbon-neutral bricks. Could biology help us make better ceramics, glass, and composites? Researchers are trying to harness these processes.

The materials we use to make up our world are themselves about to be changed.

With increased transparency, consumers will select products based on the entire cost—and impact—of what goes into them.

COMMU

CHAPTER 5

INITIES

Around the globe, a new class of entrepreneurs, artists, dreamers, and tinkerers is congregating to experiment, build, learn, and share. What defines them is not just the unprecedented access to the new technologies of making.

Their shared optimism, open attitudes, and belief in any person's ability to imagine something new, prototype it, and then build it with their own hands is unleashing creative energy and enlivening neighborhoods. They have rediscovered that there are few things as satisfying as coming up with a good idea and making it real.

Some call this the Maker Movement. People from all stages of life and all skill levels are building things, unleashing a torrent of innovation. Armed with soldering guns and tablet computers, sewing machines and table saws, Arduino microcontrollers and personal 3D printers, makers are building everything from pizza-making robots to advanced X-ray equipment for hospitals, from baby incubators to fire-breathing mechanical dragons worthy of Burning Man.

In many cases, they are gathering in shared and communal spaces that facilitate that work. For some, making provides a way to activate their entrepreneurial spirit. For others, it drives social change—building a sense of community to solve local challenges. And for others, making is simply a way to express themselves; participating in the pleasure of coming up with an idea, working with your hands, and being able to say, "I made that."

What unites them all is their vibrant spirit of trying, tinkering, building, and sharing.

WHY NOW?

The Maker Movement is being powered by three forces: technology, economic changes, and shifts in society. Technologies are crushing the barriers to making. Simple design and production tools give anyone cheap ways to make anything. Many makerspaces produce DIY kits that give crash courses in specific technologies. You can learn the basics of welding or 3D printing in an afternoon and start your project that day.

While makerspaces are providing access to a wide array of technologies, online services explain how to use them in exquisite detail. Web sites such as Instructables have detailed instructional videos on how to make anything from VR headsets to Christmas cakes, sharing tens of thousands of projects with more than two million members. Sites such as these multiply the spirit of making across many communities.

Makers are also responding to changes in the economy. Today, 40 percent of the U.S. workforce is composed of freelancers, consultants, and other contingent workers. Talent used to be about stability. Now it's about mobility—and creating your own business. It's much easier to take advantage of online and community tools to build, sell, and scale your idea. You no longer need the full infrastructure of a complete business. You simply take advantage of services to do what you need.

Many communities are using makerspaces as ways to revitalize their communities. They are incentives to create incubators for individuals and small businesses to create jobs, one at a time, and to build the spirit of creation. Economic growth depends on entrepreneurs as well as intrapreneurs, who are also taking advantage of these spaces.

Finally, makerspaces generate qualities that we value in society: curiosity, passion, and creating to meet necessity. Makerspaces are creating the room for people to discover their passions, figure out what they are good at, and develop their skills. This is infectious. Small groups of talented, passionate people with a mission to make better things can have a huge impact on a community, small and large.

SPACES FOR MAKING

It used to be simple: There were people who made things and people who bought things. Those who made belong to groups that designed, machined, sewed, sold, and distributed things. Those who bought went to stores and selected the things that suited them.

Now all that is changing. The entire supply chain is becoming democratized and many platforms are connecting the worlds of designing, sharing, learning, funding, pitching, making, selling, marketing, distributing, warehousing, and buying. Making is now a viable, accessible business.

Making is creating both tangible and virtual communities. It unites people who share common goals and activities. For most of humanity, the formation of communities was limited by geography. You belonged to

When powerful, easy-to-use technologies meet creative, inspired people, magic happens. Tools that were once available only to professionals are now accessible to almost anyone, releasing a torrent of creative possibilities.

groups that were close together. With the exponential power of digital communication, new communities connect together because they share interests and passions.

These communities are giving companies access to a vastly larger pool of talent than in the past. Imagine the flexible resources these people can bring to bear on any challenge. Just as we should embrace new technology, we should be welcoming new kinds of talent.

MAKING FOR PLACES

There is another way in which communities are being affected by making. Professional designers are working to engage local communities in unprecedented ways. The old ways of making—whether architecture, infrastructure, or products—were almost always top-down.

A designer created something and a factory or a traditional building system made it. This process was essential to the first industrial revolution—and the second, and the third. At the beginning of the fourth, though, it is no longer the only way. Designers are now collaborating with communities to make things in new ways, respecting the communities' unique qualities and empowering them at the same time.

Maker culture emphasizes informal, networked, peer-led, and shared learning. It's fun and fulfilling. And it's also a way to bring a community together to co-create something that's important to it. Professional designers are now engaging more people to participate in the design, construction, and operation of all kinds of things—gardens, community centers, even schools and hospitals. The shared ownership makes a huge difference in the life of the community as well as the end result, the product. A feeling of ownership changes everything.

When powerful, easy to use technologies meet creative, inspired people, magic happens. Tools that were once available only to skilled professionals are now accessible to almost anyone, releasing a torrent of creative possibilities.

A Global Network of Makers

Incubators, workshops, makerspaces, tech shops: Creative makers are coming together to share tools and forge a new world.

In 2005, a new publication, *MAKE* magazine, began identifying hobbyists, backyard inventors, and DIY enthusiasts who celebrated handwork and tinkered for the fun of it. Before long, these so-called *makers* organized fairs to showcase their work and congregated in dedicated spaces with simple tools like lathes and saws, as well as the emerging technologies of making—3D printers, CNC machines, and other digitally mediated tools. The participants in these community spaces celebrated (and continue to celebrate) creative thinking and improvisation, much like the first tech innovators did in Silicon Valley garages.

Communities of creative people can be found in cities and rural areas, and in industrialized and developing countries. As the cost of high-tech tools and equipment goes down (and when companies see the benefits of creating these workshops), people of all ages, incomes, and education are gaining access to machines that were previously unaffordable. Whether these spaces are known as a Fab Lab, a makerspace, or a genre-busting, multimillion-dollar workshop, the phenomenon of places where a community of people gathers to make new things reflects a new era of craft and innovation that brings together digital technology and social

Some spaces are customized for biotechnology, some for fashion.

connection. Community spaces offer opportunities for anyone to learn about making; the resources to fabricate more sophisticated objects; and the chance to share tools and knowledge and collaborate with like-minded people.

As such, these spaces are diverse, reflecting different environments and interests. Some are customized for biotechnology, some for fashion design. Community members address social issues like affordable housing and transportation. In India, makers pursue a type of homegrown frugal innovation adapted to a resource-challenged environment. In western Africa, they build on a traditional DIY culture to make things that improve people's lives and livelihoods. In China, many community and DIY spaces are linked to the country's massive electronics and manufacturing sectors in a way that allows fresh product ideas to flow directly to factories.

Corporations with an interest in design also recognize that individual innovators can be a source of originality and inspiration. In Detroit, Ford has funded a TechShop for its workers and the community. In San Francisco, Autodesk's Pier 9 has redefined the role of an innovation space, fostering a robust artist-in-residence program while providing its employees and partners with what may be the most advanced additive and subtractive manufacturing and prototyping workshop in the world.

Everywhere, and in so many different ways, communities of creative people are shaping the world.

GEARBOX
NAIROBI, KENYA

African makers have long been adept at transforming found materials into low-tech and community-oriented objects, like solar-powered cookers or a device made of corrugated iron and sisal that keeps camel milk cool in hot climates. It is a practice founded on "self-sustenance, bootstrapping, relying on yourself, and working with what you have and building from there," says Emeka Okafor, a cofounder of Maker Faire Africa, which debuted in 2009.

The fair seeded maker communities and a loose network of mostly self-taught inventors and craftspeople around the continent. Now, fully equipped makerspaces have emerged, and the movement is evolving from jerry-built inventions to sophisticated products and start-ups seeking venture capital.

When Facebook CEO Mark Zuckerberg visited Nairobi's Gearbox on his trip to sub-Saharan Africa in September 2016, it confirmed not only the tech world's growing interest in Africa but also this makerspace's success as a launchpad for innovative products. When it opened in 2010, Gearbox was East Africa's first rapid prototyping, design, and manufacturing facility, part of the iHub tech platform in Nairobi.

previous pages: Maker's Asylum in Mumbai, India, built this "tuk tuk" outfitted with workbenches, a 3D printer, and other tools, to visit low-income neighborhoods and universities. **opposite, bottom:** Facebook CEO Mark Zuckerberg visited Gearbox, a makerspace in Nairobi, Kenya, in 2016.

Number of Makerspaces Worldwide

1,500

1,000

500

0

ACTIVE OR PLANNED
1,393 spaces

EUROPE
556 spaces

NORTH AMERICA
483 spaces

REST OF THE WORLD
354 spaces

2006   2008   2010   2012   2014   2016

Founding Date

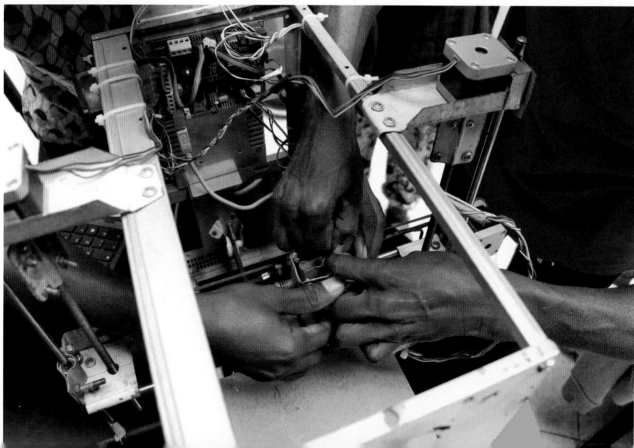

Today, some two dozen Kenyan start-ups use the space to develop and test new products, including two that were on Zuckerberg's must-see list: a solar-energy-producing roof tile and a pay-as-you-go cooking gas delivery system.

WOELAB
LOMÉ, TOGO

The "small digital republic" WoeLab opened in 2012 in the capital of Togo and quickly achieved celebrity status when a makerspace member, Kodjo Afate Gnikou, prototyped and crowd-funded a 3D printer constructed entirely of e-waste. (West Africa has several large digital-waste dumping sites; the worst are not in Togo, but plenty of e-waste winds up there.) "The concept for WoeLab is to make 'low' high-tech," WoeLab founder, Togolese entrepreneur Sename Koffi Agbodjinou, told Vice's Motherboard. "To develop very high-tech projects but with what we have in our hands."

The makerspace is open to everyone in the community, from street vendors to engineers. Part of the global Fab Lab network, WoeLab also incubates early-stage start-ups and is leveraging the e-waste printer to launch 3D-printer cybercafés and education programs.

MAKER'S ASYLUM
MUMBAI AND DELHI, INDIA

Residents of Mumbai and other Indian cities are used to seeing three-wheeled auto rickshaws sputtering through the streets, but none like the "tuk tuk" customized by Mumbai makerspace Maker's Asylum. Outfitted with folding workbenches and tables, storage, a 3D printer, and tools for woodworking, soldering, and general tinkering, the auto rickshaw will travel to low-income areas and universities around the city and

offer free maker workshops in partnership with community groups.

Maker's Asylum cofounder Vaibhav Chhabra hopes the auto rickshaw will "start a conversation about makerspaces and showcase the power of tinkering." He also wants to connect the nascent maker movement to India's traditional maker culture *jugaad*, meaning frugal innovation or a quick fix to a problem. Initially, India's maker movement was stymied by the high cost of equipment and the lack of a strong manufacturing and R&D base in the country. Maker's Asylum opened in Mumbai in 2014 on a shoestring and added a second location a year later in Delhi after receiving corporate backing; each has 50 to 60 members. Start-ups use the Mumbai space for making laser-edged skateboard decorations, designer leather bags, and handcrafted wooden eyeglass frames, among other things.

Chhabra says that makers must first understand how to "take jugaad to the next level, make real products, and pass on that knowledge and creativity to others."

XINCHEJIAN
SHANGHAI, CHINA

China's first makerspace, XinCheJian, or "new workshop," was founded by David Li in Shanghai in 2010. It carried only basic tools and equipment and catered mainly to hobbyists who wanted to make things for fun. Today, more than 100 makerspaces operate across the country as community spaces, hardware accelerators, open-access labs, and kids' education clubs. As China's makerspaces evolved, they forged strong ties with university research centers, entrepreneurs, and industry. Another boost came with official government backing: Makerspaces and homegrown innovation are regarded as pivotal to

opposite: WoeLab, a makerspace in Lomé, Togo, celebrates "low high tech," evidenced by a 3D printer its members made using e-waste. page 260: Maker's Asylum's setup (top) at an outdoor event, part of its goal to bring making to the public; a group at Maker's Asylum works on a design problem (bottom). page 261: A motorized skateboard (top) is one project to emerge from XinCheJian in Shanghai, China, the country's first makerspace (bottom).

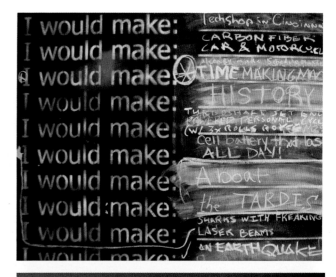

I would make: Techshop in Cincinna
I would make: CARBON FIBER
I would make: CAR & MOTORCYCL
a would make: TIME MAKING MA
I would make: HISTORY
I would make:
(w/ 3x ROLLS ROCKE
I would make: Cell battery that las
ALL DAY!
I would make: A boat
would:make: the TARDIS
I would make: SHARKS WITH FREAKING
LASER BEAMS
I would make: an EARTHQUAKE

Instead of hackathons, Genspace hosts classes in synthetic biology.

transitioning China's economy from mass manufacturing of low-cost goods to mass innovation and higher-value products. Increasingly, big Chinese companies look to makerspaces as a source of fresh ideas and products, or they set up their own in-house labs, as consumer electronics giant Foxconn has done.

XinCheJian retains its focus on hobbyists having fun making things, although it sometimes goes commercial—developing, for instance, an affordable, Kickstarter-funded electronic skateboard called STARY.

GENSPACE
BROOKLYN, NEW YORK

Michael Flanagan, CEO of a tiny start-up called FlanaGen, has a concept for producing artificial cellulose from bacteria. In the past, a small company like his would have been stopped by an unmovable obstacle: Biotech labs are very expensive. Flanagan and other scientist-entrepreneurs have a new solution: Genspace, one of a handful of biotech makerspaces in the United States.

The 700-square-foot community biolab opened in 2010 in a downtown Brooklyn building. It attracts students, hobbyists, artists, teachers, scientists, and entrepreneurs like Flanagan. "It's a platform for people who want to get their hands on machines in a safe and open environment," says Dr. Ellen Jorgensen, Genspace's general director and cofounder. Members use lab equipment like a freezer set to -80°C and incubators for genetic engineering to conduct "living" experiments that need constant monitoring and tending—like

growing fungus for sculptures—and a secure biosafety environment. "It's not your average open hacker space," Jorgensen says. Instead of hackathons and 3D printers, Genspace hosts classes and workshops in synthetic biology, CRISPR genome engineering and advanced fermentation techniques, and a biohacker boot camp.

TECHSHOP
DETROIT, MICHIGAN

TechShop, a for-profit DIY and fabrication franchise founded in 2006, provides tools, resources, and classes for members. Equally important, it has created supportive communities. "It's not so much the material resources," says Naganand Murty, codesigner of the Embrace baby warmer, prototyped at a TechShop. "It's the community of people that keep you company during the late nights when you're chipping away at a problem only you and a small bunch of people believe in."

These well-equipped spaces around the country have provided fertile ground for start-ups and solo entrepreneurs that need space to tinker. In addition to Murty's low-cost, portable infant warmer (now being distributed by GE Healthcare), the Square credit-card reader was prototyped in a TechShop open-access workshop, as was the Oru folding kayak and the Emberlight smartphone-controlled dimmer.

Big companies have taken notice of the inventions and are partnering with TechShop to boost innovation. Ford bankrolled TechShop Detroit, a 33,000-square-foot facility adjacent

opposite, clockwise from top right: Inspiring ideas for making at TechShop in Detroit; a TechShop member works on a cello; a maker at Genspace in Brooklyn, New York, explores biological design; other Genspace members learn more at the unique communal biolab.

to the automaker's Dearborn product-development campus, to inspire employees to experiment and prototype concepts outside of the company's established development pipeline. The location also focuses on science, technology, engineering, art, and math education initiatives for schoolkids in the area.

PIER 9
SAN FRANCISCO

Autodesk's Pier 9 is a creative workshop where engineers, programmers, entrepreneurs, and artists explore every stage of the process of making things.

Housed in a historic 12,000-square-foot pier on San Francisco's Embarcadero waterfront, the workshop hosts some of the most advanced production tools, which share the space with traditional machinery like industrial sewing machines as well as a professionally equipped test kitchen that once featured a 3D printer capable of making hummus. There is a well-stocked electronics lab as well as metal, print, CNC, textile, and wood shops.

Since opening in 2013, Pier 9's advanced tools have helped turn out an aerodynamic prosthetic leg for an Olympic cyclist and the world's first industrial tattoo-making robot, and re-created statues and archaeological artifacts destroyed by ISIS, among dozens of other projects.

What all these activities have in common, says Noah Weinstein, Pier 9's senior creative programs manager, is that they bring together the worlds of hardware and software. "We are able to develop connections between software and hardware, the materials, the tools, and the people who are empowered to use them," he says.

The facility has around 1,200 certified users, including 900 Autodesk employees and some 300 creative partners and artists, who rotate in and out as part of an artist-in-residence program.

Pier 9 encourages collaboration and crossing domains. "The experiences of the past might not always hold true here because we are inviting people to try something different," Weinstein explains. The results are often surprising and insightful, as engineers and artists experiment with tools, equipment, and software they hadn't encountered before. Artist Alex Schofield, for example, used a CNC milling machine to make objects out of coffee grounds as a way to rethink waste products. A 3D-printed model of San Francisco was fabricated and projection-mapped to help urban planners imagine how new buildings and civic infrastructure would affect the city.

opposite and following pages: Designers, engineers, and artists in residence make Autodesk's Pier 9 a vibrant, creative workshop; it is outfitted with physical and digital tools to explore almost every aspect of design and fabrication.

The results at Pier 9 are often surprising, as artists experiment with equipment and software they hadn't encountered before.

Metropolis magazine suggested that Pier 9 represents a millennial version of industrialism, with its sharp focus on "minds, machines, and computers." Weinstein agrees, in that Pier 9 wants to initiate conversations about the future of technology and its impact on society. Also important are questions about how we use these new and powerful tools to inspire creativity. "Tools not only shape the materials," he says, "but are part of a transformational experience to make the world a better place."

Connecting hardware, software, and materials is at the core of Pier 9's vision. It is a place where individuals and teams can explore those connections, and feed them back meaningfully into software.

Many advances in manufacturing processes and techniques will be predicated by this tight integration. This is most apparent in additive manufacturing, where hardware, software, and materials must all intimately dance together. It's a challenge that attracted the attention of an interdisciplinary group working at Pier 9; the result, known as Autodesk Collaborative Control (and born under the code name Project Escher) reveals the potential of these connections.

Fused deposition modeling (FDM) is probably the most common additive manufacturing technique because of its low cost and consumer availability. In FDM, thermoplastic is melted, forced through a nozzle, and deposited. The technique allows for the use of some engineering-grade materials, but offers a strict trade-off between resolution and speed—bigger nozzles offer higher throughput, but at the expense of resolution. In essence, FDM is a surface area problem: All of the deposited mass needs melting.

The Pier 9 team's approach was to increase the number of nozzles while keeping them properly sized for high resolution, and carefully controlling their combined movement with software. An object is split into several toolpaths, and the motion of the nozzles is orchestrated along those toolpaths in a coordinated fashion.

"Think of it as an orchestra conductor who makes sure all the players are in the right tempo and come in at the right time," says Andreas Bastian, an Autodesk research scientist who came to Pier 9 as an artist-in-residence in 2014 and advised the Escher team. Bastian imagines Escher's parallel processing technology being used to "unlock a huge class of applications," including manufacturing lightweight drone fuselages and auto assembly-line parts with high-performance materials including magnesium, titanium, and aluminum.

Designing Through Full Immersion

To design a remote primary school, MASS Design needed to make it appropriate for its users—and for the people who would build it.

In the spring of 2013, Andrew Brose traveled to the village of Ilima in a remote part of the Democratic Republic of Congo to help the local community design and build a much-needed primary school. Brose, a 30-year-old architect from the public interest design firm MASS Design Group, had lived and worked in Africa for many years. But as he made his way to Ilima, by bush plane and along rutted mud paths on the back of a motorcycle, the neglect and lack of infrastructure took him by surprise.

This is one of the most isolated places on earth. Building a school here would pose a challenge not only to the community of Ilima, but also to the team at MASS Design, a nonprofit dedicated to, in Brose's words, "bringing architecture to people in parts of the world that feel abandoned by the rest of the world." At the school site, for instance, there was no electricity, no running water, and few building materials or equipment except for axes and manual saws to cut and fell huge trees. Handmade bricks would have to be fashioned from clay and sand gathered from anthills. The 3,000 people who live in the area are mostly subsistence farmers with only basic literacy and carpentry skills.

Founded in 2008 by Alan Ricks and Michael Murphy, students at Harvard University's Graduate School of Design, MASS Design has never shied away from tackling projects in difficult environments. Over the years, it has built hospitals and clinics in Rwanda and post-earthquake Haiti, among other projects, as part of its mission to promote architecture based on human-centered design principles and community engagement. A central tenet of that ethos is that design is a singular vision arising from a collaborative community the client, MASS Design focuses on social impact design—a field of architecture that conveys values, promotes social justice, and is deeply rooted in what social benefits good design can, and should, bring to communities.

For MASS Design (its name stands for Model of Architecture Serving Society), the first step in any project is partnering with an organization, foundation, or government agency that has a social impact goal, knows the conditions on the ground, and has relationships with the target community.

A central tenet of MASS Design's ethos is that design is a singular vision arising from a collaborative process and a shared language with the community.

process and a shared language with the community. For a building to be successful and truly serve community needs, the firm believes, architects must be fully engaged with that community and also furnish its members with skills and expertise to help construct the building and maintain it long after the designers have gone away.

The traditional business model for architecture, however, favors the wealthy and the privileged, and not the 99 percent of people who can't afford design but need it the most. "Why do affordable housing when you can build luxury condos?" Ricks asks. By flipping that equation and making the

"We proactively seek out the change agents in the world and ask them how we can use architecture to catalyze and amplify their mission," says cofounder and COO Ricks, in an interview in the firm's Boston headquarters.

For the Ilima Primary School project, MASS Design teamed with the African Wildlife Foundation, an organization that fosters relationships with business leaders and rural communities to manage Africa's living and natural resources. In Ilima, the foundation had arranged to build a school for the community if it could initiate environmental and conservation programs in the area and introduce a conservation

curriculum at the school "to teach young kids about the importance of protecting the ecosystem," says Brose. The long-term goal was to help curb the deforestation and slash-and-burn agriculture that is threatening endangered species in the region.

With the partnership established, Brose went to Ilima with his wife, Rachel, and two Congolese architecture interns, for what MASS Design calls "full immersion" within the community. Instead of architects or the building's sponsor determining the design, close relationships are established with community members to discover needs. It is part of an information-gathering exercise unique in both the development and design worlds, according to Chris Scovel, a MASS Design architect in Boston. "There is a model of development in which a benevolent organization flies over in a plane and drops a building like a bomb and then flies away, leaving the people on the ground to wonder what the building is and what to do with it," he says. "That is the opposite of what we do."

In Ilima, the MASS Design team asked students of all ages what they wanted for their school and to draw an ideal school building. They indicated a preference for blackboards at the right height for their size, windows they could see out of, and benches that were not too cramped and close together. Girls said they wanted separate bathrooms rather than facilities shared with boys to ensure privacy. Mothers in the village said they would like a shaded community space where they could feel comfortable sitting and talking or cooking together and watching the children.

On the logistical side of things, Brose discussed with local men what materials and equipment they would

be able to transport on a bike from the closest river port. The conclusion: Not much would fit on the narrow path to the village. This led Brose and his team to shift the roofing material from sheets of corrugated tin to local wood.

Using the on-site data, MASS Design worked through an iterative design process to figure out what the size and foundation of the building could be and tested its structural soundness in consultation with its staff in Boston as well as the AWF and architects in Kinshasa, the capital of the Democratic Republic of Congo. "Our intention was a singular building with a roof that covered the entire facility so you get a lot of space for interactive moments and discussions between teachers and students, and also have a place for them to sit and be protected from the tropical sun and rain," Brose recalls.

The design that emerged was driven by the conversations with the community and the realities of building in a place where "you can't just go to the lumber yard and buy kiln-dried wood," Brose says. It would also embody the project's mission: to build a school that teaches respect for the environment and conservation, as well as agriculture, the community's primary activity. As seen in early sketches, the shape of the building—two opposite-facing arcs that gently touch at the curve's midpoint and spread outward—represents these two aspects of the community's life.

Responding to student concerns, the architects put in light-filled classrooms and a library cooled by natural ventilation through abundant windows; floor-to-ceiling wood-framed doors featured screens of woven and dyed vines, a traditional craft of local women. There were separate toilet blocks for boys and girls, as requested, and benches and

Local-sourcing of materials, labor, and ideas is part of an approach MASS Design calls Lo-Fab.

desks for students of various ages; outside, kids could enjoy a play area near a space for community gathering.

For the roof, the architects drew a sloping, shingled wooden structure supported by an intricate network of timber trusses, rafters, and beams. All these elements would be hewn by community workers from nearby trees, the only sturdy material available. This local-sourcing of materials, labor, and ideas is part of an approach MASS Design calls Lo-Fab, short for Local Fabrication. Incorporating these into design and construction provides the workers with skills and engenders a "sense of ownership by the community that is the surest form of sustainability," says Sierra Bainbridge, an architect and senior director at MASS Design.

Construction began when Brose returned to Ilima in December 2013. On the way, he stopped in Djolu, about 50 miles away via primitive roads and the closest big settlement, to hire more-experienced masons and carpenters. These tradesmen would become team leaders and teach new skills such as brick joining to local workers. The constraints of building in a remote rural location often complicated planning: Nails, tools, and fasteners, for example, had to be brought in by river barge from Kinshasa, more than 500 miles away. A special color-coding system was devised to render complex two-dimensional architectural diagrams easier to

understand for workers with minimal knowledge of design. And with upward of 200 locals working on the site at any one time, shifts were adjusted to accommodate those who needed to farm their land.

The jungle was cleared for the site; workers hauled away large boulders by hand while men spent a half day chopping down a tree with axes, and then used saws to split it into smaller pieces, and finally into roof shingles. The bricks were made and dried, and boiled palm oil was added to the mix to make them more water-resistant. Brose worked with masons, building practice walls with mortar to ensure the joints were correct. Slowly, the contours of the Ilima school took shape.

The building opened in 2015. Today, around 300 students attend school in a beautiful building with curved walls of white, earth-covered plaster instead of the flimsy shacks they previously used. The school has a new director and new teachers, and more children attend classes; a conservation curriculum is in place. Moreover, much as the designers intended, the school has become a focal point for the community and a source of pride. And when repairs are needed, workers from the community who helped construct the school and learned new skills know what to do.

The Ilima school joins a roster of around 50 MASS Design projects that are completed or underway, including

opposite: Completed in 2015, the school now educates about 300 students.

COMMUNITIES / DESIGNING THROUGH FULL IMMERSION

the celebrated Butaro hospital in Rwanda and pioneering cholera and tuberculosis clinics in Haiti. It's a great achievement for a small, non-profit firm with a total staff of around 50 people (30 in Boston and 20 in a regional office in Kigali, Rwanda) and an annual operating budget of $3 million financed from foundations (including the Autodesk Foundation), governments, NGOs, and in-kind donations from companies.

A big question facing MASS Design is how to scale operations and increase awareness of how social impact design engages communities and improves people's lives. Part of its mission is "to advocate for those values being adopted globally," Ricks says, and now it is creating an institution to promote those ideas. In September 2016, MASS Design opened the first African Design Centre (ADC) in Kigali, offering a two-year postgraduate fellowship program for architects in human-centered design.

The ADC stems from the recognition that while Africa desperately needs more architects—there are four times as many architects in Italy as there are on the entire African continent—new graduates are, for the most part, not being trained to address the specific challenges facing Africa. In African cities, for instance, which are expected to reach 1.2 billion people by 2050, from 400 million today, rapid and unplanned development is repeating the mistakes of the past, displacing communities and destroying the environment.

"A rapidly growing market demands that architects resolve problems in the easiest possible way, and that means putting up many projects every month," says Christian Benimana, a Rwandan architect and founding director of ADC. "New graduates are being sucked into

systems of practice that are not prepared to tackle these challenges," he adds. "This type of practice is hurting us. It is not sustainable."

The first 10 ADC students, all from African countries, will get experience in the field and in workshops, and learn from MASS Design staff, visiting architects, and professors to complement their traditional education. In the future, a network of such centers might exist across the continent to train a new generation of African architects. Eventually, Ricks foresees these architects taking up positions in government ministries, higher education, and private practice, where they will seed ideas about social impact design. "They will be able to exponentially expand their reach with a different kind of thinking about design and a different model."

What is equally important, Brose reckons, is that the Ilima school has started an important conversation in the community. "There's more at stake than just the building," he says. "It's about the environment and how we live, and how the unique design and building process makes us more considerate of the environment and taking care of what we have."

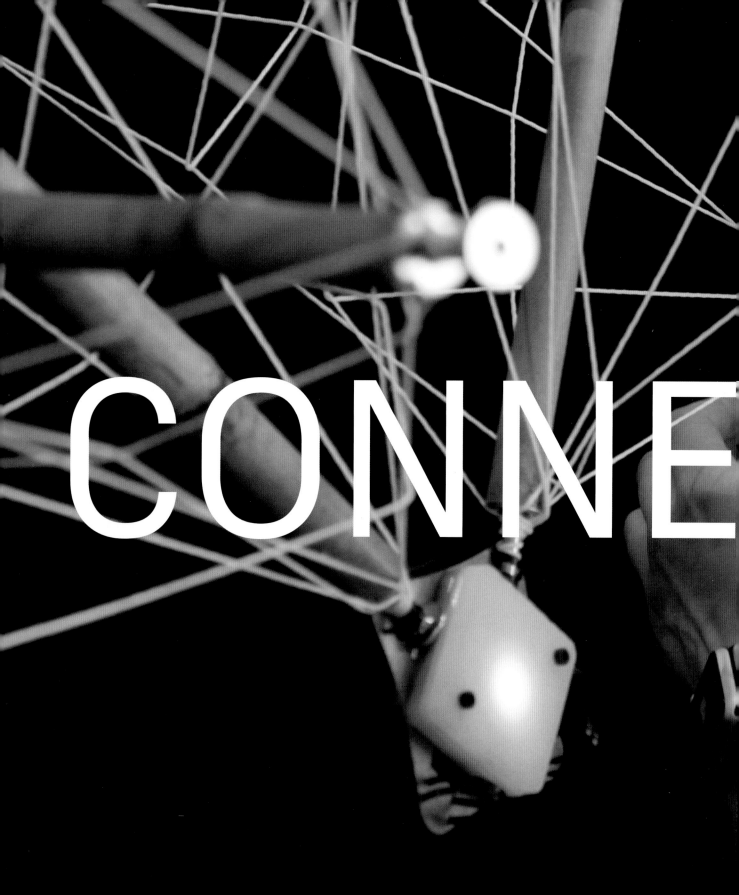

CHAPTER 6

CTIONS

As the line between our digital world and physical world blurs and erodes, we are not only making things in more connected ways, we are making things that are themselves more connected. The fabrication of inert objects is being replaced by the design, production, and management of interconnected flows of materials and information. This is precisely where new types of value are emerging.

The fourth industrial revolution is rapidly unifying every stage of making. As technology fluidly shuttles information between people, processes, and products, the once disconnected phases of design, fabrication, and operation are becoming bound together in connected systems.

What will industries look like when they are fully connected? How will we make buildings, cars, or everything else when these technologies are fully operational?

Systems emerge from connections. Now that we can see, model, and compute these connections, we can produce increasingly sophisticated big-picture views that link any and every part. And in doing so, these systems improve efficiency, increase flexibility, and generate fresh business models. Each system will create value based on the connections and feedback loops contained within.

Connected systems optimize performance. Imagine systems that connect customer preferences with manufacturers' capabilities—we will see personalized consumer electronics, clothing, furniture, and cars. New systems also promise products that are less expensive and available more quickly. More value is squeezed out of a process or product or business.

The underlying digital infrastructure for making is consolidating some industries and fragmenting others—and sometimes doing both at the same time. Consolidation happens through the large software platforms that act as hubs for makers. These common design tools, collaboration techniques, and funding, marketing, distribution, and learning tools give everyone an equal footing.

Fragmentation happens as more makers become free agents to develop new products and can bring these products to market quickly and outside of traditional channels. The full scope of innovation can now be done in a garage or shared space at lower cost and risk. More and more people are participating at scale because they can access these platform tools.

When combined, consolidation and fragmentation reinforce and amplify each other. We wouldn't have today's scale of fragmentation if we didn't have enormous consolidation.

Already, we are glimpsing what connected organizations and industries look like. What follows are seven snapshots of innovative companies that are reinventing their own industries by taking advantage of the platforms of innovation while carving out distinct places for themselves. Each in its own way creates "wow" experiences to delight its customers or "uh-oh" experiences to block its competitors. And each invests in sustainable and protectable business models—timeless qualities of any business strategy.

The implications of the fourth industrial revolution are still unfolding. What will robotics mean for jobs? Who owns a computationally generated design? Who is responsible for it working, or not working? What about the human element? How can we ensure that we are solving problems that are relevant to people today?

In "Connections," we look at hints of how the future of making is emerging. These snapshots reveal where different trends are already converging. We also meet seven thought leaders who explore the implications of the future of making, and several leaders at Autodesk who explore how our world might evolve.

Of course we are still in the infancy of this future. The tools of digitization and materialization will continue to improve and accelerate. What might we make in two or three generations? What might the world of making look like? And what might our world look like?

Connections Stories/

Seven snapshots reveal how the future of making things is already here.

A Bridge Assembled in Midair

In Amsterdam, a city full of canals, managing foot traffic is tricky; rerouting pedestrian habits often requires building a new bridge. MX3D, an Amsterdam company pioneering robotic 3D printing technology, and Dutch artist and designer Joris Laarman are working to build an entirely new kind of footbridge across the picturesque Oudezijds Achterburgwal canal. The bridge will be constructed by a pair of robotic 3D printers that can print in metal in multi-axis, 3D space.

"A design usually starts from a technical experiment or a vision," Laarman says. In this case, the vision is of robots printing new structures on-site in a miraculous dance that has them meeting up at midpoint, balanced above the canal. (This bridge will be printed elsewhere and transported to the canal for installation.)

The construction method is spectacular, but so is the design process. Laarman used the generative design tool Dreamcatcher, which supplied ideas for a better and stronger structure. He then combined the computational suggestions with his own aesthetic, allowing for a radical new design. "Different geometries morph into others to address functional necessities and technical limitations," he says. "It's kind of like a tree, where the tubular supports branch out into smaller ones that morph into a canopy-like handrail."

"It's very, very intricate," says Maurice Conti, director of strategic innovation at Autodesk. "There's not a straight thing on it."

Indeed, the supports intertwine in so many ways that they couldn't be manufactured in separate pieces and assembled. Laarman's multi-axis 3D printers add the steel substrate in one continuous process. "It would be close to impossible to create this object with traditional methods," he says. "I consider the bridge and all its functional areas as one single organism."

CONNECTIONS / CONNECTION STORIES

Desire in the Digital Age

Who needs a wristwatch with a perpetual calendar and a double-moon phase so you can track the moon's position in the northern and southern hemispheres? The surprising answer from Georges Kern, CEO of IWC Schaffhausen, which produces just such a wristwatch, is: nobody. Nobody needs that.

And yet the legendary watchmaker continues to make and sell its beautiful and ever-more-complex creations. The story of IWC Schaffhausen's success is not one of the latest fabrication processes; rather, it is a look at how craft and desire can thrive even as how we make, distribute, and sell goods is transformed.

"We are living in a globalized world, so we have generic products all around us," says IWC Schaffhausen creative director Christian Knoop. "Yet there is a growing interest in more authentic products." For Kern and Knoop, it is the finest luxury products that deliver that. One function of a watch is mechanical, Kern says, "but the other function is the carrier of a dream."

"The way we bring those dreams to life will change in the digital world," continues Knoop. Some of that change is in production, which now includes 3D printed prototypes and new ceramic materials. Crafting the public image of the watch has also been transformed; the model seen here, the Portugieser Perpetual Calendar Single Moonphase, is actually a purely digital rendering.

For Kern, such tools cannot dominate the process. "Robots can only work with stuff that exists," he says. "Can they create emotional products? Here I think humankind will always be stronger than the robot."

That focus on human-ness is key. It marks the difference between a great technical product and something that can become an heirloom. Knoop returns to the perpetual calendar, which tracks days through at least 2499. "I think there is a certain need in human nature to have something that remains even after your death," he says.

CONNECTIONS /

The Augmented Office

Sensors have been part of our workplace for more than a decade: the familiar motion detectors that darken empty offices, climate monitors that keep temperatures steady, and light sensors that, in the case of Al Bahr Towers, adjust the exterior of the building.

At Steelcase, the promise of sensors and the data they can provide points toward collaborative, creative workspaces that reduce the friction of work and augment the abilities of the people who work in them.

And not a moment too soon. "We're driving 21st-century cars to 20th-century workspaces," says James Ludwig, vice president of global design and product engineering at Steelcase. "We have the opportunity to propel these spaces forward to become some of the smartest, most connected spaces on the planet."

Ludwig's focus is to make the social experience at work better so people can take advantage of "the massive neural network of many minds working on one problem, which is how we solve problems today."

To do that, the firm is combining sensors—inexpensive, off-the-shelf technology—with deep research to create new systems that let a workspace communicate with its users. Ludwig lists some of the information a space can collect and communicate: "Did the five people that said they were going to use that room actually show up? Who didn't show up? Are they coming? Should I start the meeting? What if we could remove that friction—how much value would be recaptured in that whole equation?"

Further down the road, he says, after we have become more comfortable with AI, workspaces can augment our days even more. "Imagine your room sensing that the brainstorming session was losing steam, and it finds a way to slightly adjust the lighting or the temperature in a way that can reanimate a group, like a break or a round of refreshments can do."

Bullitt's New System

Creating a new home for the Bullitt Foundation, an environmental advocacy group based in Seattle, was a chance to explore "the path of genuine sustainability and restorative design and architecture," says Bullitt president Denis Hayes, rather than making a building "with green features bolted on to it."

The result, the world's greenest office building, depends on a "living system" of integrated components. That is in some way a product of avoiding existing green building regimes such as LEED; Bullitt instead pursued the Living Building Challenge, or LBC, a certification that requires criteria in seven areas, including site, water, energy, health, materials, beauty, and equity.

The heavy timber used for framing is 100 percent Forest Stewardship Council certified and sourced within 1,000 kilometers of the building (all steel and concrete was sourced within 500 kilometers), making the Bullitt Center deeply rooted in its location. LBC's performance requirements drove the building's aesthetic, as well as an integrated design approach. From this perspective, the building is regarded as an interdependent system composed of multiple components. Particularly challenging was reaching net-zero energy, which means ensuring the total energy used is roughly equal to the total renewable energy created on-site—in this case, a 52,000-square-foot commercial building in one of the cloudiest American cities.

Most of the products in the Bullitt Center's systems are off the shelf. The innovation was how the design team linked the products with control systems that are always monitoring, sensing, and doing things. Corey Reilly, the building engineer, keeps an eye on those systems from his desk. From his screen he follows real-time data on energy use and production, temperature, and window positions, and is able to control the heating and cooling systems, HVAC, windows, composters, and the water system, as well as pre-chilling the building's concrete slab floor when the next day is expected to be hot.

CONNECTIONS /

Tesla's Robot Partners

Brilliant orange robotic arms, and their human counterparts, cut, mold, weld, and polish raw aluminum into brand-new Teslas at the company's Fremont factory.

What its 1.9-million-square-foot bigger brother boasts in scale—Reno's $5 billion "Gigafactory" will grow to 10 million square feet in the future, nearly doubling the world's production of lithium ion batteries—this plant has in finesse, producing 400 Model S cars each week with only 3,000 human workers and 160 robots. It's relatively slow, compared to car-a-minute plants like Ford's, but it's futuristically efficient. Other factory robots do one task only—and do it fast. Tesla's are slower but smarter. One orange arm might seamlessly switch from angling seats into a roadster frame to carefully gluing front and rear windshields onto a nearly finished car body.

Cutting-edge software and light, nimble mechanics turn robots from drones into collaborators, adapting to new jobs as they follow cars and coworkers down the magnetized assembly line, from 20,000-pound coils of raw aluminum to the final painting bay. This multifunctionality allows Tesla to control almost the entire Model S manufacturing process from one central campus.

The Fremont factory houses business teams, design staff, line workers, and all-purpose robots in its 4.5 million square feet of space: a revolutionary approach to previously decentralized routines, in which networks of specialized plants work independently. Tesla's factory makes more than cars; it models a future of manufacturing.

CONNECTIONS /

A Robot for Anyone

Platforms are everywhere. A variation on Marc Andreeson's famous quip "Software is eating the world" is that platforms are eating software. Modbot, a Bay Area start-up led by Daniel Pizzata and Adam Ellison, aims to create a modular platform for robots.

With interchangeable components that fit together with a nice "clunk," a user combines a robot's muscles (servo motors), joints, base (wheels, if you need them), and functional pieces like a drill or a camera or a manipulating tool. All controlled by a mobile app.

Modbots are not going to replace the giant robots Tesla and other carmakers use; that generation of robots, Pizzata says, "are single-purposed, kind of dumb, reasonably dangerous, and only accessible to people that have money." Our goal, he says, "is to make robotics massively accessible."

The platform is meant to bring the power of robotics to huge new audiences. From small manufacturers to schools to hobbyists to filmmakers, there is an unquenched need for custom, inexpensive robots. "It's like handing people a new tool," Pizzata says. "We're not giving them a robot. We're giving them the tools to make their own robot. We are doing all of the really heavy lifting—the communications infrastructure, the software design, the mechanical development, the couplings, the cabling, the harnesses. So people can focus on the task or on the problem that they want to solve rather than how the tool is going to solve the problem."

Once adaptable robots are in people's hands, we will find endless new uses for them—and new capabilities. Modbot's founders envision users adding their own components via 3D printing, making the platform not only accessible, but also infinitely adaptable.

CONNECTIONS /

Clothes in Size "Me"

Get ready for an era of radical customization in what you wear. Clothes that match your taste, your activities, and your exact proportions. That's the message of Nathan Sivagananathan, chief growth officer of MAS, a major apparel manufacturer based in Sri Lanka, with clients around the globe.

With factories adopting new, adaptive digital technologies, manufacturers will soon be able to produce on-demand clothes. "The future of apparel manufacturing harks back to the earlier model of tailoring-to-order," says Sivagananathan. "The consumer once again will be central to the whole process. Digitization and autonomation allow this to be possible."

He compares the future process to the "farm to table" movement: more transparent, closer to home, and adapted to individual tastes. Consumers will demand to know where materials come from (ideally nearby), and they will also want a voice in what their clothes look and feel like. "Clothing that feels more personal," he adds. "With changes in color, size, and function made by the wearers themselves."

As more and better data comes back to manufacturers, from the supply chain as well as via sensors that are part of the Internet of Things, clothing makers will be able to better predict consumers' desires based on their lifestyle needs. MAS's factories will be able to "make to demand" rather than "make to order." This will mean some fundamental shifts in how and where apparel is made. "Manufacturing clothes will become a service that has a smaller global footprint and is closer to where consumers are," adds Sivagananathan. "The factories of the future will be fragmented rather than concentrated in one area of the world. They'll be smaller, use more connected systems, work with smaller minimum orders, use on-demand sourcing, and embrace the circular economy, reusing and recycling materials."

CONNECTIONS /

Consequences/

Seven thinkers, designers, and leaders look at the impacts of the future of making things—from thinking like a machine to remaking our bodies to the morality of our algorithms.

DR. CATHERINE MOHR is vice president of medical research at Intuitive Surgical and an expert in the field of robotic surgery.

Most of The Future of Making *focuses on industrial topics. How does medicine fit into this realm of making?*

Every surgeon who sits down at one of our consoles is using it as an act of creation. They are taking the raw materials of the person's body and reassembling it in a way that allows the person to heal. So I think of it as an act of creation.

Surgery is more like gardening than it is like other forms of making. The person is not healed when you're

For example: If you repair a hernia with these new sheets of biological material with proangiogenic [pro-blood-vessel-growth] factors in them, what happens is the cells go, "Oh, I ought to be replacing this. These signals are saying, Grow blood vessels." The cells come racing in and replace this material with your own body tissue and grow blood vessels into it.

These new materials talk to the body in a way that synthetics don't. You can surgically repair a part of the

> "These new materials talk to the body in a way that synthetics don't. You can repair a part of the body so that it's repairing itself."

done with the surgery; instead, the person is in the best position to *start* the healing process. These are long-term plans. Sometimes surgery is like planting a tree, because the final end result may not be there for years. Especially in pediatric surgery.

The body represents "raw material." Are there also new materials in medicine that are transforming its practice?

Yes. New materials in the robots we make and new materials in the person.

There have been breakthroughs in understanding how to make cells and blood vessels grow into a material. There are people walking around today with blood vessels and tracheas and bladders that were grown from their own cells and put on external scaffolds like electrospun fibers. They were grown outside of their body and then were put into their body.

Some of the new materials that we have are variations on the old—there's this stuff called an acellular matrix. It's an animal tissue–based scaffold composed of the kind of collagen that is in your connective tissue. The newer ones are washed in such a way that all the cells are gone, but the chemical compounds that are progrowth factors are left behind in that matrix.

body with a material that chemically tells it to start repairing itself. We'll take a little bit of you, we'll build a scaffold, we'll put the bits of you into it, and the scaffold will have the instructions necessary for you to regrow an organ.

Is new technology changing what we mean by medicine?

Every intervention that we make degrades the organism a little bit. Whether it's a drug that we give or a surgical intervention. The future is, we make surgery less and less invasive and more and more capable of working with this active creation, the tissues themselves. Repairing them in such a way that the person heals with no foreign bodies still inside their body. We'll be able to heal them with either their own selves or with a material that gives them the signal to replace it with their own material. That kind of surgery is a return to wellness.

We're not making these technologies and then looking around to see if there's anything we can apply them to. The real goal of health care is wellness. It's preservation of a pain-free, functional, happy life as long as one can.

CARLA DIANA is a designer, author, and educator who explores the impact of future technologies through hands-on experiments in product design and tangible interaction.

What problems does designing connected objects bring up?

We're starting to develop a lot of "connected" products that do object-to-object communication. But they still don't have the knowledge that a human has or the ability to take into account all situations.

One example is the thermostat which is a learning device. It remembers your patterns. And it will often seem to do something that you don't want it to do. It doesn't quite get it right. It's trying to do everything without us intervening. But it seems we still need to intervene. Getting those intervention moments right is

You've written about designing for a world that needs to be understood by both humans and robots. What new skills do we need to do that?

What's tricky about this new world of connected objects and machine learning is that we have in our minds the model of being a human being. And it's getting us into trouble.

A colleague of mine, Tom Guarriello, is trained as a clinical psychologist, and he's bringing some of that insight into human-robot interaction. He likes to use the term "robot whisperer." Designers may need to get really good at being robot whisperers.

> "What's tricky about this new world of connected objects and machine learning is that we have in our minds the model of being a human being. And it's getting us into trouble."

what contemporary design needs to focus on.

What is not happening right now in these is what we call the handoff. How does the machine let us know when it needs us to step in? How do we gracefully let it know we want to step in?

In other words, the challenge is: How do humans and machines work side by side to make the best of each other's abilities?

That's the interesting design problem. We're interacting with these autonomous machines, call them robots or whatever you want, in a way where they're like partners to us.

We need to put ourselves into the mind of the computer. We need to understand how the machine thinks. We might need to understand that this is a machine that has a camera, it can understand depth, it can understand the speed at which I gesture.

We should capitalize on what the machine is good at and let people really understand what it sees and what it hears. A robot isn't a thing that's been programmed to be human; it's a thing that has a machine brain. And what is a machine brain? What is machine sight? What is machine hearing? What is machine touch?

THOMAS L. FRIEDMAN is an

internationally renowned author, reporter, and columnist—the recipient of three Pulitzer Prizes and the author of seven bestselling books, including *Thank You for Being Late: An Optimist's Guide to Thriving in the Age of Accelerations.*

What are the forces shaping our world now?

What's shaping more things in more places in more ways are the three largest forces on the planet: the market, Mother Nature, and Moore's Law. All of them look like a hockey stick now.

When the market, Mother Nature, and Moore's Law all go into hockey stick, it has huge implications. The way I frame it is that average is now officially over for every worker, average is over for every leader, and average is over for every country.

I use Syria as my prime example. The Syrian revolution happened. Syria got hit with the worst four-year drought in its modern history in the four years preceding the revolution. Mother Nature set the table, and then Moore's Law came along and connected a million climate refugees, and they blew the lid off the place.

They've created a release of energy that is the greatest release of energy since fire. This supernova has five properties:

It's an incredible **solvent**. It breaks bonds everywhere....
Second, it's an incredible **adhesive**. I can now connect up with people....
Third, it's an incredible **propellant**. It empowers makers and breakers like never before....
Fourth, it's an incredible **transparent**. I can see inside you now. I can see inside things like never before....
Lastly, it's an incredible **accelerant**. It accelerates the exchange of ideas.

I'm a huge fan of the historian William McNeill, who asks, What is the driver of history? Is it the rise and fall of civilizations? Is it the quest for freedom? He says no,

"The processor, the storage chip, the sensor, the network, and software experiencing Moore's Law together have created what I call 'The Supernova.' They've created a release of energy that is the greatest release of energy since fire."

How does Moore's Law—technology—have such a big impact?

Computers are made of five parts: the processor, the storage chip, the sensor, the network, and the software. All five are going through a Moore's Law move.

Those five things experiencing Moore's Law together have created what I call "The Supernova."

the driver of history is contact between strangers.

You and I are driving history. Two strangers meet, and we exchange ideas. This system is accelerating that contact between strangers unbelievably.

HOLLY O'DRISCOLL is a champion

of human-centered design and innovation at Procter & Gamble, where she is a design-thinking leader.

How are the technological advances of the future of making things affecting P&G's work?

The mindset of prototyping, rather than the relentless pursuit of the *one right answer*, is one big shift. We're getting better at holding multiple solutions in mind. Instead of testing one idea, how do we test five ideas, twenty ideas, and not be married

scale—everybody's going to get trained on how to do design thinking workshops, how to facilitate, how to do framing exercises, empathy exercises....It was something special that you went off-site to do. But we found that people would go back to what Joseph Campbell would call "the ordinary world," and their behavior wasn't changed.

"The activity of design thinking unleashes the spirit that everybody can do this. The language of prototyping invites that."

to any of them? That's a real shift for us—the idea that there is likely more than one solution invites learning.

The ability to physicalize an idea, to do it really quickly, is immensely valuable at advancing the conversation and allowing us to make decisions in our business faster. That's so powerful because it provokes meaningful conversation that goes beyond the one-page memo. One of the very first trainings you have at P&G is how to write a one-page memo. But I can't tell you how many times I've handed people a marker to start to sketch their idea and they start to sweat. I'll ask, "What's going on here?" And they'll respond, "Well, I can't draw. I can't do this very well."

The activity of design thinking unleashes the spirit that everybody can do this. The language of prototyping invites that. Everybody can bring an idea to life that lives outside the context of the one-page memo.

You helped bring the practice of design thinking to P&G. How has that changed in the years since? How is it affecting the company's work?

We started in 2007, largely driven by design-thinking methods. We were very much about driving

About four or five years ago, we made a shift to the application of design thinking to everyday P&G life. We started really playing with the idea of mindset more effectively. The method was the mechanics; the mindset is, This is a way of life, a way of being, a way of approaching problems and examining the possibilities for solutions.

We are now in a world where, in general, everything works. The idea of "20 percent cleaner" isn't as relevant as it used to be. If you're not rolling around in the grass every day, you're probably not getting that dirty. So while superior product performance is important—the brand experience across all touchpoints is an important differentiator.

How do you differentiate? The idea of brokering a human connection—a lot of interesting things are starting to emerge in this space. There are a lot more conversations around holistic product experiences and pushing into that emotional space. It goes, again, back to that mindset shift: one conversation, one behavior, one interaction done differently tomorrow than today, one small step leading to something more meaningful on a grand scale.

GEOFF MANAUGH is the founder of
BLDGBLOG, one of the most popular architecture sites on the Web, and author of *The Burglar's Guide to the City*.

How will we see generative design expressed in our built environment?

I think it is already happening. A lot of designs coming out of architecture school right now, for example, look like plants or vines in an alien rainforest, and these buildings are basically expressions of particular software programs.

This is leading to radically different building forms that seem detached from the linear history of aesthetic development. Could a human being actually sit down and determine, by hand, all of the strange-shaped pores and cavities and pillars required to support this sort of thing? Were those details determined based on

That's a pretty false assumption. Some basic examples are how our news feeds are now filtered, or how Instagram photographs are now ordered or prioritized in ways that remain opaque to us.

What's more interesting, however, is when you look at where algorithms are creeping into the everyday environment. Look at simple decisions, such as the amount of time a crosswalk gives people to cross the street. You could imagine that by programming longer times for pedestrians, you'd be helping the aged get around on their own. But if your algorithm prioritizes different forms of transportation because they are perhaps more efficient from a logistics point of view,

"Some writers have suggested that we are moving into an almost ethics-free world because we have handed everything over to algorithms."

historical rationality or was a computer simply thinking through things algorithmically?

It remains to be seen if this type of aesthetic is going to be accepted as humanist—that is, where we can actually engage with a building in a way that makes sense to us as human beings. Perhaps, instead, it will be as if we've encountered a kind of alien algorithm in the shape of a building and it will remain unclear how we should proceed.

Recently, there has been more attention for the idea that our algorithms are not neutral. Is there a morality involved in design based on algorithms?

Some writers have suggested that we are moving into an almost ethics-free world because we have handed everything over to algorithms that aren't clouded by partisan or political interpretations, and so on.

then your traffic algorithm is going to decide against something that would benefit the elderly. Details like this show how prejudices can be mathematically programmed into the urban environment.

Another example: One of the things you see in policing today is a reliance on the statistical modeling of crime. Police will come back to a particular neighborhood, even a specific block or corner, based on algorithmic predictions of criminal activity that may or may not be about to occur there.

Police might get to a crime scene faster than before, of course. But this technique also gives the sense that you live in a neighborhood under constant surveillance and that you have lost the ability to be an equal part of the city. You are singled out by an algorithm and, as a result, treated differently by police.

DANNY HILLIS is an inventor, scientist, author, and engineer known for pioneering the concept of parallel computers. He is cochairman and CTO of Applied Minds.

What does it mean that our designs are becoming more and more complex?

We are now making systems that are so much more complex that they have emergent behavior that nobody designed into them.

As we make more complicated things, they're increasingly beyond our ability to understand them in detail. Who is really accountable if your network connection is flawed? The answer is, nobody. You can't really figure out why it's happening. There are pieces of it made by lots of different people, and your experience with it is how all of those pieces work together. It's not the function of any one piece.

One of your most famous projects is the Clock of the Long Now, which will keep time for 10,000 years. How should designers think in terms of such a long time frame?

We have the power to shape the world around us to be anything we want it to be. We have to ask, what do we want to shape it into?

We have to recognize that we're not just designing objects, we're designing the world. I think that obviously raises a whole bunch of questions that we're not used to asking. It can't just be local economic forces that shape that. As we become more connected, the things we do have consequence for larger numbers

"Being a designer, you're fundamentally participating in a political process in a way you weren't as a designer a hundred years ago."

This is a fundamental shift in our relationship with things. I think it's more like our relationship with natural objects. In some sense, our designs are becoming more biological. At the same time, we're actually beginning to use real biological organisms to do the manufacture.

So we're coming closer and closer to biology. I think we're eventually going to get to the point where the distinction between natural and artificial is not clear, when you can't say whether something is designed or is grown.

of people. That means that being a designer, you're fundamentally participating in a political process in a way you weren't as a designer a hundred years ago.

In some sense, what we're designing is—we're designing ourselves. We're designing human society. We are designing what it's like to be alive.

JUAN ENRIQUEZ is a bestselling author,
businessman, and academic, and a leading authority on the economic and political impacts of life sciences. He is managing director of Excel Venture Management, a life sciences VC, and the founder of Biotechonomy.

What's next for how humans design and make things?

If you think of a design school circa the 1980s, there were probably a few crazy professors saying, "Let me show you this new device called a computer. It's

Even getting to the closest star system, which is about four light years away, you're going to be on the starship for close to 14,000 years at current speeds. You fundamentally have to redesign a body to live for

"Biology will likely become the established manufacturing method in the next few decades. It may make the industrial revolution look very small."

clunky, but someday you're going to be able to design and make stuff with it." Students who paid attention to these new technologies broke the rules of design and began designing in a very different way.

Apply that idea to biology moving forward, because biology is going to drive how we make things. And biology is so much more powerful than anything we've been playing with in terms of making stuff. Once we start harnessing biology, then things are going to change. Slowly at first, but then on a scale that is completely different from the scale that we're used to. This software makes its own hardware.

Biology will likely become the established manufacturing method in the next few decades. How we make things and where we make things is undergoing a massive evolution as we speak. It may make the industrial revolution look very small.

You've talked about redesigning humans and other creatures. What kind of redesign are you talking about?

Space is a very nasty place for human beings. The radiation that you get hit with by going just to Mars is astronomical. So you have to redesign the body to be able to repair that damage. You have to adapt to a different atmosphere, or to other parameters. That's nontrivial.

tens of thousands of years to continue to get smarter, to live in very different atmospheres, to consume far less oxygen, far less food. So you have to think about the parameters of life and where it's going.

Why do we need to redesign our bodies for space?

Because extinction is common and natural. Most lifeforms on earth have gone extinct many times.

Right now, we're betting on a very, very, very small dot. If you don't redesign humans, and if you don't get them off this planet, then we are going to go extinct.

There are certainly ethical challenges. There are certainly moral challenges, there are certainly risks to altering biology. But the consequence of not acting is, we go extinct. I don't know when, I don't know how, but the fossil record tells you there are periodic, and normal, and natural extinctions on earth.

You want to diversify the bets as to where humans live. What you want to have happen as you look out at the stars—not next week, not next month, not next year, but in the next few thousand years—is that you want to be able to say, "Human beings are here, and here, and here, and here, and here." If you don't do that, then you're betting on a single, large number on a roulette wheel. You can lose everything.

The Future
of the Future/

Five leaders at Autodesk
share glimpses of
the future of the future
of making.

Reordering the World

Jeff Kowalski,
Chief Technology Officer

We're starting to see that the cloud quite literally is coming to collide with earth. It is reorganizing our world according to computation.

One way to look at the Design Graph is that something's hidden inside of a computer, and the supply chains and things like that are these sort of virtual depictions of relationships between people and things and goods. I'm trying to be even more literal. When you open your front door in the morning, the world is going to look different. It's not virtual at all; it's actually shockingly physical.

For example, if you play out autonomous vehicles, the big news is not the vehicle, it's the way that we reorganize for autonomous vehicles. We don't need outright ownership. It gets even more physical then: Autonomous vehicles don't crash. Not if they're communicating well with each other. So the safety systems that we have in cars are no longer required. You don't need seatbelts. We don't need traffic lights. We don't need traffic signs. We don't need speed limit signs. You don't need crash prevention. So the cars are substantially lighter. If you are confident that the car is not going to crash, it looks entirely different and is composed in a totally different way.

So the infrastructure itself looks fundamentally different. When I step outside my house in the morning, the road will be physically different. That's what I mean. The impact of computing is starting to alter our environment.

It's not so much that you have a supercomputer in your pocket. It's that computing is actually going to change the things that you bump into every day.

We've got enough computing power that the models are starting to appear more and more like the real thing. We will actually start computing in and with the real physical environment; no longer simply representing things, but actually acting with them.

We're going to have a direct connection between the things that we are making and the computers that are making them. So I don't think that we will wind up having a simplified cyberworld. I think we will end up acting directly in the world—and the computers will be in and among the things that we have.

AR, VR, and the Importance of Fluency

Brian Pene, Director of Emerging Technology

We can really no longer afford the conduit between computer and our world to be as narrow as the bottleneck we are experiencing with keyboard and mouse. Augmented and virtual-reality devices are like a new wave of computing. The big question is, What does it mean when humans merge with machines?

This will give humans the ability to interpret really large, continuous, complex data sets—information correlated with the physical world—in a very immersive state. Just like we do in the physical world.

As a result of that, we're able to save tons of money, materials, carbon. We'll enable people to collaborate all over the world in connected, immersive environments. We'll be able to filter all of that complex information and have entirely new ways of looking at things.

This is going to change the way we think about how design is done, how it's done collaboratively, how it's much more intuitive. It's going to change the way we think about engineering because we'll be able to assimilate digital information to predictively understand how something will perform. We'll be able to do things better from a storytelling perspective.

The real opportunity for the future is fluency—bridging the gap among humans, machines, information, and the real world. In the future, whoever is more fluent with technology is going to win. People who are fluent with technology are going to look superhuman against people who aren't. It will be a huge gap in capabilities of what humans can do just based on how well we can integrate with these different technologies and how fluent we can become.

Today, I can talk to my Alexa. I'm just having a natural conversation. It's enabling a dialogue between humans' digital information in the real world. I think that's what a lot of AR and VR technology will enable.

I hope that it takes us to a place where life is simpler and we understand the implications of the things that we do. I don't think that we do that today.

There's also a social anomaly that's happening with the "swipe generation." Children are losing empathy. Their motor skills are not as good because they're swiping phones at a young age. I think that's because they're looking at this flat device, and their situational awareness is off. But when the world becomes my interface and display, I'm not as lost in my technology. These technologies can enable more connectivity between people, between information and understanding.

Don't Build Things— Grow Them

Andrew Hessel, Distinguished Research Scientist

The future of making things is going to be based on biological systems. If not bio directly, then bringing the dynamics and the mechanisms of biology into the manufactured world.

You can biomanufacture glass and crystallites, for example. You can make glues and adhesives. There's an incredible array of molecular structures that can be encoded in code, and realized by self-assembling molecular machinery, which we call life.

As we start to get mastery over these processes, it's revolutionary. Through all of human history, our ability to manufacture has been crude and toxic and, ultimately, unsustainable. The shift to these technologies will be driven based on the only sustainable technology that we're aware of, which is life.

This will touch every area of humanity, every area of manufacturing, every sector that we can imagine, because life is the thing that connects everything on this planet.

Right now, we have garbage everywhere. That is a giant problem. We have toxins and garbage. All that's going away. Anywhere you see waste today, it is going to be digested and turned back into the elemental materials that it was made from, and reprocessed into something a lot more valuable. Garbage goes away. Air pollution and those things go away. All the next forms of manufacturing are nowhere near as toxic.

The Project, Not the Data

Brian Mathews, Group CTO, Information Modeling and Platform Group

With the cloud we can integrate different data sources together and get connectivity, much like what Google does for textual information on the Internet.

Think about the Internet before and after Google. The focus of the Internet used to be on the specific documents, specific pages. You used to have to know where to go. Yahoo! used to make a big table of contents for everything on the Internet. And then when Google came around, it put the data at the center of your experience.

Design is late to the party here. With CAD, we've had this librarian mentality, that we were going to have a big database in the cloud, and we were going to organize the folders and put all of our data in one centralized place.

Design, on the one hand, is really high-tech—confrontational fluid dynamics, hard math, that kind of stuff. But in another way, design is actually behind. While everyone else has been creating platforms, what is the platform for doing design?

Something similar is going to happen in design, where we used to have a very choppy workflow, where there were people who did detail design, construction, and operation, and so on. And what the cloud and subscription models are allowing us to do is put the project at the center. One set of data. It's a singular way to navigate a design.

That's important, because it allows more people to participate. No matter what your role is, you can come into this hospital, if you think of the hospital as the user interface to all these different applications. If I'm a contractor, I say: What do I need to build today? If I'm a finance person, I see a spreadsheet and can ask, Where are my cost overruns? If I'm an architect, I see a three-dimensional model.

There's no next big thing. It's the combination of trends already happening. It's the integration. It's federating all these different pieces together. I'm not even sure how we talk about that, other than through examples. The closest thing we come to in our space is this concept of the project at the center.

Looking to Regenerative Design

Dawn Danby, Senior Sustainable Design Program Manager

There's a huge opportunity to be looking at the deep future of manufacturing. But in the near timeframe, the opportunity is, How do we hack the remainders of the 20th century? The majority of the buildings we're in, how do we modify those systems? We need to be looking at really mining efficiency. That doesn't mean just shaving 10 or 15 percent off of things. That means looking at really high-performance buildings, net-positive buildings, buildings that are so efficient that they're able to generate their own energy and then make more. You can create buildings that are so efficient that you eliminate a lot of the mechanical systems completely.

Machine learning and artificial intelligence can help assist designers and engineers to make much smarter decisions. Right now, a lot of it requires skill building. Traditionally, people have had to become specialized—how to do simulation for products, or how to do whole-building energy analysis, or how to do simulation for building performance.

Now we're starting to build capacity to assist people in making those decisions, without having to completely change their mindset. That may mean relinquishing the notion of yourself as just being the full designer. You're designing with machine intelligence.

Change, whether it's technological change or social change or population change, those things are all inevitable. Frankly, the ecological changes around climate are also inevitable. They're happening to us now.

When we talk about sustainability, a lot of the time it means just keeping things in a state of stasis. But we use more than we give back as a species. What we need to be doing is supporting the ecological health of the planet.

We need to be moving into a world where the designs that we create are a net benefit. Regenerative design is a way of looking at different things that we can do to support and actually build ecological health. Looking at how do we keep carbon in the ground, how do we maintain and enable forests and grasslands and watersheds and oceans to thrive as best they can? Regenerative design can mean looking at how we design land management, or how we design buildings, or how we look at infrastructure. Instead of paving everything, how do we work with green infrastructure?

CHAPTER 7

Our digital tools give us near-infinite vision, insight, and expressability. In this new era, if something can take shape in our imagination, it can be given form in the real world. This remarkable power frees us to focus on decisions of what we should make—and why.

Instead of *limiting* our imaginations, emerging tool-sets will *augment* our abilities and help us to *amplify* our ideas.

We now have a growing arsenal of superpowers: X-ray vision to see the physical world and understand its dimensions and patterns more clearly. Limitless thinking power to discover brilliant solutions and envision better outcomes. Magic tools that move materials around in just the right ways to express our ideas. Persistent connections with people and things to ensure that our systems flow smoothly and intelligently.

What was impossible yesterday is possible today. What is impractical today will be commonplace tomorrow. As the future rushes toward us, exponentially growing technologies will stretch our thinking and our capabilities. It will be daunting—and exhilarating.

Armed with these superpowers, we can design and make anything. But what do we want to see in the world?

Should we make things that last longer? Or things that cost less? Should we make things more efficiently? Or should we make things that are created just for you? Should we make things that consume less energy? Or produce them in fewer steps? Do we make things that satisfy what people want right now? Or create things they will want tomorrow?

Every designer, engineer, architect, or other maker will ask themselves these kinds of questions. The ones we choose to ask reflect our values. We build what we think is right and important. But with our new superpowers, we no longer need to make binary choices or succumb to the usual trade-offs. We can pose bolder questions that provoke, expand, and inspire. What will bring us profit *and* create a healthier world? How can we design to serve the needs of people today *and* tomorrow? What might we make that will take advantage of the emerging tools *and* embody craftsmanship?

This should be a source of hope. As the space between our intentions and outcomes shrinks, the role of designers, makers, and builders becomes more important than ever: to develop daring ideas that make a real and lasting difference. The strongest of our superpowers is understanding why we should make things and how that will serve the people we do it for. We will understand this in ways that are deeper and broader than we could have ever imagined before.

HOW WILL WE PUT THESE POWERS TO GOOD USE?

We must be prepared to take big steps. When people moved from wood tools to stone, they created such an advantage for themselves that they never went back. The same was true for the shifts from stone to bronze, from bronze to iron, from iron to steel, from manual tools to powered ones, and from powered tools to digitized, connected, adaptive technologies. Each step is irreversible. Once we experience the future, the past just doesn't look that good. These changes left no way to go back.

Our mental models will need to keep pace with the changes in the world. We must be prepared to learn continually. In every transformation, success depends on understanding the forces at work and learning to flow with them. The surfer learns to ride the big waves.

The irony is that the wizardry of the digital, mechanical, and biological advancements actually exposes and magnifies our humanity. To be human is to feel, to be moved, to be inspired, and to channel those feelings into what we do: create art, tell stories, and build things.

Never before have we had such an abundance of opportunities to do all of that. Never before have we had the power to create better, more elegant, and truly extraordinary things. Never before have these resources been more available to more people in more places.

Right here, right now, we are living in the earliest moments of an amazing new chapter in the history of making things.

The Shape of Things to Come: A Manifesto

When we combine sensing, computing, and physical expression with new materials—and help equip communities to make things they are passionate about—magic happens. The result is a tremendous release of energy by the people who design, make, and operate things that will revolutionize our world. What follows are some rules for working on that revolution.

RIDE THE CURVE.
Equip yourself with exponential tools to move from guessing, wondering, and approximating to knowing, solving, and expressing precisely.

CONNECT WHAT'S IMPORTANT.
Identify how isolated parts of something connect with and inform each other to make systems flow better.

KNOW LIMITATIONS.
Seek to move away from extraction to embracing aggregation and regeneration.

DESIGN SYSTEMS THAT ADAPT.
Learn from biology to shift from building to growing or farming things.

SEEK EMPOWERMENT.
Find the people who share a common vision and passion to learn, share, and make things that are important.

APPLY INTELLIGENT TOOLS.
Take advantage of the phenomenal power of learning algorithms to go from demanding obedience in our tools to valuing their autonomy.

Go Forth. Make Anything.

ACKNOWLEDGMENTS

The ideas presented in *The Future of Making* were gathered through many interviews with dozens of talented and passionate individuals within Autodesk as well as those in research, industry, government, and nonprofits. Each deserves a warm thank-you.

The Autodesk senior leadership team embraced the project fully, using it as a tool to clarify our long-term vision for the future of making and giving it broad direction. They also extended the freedom to pursue a wide range of ideas. Carl Bass, Amar Hanspal, Andrew Anagnost, Chris Bradshaw, Jan Becker, Jeff Kowalski, Moonhie Chin, Scott Herren, Steve Blum, and Steve Hobbs encouraged us to push the technology forward as well as to humanize the stories.

Our thought leaders deserve thanks for providing their expertise and guidance. Jon Pittman, Azam Khan, Brian Pene, Brian Mathews, Diego Tamburini, Dominic Thasarathar, Mickey McManus, Mike Haley, Phil Bernstein, Tatjana Dzambazova, and Terry Bennett consistently unpacked complex subjects, revealed insights, and pointed to surprising implications.

The office of the CTO provided tack-sharp feedback from Maurice Conti, Arthur Harsuvanakit, Bill O'Connor, Darren Brooker, David Thomasson, Evan Atherton, Heather Kerrick, Hui Xylo Li, Jonathan Knowles, Kerry Ann Levenhagen, Lisa Rotzinger, Lucas Prokopiak, Shaan Hurley, and Zachary Miller.

Autodesk Research pioneered many of the topics depicted in this book: Gordon Kurtenbach, Eli Groban, Francesco Iorio, George Fitzmaurice, Jos Stam, Larry Peck, Tovi Grossman, and many others. Thanks to specific contributors and reviewers: Mark Davis, Daniele Grandi, Dianne Gault, Erin Bradner, John Schmier, Merry Wang, and Michael Bergin.

Our production team of Scott Sheppard and Genna Tricarico ensured the book progressed on track, on schedule, and on budget.

Autodesk's brand team, Heike Rapp, Alain Bolduc, Allati El Henson, Hoagy de la Plante, and Keith Chamberlain, did an outstanding job creating amazing design language and producing stunning imagery. Keith also produced the intricate generative design patterns for the cover and opening pages of each chapter.

Autodesk's ReMake team worked with the Smithsonian Institution to create beautiful new images from their project to capture the Apollo 11 Command Module.

Our marketing, PR, Redshift, and sales teams helped guide our efforts: Greg Eden, Carolyn Rohrer, Caleb Garlin, Clay Helm, Erin Emery, Jason Medal-Katz, Jessica Schonwasser, Joseph Wurcher, Julia Papapietro McFarland, Joy Stark, Matthew Tierney, Noah Cole, Pam Moon, Rama Dunayevich, Rey Ledda, Roddy Wykes, and Taylor Jacobs.

Our Autodesk Foundation and sustainability team steered the book towards many important questions about renewability: Lynelle Cameron, Ben Thompson, Bobbie Casey, Catherine Wolf, Dawn Danby, Jake Layes, Joe Speicher, Katy Evans, Paige Rodgers, and Susan Gladwin.

Other contributors included Tatjana Dzambazova, Beth Trakimas, Ben Schrauwen, Chris Romes, Dan Silmore, David Benjamin, Joel Pennington, Jordan Brandt, Justine Crosby, Kevin Schneider, Liz Lynch, Mary Hope McQuiston, Robert "Buzz" Kross, Rolland Zelles, Shalom Ormsby, Tanya Liu, Thomas Heerman, and Tom Joseph.

Our book designers, Scott Thorpe, Brett MacFadden, and Laura Bagnato, worked tirelessly to refine the book's look and feel.

Melcher Media, once again, did an amazing job producing the book. A special thank-you to Charlie Melcher, Bonnie Eldon, John Morgan, and Susan Lynch for their generous spirit and uncompromising pursuit of quality. Melcher Media also thanks

IMAGE CREDITS

Callie Barlow, Jess Bass, Emma Blackwood, Karl Daum, Cheryl Della Pietra, Shannon Fanuko, Luke Jarvis, Aaron Kenedi, Karolina Manko, Sarah Melton, John Morgan, Lauren Nathan, Kate Osba, Rachel Schlotfeldt, Victoria Spencer, Michelle Wolfe, Megan Worman, and Katy Yudin.

To David Brown, a great editor, writer, contributor, and friend: I always enjoyed our deep dives and fierce explorations about what was most important. This book would be just half of what it is without your extraordinary contribution.

And finally, to my wife, Sandra Muscat, whose patience, love, support, and encouragement made the journey of writing, managing, and production much, much easier.

AUTODESK.

The authors, editors, and publisher have made extensive efforts to ensure the accuracy of the information contained in this book. Any errors brought to the publisher's attention will be corrected in future editions.

Produced by

MELCHER MEDIA

124 West 13th Street
New York, NY 10011
www.melcher.com

President, CEO: Charles Melcher
VP, COO: Bonnie Eldon
Senior Producer: John Morgan
Editor: David E. Brown
Production Director: Susan Lynch
Assistant Producer: Karl Daum

Design by MacFadden & Thorpe